African-Centered Pedagogy

SUNY series, The Social Context of Education

Christine E. Sleeter, editor

AFRICAN-CENTERED PEDAGOGY

Developing Schools of Achievement for African American Children

PETER C. MURRELL JR.

State University of New York Press

Published by

State University of New York Press, Albany

Printed in the United States of America

For information, address
State University of New York Press,
90 State Street, Suite 700, Albany, NY 12207

Production, Laurie Searl
Marketing, Michael Campchiaro

Library of Congress Cataloging-in-Publication Data

Murrell, Peter C.
African-centered pedagogy : developing schools of achievement for African American children / Peter C. Murrell, Jr.
p. cm. — (SUNY series, the social context of education)
Includes bibliographical references and index.
ISBN 0-7914-5291-3 (alk. paper) — ISBN 0-7914-5292-1 (pbk. : alk. paper)
1. African Americans—Education. 2. African Americans—Race identity. 3. Afrocentrism—Study and teaching—United States. I. Title. II. SUNY series, social context of education

LC2731 .M87 2002
371.829'96073—dc21 2001049178

10 9 8 7 6 5 4 3 2 1

Contents

List of Figures and Tables vii

Preface ix

Introduction xix

PART I: FRAMING THE WORK

1 The Wrong Frames for the Right Problem 3

2 Traditions of African American Education: A Historical Perspective 19

3 Culture, Cognition, and the Community of Achievement 37

PART II: PEDAGOGICAL THEORY FOR BUILDING A COMMUNITY OF AFRICAN AMERICAN ACHIEVEMENT

4 Overview of the Pedagogical Theory 59

5 From a Community of Caring to a Community of Achievement 75

6 Teaching as Assisted Performance in the African American Tradition 103

7 The Classroom Ecology of Culture and Language 115

8 Discourse Practices in a Community of Achievement 125

9 Teaching for Understanding, Learning for Liberation 135

10 Appraising My Own Practice: African-Centered Pedagogy in Preparing Teachers 155

Appendices 171

References 181

Index 193

Tables and Figures

Figure 1	Activity setting—Unit of analysis triangulating teacher practice, learning activity, and student performance	16
Figure 2	The basic components of the African-centered pedagogy	17
Figure 3	All components of the African-centered pedagogy	54
Figure 4	Instructional Activity System	63
Table 1	Pedagogical Frameworks Incorporated in African-Centered Pedagogy	xii
Table 2	Premises of the African-Centered Pedagogical Theory	46
Table 3	Essential Cultural practices in an African-Centered Pedagogy	52
Table 4	Specific Cultural Practices in African-Centered Pedagogy	71
Table 5	Essential Cultural Practice Analysis of Case One	98
Table 6	Glossary of Terms in African-Centered Pedagogy	170

Preface

> Education is the practice of assisting people to find agency in, and responsibility for, the struggle for freedom.

This book is a practical guide to teaching and learning. The book is written specifically for teachers of African American children who are struggling to translate contemporary educational theory into successful practice, given the demands and constraints of public schooling in urban America. I wish to reach all those who are invested in the academic achievement and personal development of African American children, including teachers, school administrators, scholars, and researchers, as well as parents and community members.

The book presents an instructional theory for successful work with African American children that integrates the historical, cultural, political, and developmental considerations of the African American experience into a unified system of practice for the educational achievement of African American children. The book brings to light those principles of good practice that already exist and links them to contemporary ideas and innovations that apply to effective practice in African American communities. The theory of teaching and learning is called "African-centered pedagogy" and has been shaped by more than twenty-five years of teaching, community organizing, and research in and around urban schools and communities. This African-centered pedagogy for effective teaching is based on a critical reinterpretation and appropriation of several key educational frameworks (e.g., constructivist teaching, responsive teaching, child-centered learning, cognitively guided instruction) and innovations (e.g., project-based learning, cooperative learning). In this book I demonstrate why these frameworks and innovations have not yet made an impact on efforts to elevate the academic achievement and personal development for African Americans. Individually, the innovations and frameworks are basically good ideas. But as *systems* of instruction they are inadequate for improving the quality of education for African American children. I therefore provide the reader with a unifying conceptual framework. I incorporate these innovations in an active theory of effective teaching—a pedagogy of success—for the achievement and development of African American children in school contexts. Finally, the book illustrates the application of the theory through case study analyses of accomplished practice in both instructional settings and professional settings to demonstrate the development of a community of achievement for African American children.

An effective pedagogy should provide teachers with a unifying framework for how they are to apply understanding of human cognition, learning, and development. The African-centered pedagogy presented in this volume does just that, but also guides teachers in how to situate those understandings in practice—and to use these situated understandings to take full account of the lives, histories, cultures, and worldviews of children in diverse urban communities. African-Centered Pedagogy is an instructional theory designed to serve as a guide to practice, as it reveals to teachers how to circumvent the deep-seated, uncontested structures of inequality in schooling that pose barriers to quality education for African American children. I will address how to recognize and confront these barriers in our own work contexts, in our own thinking and in our own training as teachers of African American children.

This work focuses on practice—the site of teaching and learning—and how to get results in the actual conditions under which teachers and students interact with one another. How do teachers acquire proficiencies and the knowledge-in-practice required for successful of teaching African American children in a culturally responsive manner? How do teachers acquire, and then use, this awareness to improve their teaching practice? What specific changes can teachers make in how they organize classroom life, assess learning achievement, and support learning activity that will result in quality education for African American children? These are the questions I take up and address in this volume.

I draw on an emerging research literature on culturally responsive teaching, incorporating what we already know about the social and cultural contexts that maximize African American children's learning, cognitive development, and identity formation. However, this effort charts a new direction by exploring what culturally relevant teaching looks like as a system of institutional and professional practice. What follows is the development of such a system for successful work with African American children. With this system, called African-centered pedagogy, you will be able to visualize and develop *accomplished practice* in your work with African American children.

The idea of *practice* is central to the African-centered pedagogy. I need to make clear at the outset that I use the term in a way different from everyday use in the profession. In teacher talk, the term *practice* is often used as an antonym for *theory*. I adopt the view that theory and practice are *not* the distinct, mutually exclusive entities that we represent as opposites in our everyday talk. When, for example, a supervising veteran teacher dismisses something the student teacher learned in her college classroom by saying "Oh, well that might work in *theory*, but in *practice* . . .," theory and practice do seem split apart. That kind of "teacher-talk" places theory and practice in opposition to one another—as if they occupy opposite ends of a continuum of professional practice ranging from the "abstract, ivory tower" to the "real world, in the trenches" level of work. In this book, "practice" means both the actions and activities of teaching on the one hand, and the appraisal and refinement of those activities in light of theoretical knowledge on the other hand. I thus bring theoretical knowing and practical knowing together in the construction of success pedagogy. In powerful, successful systems of teaching, theory and practice are always unified in the pedagogy of the teacher.

To develop this synergetic view of theory and practice (which Paulo Freire [1970] calls "praxis"), I also draw on situated learning theory, activity theory and recent developments in cultural-, cognitive-, and developmental psychology. By constructing a system of accomplished practice for successful work with African American learners in urban communities, I make accessible a number of educational frameworks that have emerged over the last two decades to those who are working to elevate the achievement of African American children. You no doubt have read or heard about a number of these frameworks, including such notions as "teaching for understanding," "constructivist teaching," and "multiple intelligences." Perhaps you have regarded them as merely the latest in a litany of "new and better" approaches to teaching that seem to have limited real world applicability to your own teaching. As you will see throughout this volume, there are elements of these frameworks that are useful to the enterprise of creating a success pedagogy for African American children. As you will also see in the pages that follow, these frameworks require a system of practice in their application—an African-centered pedagogy.

Of the many educational frameworks in recent years, five have particular relevance for the work of elevating the achievement of African American learners and deserve brief mention (see Table 1). The first framework is the idea of *learning communities* or *communities of learning*. The second is the notion of culturally responsive or culturally relevant teaching, voiced in the work of Jacqueline Jordan Irvine, Gloria Ladson-Billings, Geneva Gay, Michele Foster, Janice Hale, and others. The third is the concept of *teaching for understanding* which emphasizes meaningful and purposeful learning enterprises as the foundation of teaching. It is exemplified in the work of the Coalition for Essential Schools, as well as by the teaching for understanding framework articulated by David Perkins, Grant Wiggins and Jay McTighe, and others. The fourth framework is the notion of learning through activity based on *situated learning theory*, developed in the work of Jean Lave, Roland Tharp, Ronald Gallimore, Etienne Wenger, and others. Very briefly, this is the idea that what people perceive, think, and do develops in a social context. Learning is situated because what

Table 1

PEDAGOGICAL FRAMEWORKS INCORPORATED IN AFRICAN-CENTERED PEDAGOGY

PEDAGOGICAL FRAMEWORKS	THEORISTS AND WRITERS
Communities learning, Communities of Caring	**Deborah Meier, Nel Noddings, and Ted Sizer:** Noddings, N. (1992). *The challenge to care in schools: An alternative approach to education*. New York: Teachers College Press. Meier, D. (1995). *The power of their ideas: Lessons for America from a small school in Harlem*. Boston: Beacon Press. Sizer, T. R. (1996). *Horace's hope: What works for the American high school.* Boston: Houghton-Mifflin.
Culturally responsive, culturally synchronous, culturally relevant teaching	**James Banks, Geneva Gay, Jacqueline Jordan Irvine, and Gloria Ladson-Billings:** Irvine, J. J. (1990). *Black students and school failure: Policies, practices and prescriptions*. Westport, CT: Praeger Publishers. Ladson-Billings, G. (1994). *The dreamkeepers: Successful teachers of African American children*. San Francisco: Jossey-Bass. Gay, G., & Banks, J. (2000). *Culturally responsive teaching: Theory, research and practice (multicultural education series)*. New York: Teachers College Press.
Teaching for understanding, constructivist teaching	**Jay McTighe, David Perkins, Grant Wiggins, and Joan Wiske:** Perkins, D. (1992). *Smart schools: From training memories to educating minds*. New York: Free Press. Wiggins, G., & McTighe, J. (1998). *Understanding by design*. Alexandria, VA: Association for Supervision and Curriculum Development. Wiske, M. S. (1998). *Teaching for understanding: Linking research with practice*. San Francisco: Jossey-Bass.
Situated learning theory	**J.S. Brown, A. Collins, P. Duguid, Ronald Gallimore, Jean Lave, Roland Tharp, and Etienne Wenger:** Lave, J. (1988). *Cognition in practice*. Cambridge, UK: Cambridge University Press.

Brown, J. S., Collins, A., & Duguid, P. (1989). Situated cognition and the culture of learning. *Educational Researcher, 18*(1), 32–42.

Tharp, R. G., & Gallimore, R. (1991). *Rousing minds to life: Teach learning and schooling in social context.* Cambridge, UK: Cambridge University Press.

Wenger, Etienne (1998). *Communities of practice: Learning, meaning and identity.* Cambridge, UK: Cambridge University Press.

Cultural communities as ecosocial systems for identity development

C.A. Bowers, Antonia Darder, Fred Erickson, David Flinders, Dorothy Holland, Jay Lemke, John Ogbu, and Valerie Walkerdine:

Erickson, F. (1986). Qualitative methods in research on teaching. In M. Wittrock (Ed.) *Handbook on research on teaching: A project of the American Educational Research Association* (3rd ed., 119–161), New York: MacMillan.

Ogbu, J. (1988). *Black education: A cultural-ecological perspective.* In H. P. McAdoo (Ed.), *Black families* (pp. 169–186). Beverly Hills, CA: Sage.

Bowers, C. A., & Flinders, D. J. (1990). *Responsive teaching: An ecological approach to classroom patterns of language, culture and thought.* New York: Teachers College Press.

Darder, A. (1991). *Culture and power in the classroom: A critical foundation for bicultural education.* New York: Bergin Garvey Press.

Lemke, J. L. (1997). Cognition, context, and learning: A social semiotic perspective. In D. Kirshner & J.A. Whitson (Eds.), *Situated cognition: Social, semiotic, and psychological perspectives* (pp. 37–55). Mahwah, NJ: Erlbaum.

Walkerdine, V. (1997). Redefining the subject in situated cognition theory. In D. Kirshner & J. A. Whitson (Eds.), *Situated cognition: Social, Semiotic, and Psychological Perspectives* (pp. 57–82). Mahwah, NJ: Lawrence Erlbaum.

Holland, D. Lachiotte, W., Skinner, D., Cain, C. (1998). *Identity and agency in cultural worlds.* Cambridge, MA: Harvard University Press.

people *interpret*, how they *conceive* of their activity, and enact their *actual performance* on that activity all develop together (see Driscoll, 2000, p. 155–156).

The fifth framework is the idea of cultural and racial identity development, and the notion that an ecology of language, cultural expression and participation in classrooms is essential to the healthy identity development of African Americans and all students of color. The idea of cultural and linguistic ecology is articulated in the work of Fred Erickson, C.A. Bowers, and David Flinders. Relating this ecology to healthy racial and cultural identity development is articulated in the work of William Cross, Maria Root, Janie Ward, Andrew Garrod, Tracy Robinson, Rosa Hernandez Sheets and others.

Although these five frameworks are interesting and relevant to Black achievement, they have not yet been incorporated into a system of teaching and learning that successfully challenges African American underachievement. To my knowledge, this book is the first attempt to integrate them into a unified pedagogical theory for African American children. Because these ideas have been developed in the mainstream of educational discourse and in populations not representative of African American children, they have not yet been contextualized to the immediate and actual lives, experiences and culture of African Americans. The need, therefore, is to bring together what is of value in these frameworks into a pedagogy for African Americans. That is the purpose of this book.

Thus, my intention is not to dismiss these five frameworks as irrelevant for African Americans, but rather to examine, and in some cases reinterpret and appropriate, that thinking, within the context of African American historical, philosophical, educational, and linguistic traditions. The goal is to integrate the historical, cultural, political, and developmental considerations of African American children into a unified pedagogical theory for producing educational achievement.

The foundation of the pedagogy presented in this book is a deep-seated, working understanding of African American education, grounded in the historical heritage, value systems, and knowledge systems of African Americans (addressed specifically in chapter 2). If you are in need of a practical pedagogy for promoting academic achievement and educational attainment among African American children, this book is for you.

SUMMARY OF TEXT ORGANIZATION

The volume is organized into two parts—the first introduces the theory, the second connects the theory to current frameworks, and demonstrates application of the theory through four illustrative case studies.

The Introduction of the volume begins with a brief analysis as to why the best and most creative educational innovations of recent years do not and cannot work with African American children without a deeper understanding of pedagogical foundations of African American heritage and culture. The Introduction explains why an African-centered pedagogy is essential, and why multicultural education is inadequate as a framework for promoting achievement among African American learners. Chapter 1, "The Wrong Frames for the Right Problem," elaborates this discussion and introduces the substantive issues in Black achievement and provides the analysis on which the volume is based. Chapter 2, "Traditions of African American Education—A Historical Perspective," presents historical grounding upon which the framework is based.

Chapter 3, "Culture, Cognition, and the Community of Achievement," then explains African-centered pedagogy as a set of five essential cultural practices. I explain how the pedagogy is based upon epistemologies of learning, achievement, and schooling from the African American cultural traditions, such as the principles of MAAT (African cultural values of truth, justice, order, reciprocity and balance) and the historical tradition of literacy for freedom. The explanation of the African-centered pedagogy is framed in terms of the literacy traditions, liberation pedagogy, and intellectual traditions of African American writers, scholars and educators. Drawing on historical works (e.g., James Anderson, Cheikh Anta Diop, John Henrik Clark, Frederick Douglass, W. E. B. DuBois, and Carter Woodson), and contemporary works (e.g., Janice Hale-Benson, Marimba Ani, Joyce King, and Carol Lee), the theory is explained in terms of practice—how it applies to successful work with African children and youth.

Chapter 4, "Building a Community of Achievement in the Africanist Vein," then explains the African-centered pedagogy as it relates to the five contemporary educational frameworks and innovations mentioned earlier. This discussion anchors African-centered pedagogy within two theoretical traditions: the sociohistorical or sociocultural tradition of Lev Vygotsky and Mikhail Bakhtin and the recent tradition in social learning theory articulated in the work of Jean Lave and Etienne Wenger on *communities of practice*. The chapter begins with an explanation of how mainstream educational ideas, regardless of their promise in culturally mainstream contexts, are construed and actualized differently when experienced by someone socialized within an African American cultural context. Then the discussion presents an overview of Part II that demonstrates how these frameworks are interpreted and adapted as part of the African-centered pedagogy.

The purpose of Part II of the volume, containing chapters 4 through 10, is to explain in nonacademic language the new critical theory of "connected" urban pedagogy. In this section, each of the five educational frameworks are incorporated in the development of the African-centered pedagogy. Each chapter examines, reinterprets, and adapts a contemporary framework within the context of African American historical, philosophical, educational and linguistic tradition.

Chapter 5 is "From a Community of Caring to a Community of Achievement." This chapter lays out the pedagogical theory that includes the following key concepts, including the ideas of activity setting, practice, and community of practice. Chapter 6 is "Teaching as Assisted Performance in the African American Tradition," which applies the framework developed in chapter 5 to work with African American children. Chapter 7 develops the idea of the classroom as an ecosystem of language and culture. Chapter 8 then considers the case of the mathematics classroom and Chapter 9 the language arts classroom. Chapter 10 provides a case of African-centered pedagogy in practice.

Part II of this volume is devoted to practice, and presents an illustrative case study for a middle school, an elementary school, and two professional school settings. The purpose is to provide clear and concrete applications of the connected pedagogical theory in different settings. Through the illustrative case studies readers will be able to make meaningful connections between the theory for a connected-pedagogy (African-centered pedagogy) and their own teaching practices. Readers will also recognize the trajectory of the school's development of its pedagogical tools and practices as it moves toward more effective work with African American children. These case studies are not merely ethnographic descriptions of best practices, but constructed vignettes based on actual events and real situations where teachers, parents, and other educators have organized to create conditions for bringing about demonstrably effective, responsive, and cognitively rich instruction to African American children. The case studies also illustrate the parallel development of the school and the community as an integrated African-centered community of achievement.

PREVIEW OF PRINCIPLES

It is difficult to communicate an entire pedagogy because a pedagogy incorporates several dimensions of professional knowledge. It includes teachers' personal theories of human learning and development, their favored paradigm of instructional delivery, their understanding of how learners think and develop their thinking, and general knowledge of how the social institutions work in the world and impact teaching and learning. Talking about these varied sources of teacher knowledge as one system can be a challenge, and is precisely the challenge this book is devoted to. So to provide a preview, I offer these six points as a beginning outline of the African-centered pedagogy:

1. Accomplished teachers of African American children create the intellectual environment and cultural community in their classrooms that systematically provide the social, intellectual, and cultural tools for rich and worthwhile learning and development.
2. Accomplished teachers of African American children, to create this *figured world* of learning, inquiry, and achievement, must be able to access and understand the deep structure of African American culture, history, language, and life well enough to appropriate it in the structuring of the classroom intellectual environment.
3. Accomplished teachers of African American children understand education viewed as a broader process than schooling—as a total process of promoting the intellectual, spiritual, ethical, and social development of young people, and the stewarding them into capable, caring, and character-rich adults.
4. Accomplished teachers of African American children are critical consumers of contemporary curriculum, educational policy, and instructional practice, and interrogate them as a matter of daily practice by asking, "How does this practice or policy perpetuate the underachievement of African American learners?"
5. Accomplished teachers of African American children understand that their own daily practice necessarily entails recognizing and deconstructing the ways that traditional pedagogy and current instructional paradigms perpetuate underachievement of children of color.
6. Accomplished teachers of African American children actively research what they need to know culturally and historically in order to create the rich figured world of learning in their classroom, and recognize human development as a process occurring simultaneously in three domains—the psychological or intrapersonal, the social or interpersonal, and the cultural.

Introduction

> Teachers work is not simply about skills and techniques, or what people narrowly refer to as "how, when, and where" to do things. Rather, it is about interpretations, ideologies, and practices and the ways that these are interdependent with, and informed by each other. *Practice shapes, but is also shaped by, ideologies.* It cannot be understood as models of effective teaching, or as sometimes referred to in the current reform literature as "best practice." *Given all that we know about the diversity of teachers' and students' cultures, experiences, and ways of knowing, and all that we know about the diversity of classrooms themselves as cultures, it is extremely unlikely that there will ever be specific effective practices that are transportable full blown and whole, from one classroom site to another.* [italics added]
>
> —Marilyn Cochran-Smith, address at AERA

In the midst of national conversations and initiatives concerning how to improve curriculum in our increasingly diverse urban public schools, African American children continue to be the most severely shortchanged. It is not news to you that in virtually every major urban school system, African American children, particularly males, fare less well than their European American counterparts. Somewhere between the first and the fourth grade, African American children, especially males, begin to disengage and lose enthusiasm for learning in school. They gradually give up expecting school to make sense in the context of their lives. African American children, more than their European American counterparts, begin to experience schools as places that merely control, coerce and demand conformity, rather than as places that encourage learning, inspire creativity, and enable thinking. This phenomenon of disconnection and disengagement is well documented by research that also shows that the longer Black children, particularly males, remain in school, the more their enthusiasm for learning and educational achievement diminishes (Kunjufu, 1985, 1996; Comer & Poussaint, 1992).

This phenomenon of disconnection and disengagement is not in the least slowed by the advent of multicultural education, which is too often viewed as a palliative to shortcomings in the educational experiences of African American children.

WHY NOT MULTICULTURAL EDUCATION?

Let me say at the outset that the development of the African-centered pedagogy is an implicit critique of multicultural education. Although I would not disagree with those who argue that multicultural education has been important in the movement for equity in education, I believe that as educational practice, it nonetheless presents more impediments than advantages to the challenge of elevating African American achievement in contemporary public schools in America. The pedagogy presented in the following pages exposes many of the impediments to effective work with African American children that inhere in the contemporary applications of multicultural education to teaching and learning. Many of these impediments occur under the aegis of multicultural education practices. The use of children's literature is one example that I will illustrate presently. Let me introduce this discussion by asking you to reflect for a moment on a couple of critical questions: "Who is multicultural children's literature really for?" Or more specifically, "who is multicultural children's literature designed to benefit educationally?"

There is now a significant and growing multicultural children's literature for a variety of different ethnic and cultural groups. Much of this literature is written for white children to expand them culturally—to broaden their thinking and perspective. Among other things, this kind of literature prepares them for a diverse world and helps them to appreciate differences. As valuable as this literature may be for white children, "experiencing diversity" and "appreciating differences" are not predominate needs for most African American children. To expect them to benefit from this literature in the same way as white children may actually be a detriment to their literacy learning. Under the banner of multicultural education, "teaching for diversity" is too easily equated with pedagogy for African American children. But it is sometimes, perhaps often, counter to what is pedagogically best for the African American child. Let me briefly illustrate this with an example.

Consider the classroom of a "good multicultural teacher" developing a literacy learning program in an urban, underresourced fifth-grade classroom. This teacher is having a portfolio conference with one of her students, an African American boy. This teacher does a great job in setting up the program and children excitedly talk about the contents of their "written responses to the writers" section of their language arts portfolios. These fifth graders are asked to include in their writing portfolios three book reviews on novels they selected from an assigned set provided by the teacher, and then they were to make three additional selections on their own from an open selectives list.

Now, even though this young white teacher had done a superb job of composing a reading list of multicultural children's literature for both the assigned list and the open selectives list, her insistence on diversity was not in the best pedagogical interests of at least one African American student. One young man, having chosen all African American writers from the assigned list, now proposed to read and report on three more for his selectives. The teacher gently tried to persuade the young man to select from among some of the Asian, Puerto Rican, and Native American literature she had skillfully placed on her open selectives list. The young man was adamant in his three additional selections, all by the same African American author—Mildred Taylor. In a final attempt to coax the young man she said, "After all, we're a multicultural school here at Horace Mann. There are all these other cultures to learn about." The young African American boy retorted emphatically, "I *know*, Miz L. But I'm not *multi*. I'm *Black*!"

This vignette illustrates a subtle, but important, critique that this volume makes about multicultural education as it is applied to work with African American children—namely, the detrimental influence that a pervasive diversity agenda has when it eclipses the critical identity work that undergirds powerful literacy learning for African American children. Knowing about diverse people and experiences should not supersede a child's own understanding of self and culture when they are learning (to use Paulo Freire's phrase) to "read the world." Young people need to find meaningful connections among language, literature, and their lived experience. If this young teacher had insisted on the diversity agenda in her multicultural reading program, she would have missed the opportunity to make connections with, and for, this student.

The young man, in his insistence that he was "Black" and not "multicultural" was making his need for a connected pedagogy explicit. By continuing his reading of the series of Mildred Taylor novels, he was doing more than acquiring historical knowledge of the American South during the depression years in his persistence with Mildred Taylor's series. His continuing interest in the saga of Cassie Logan represents identity work—discovering himself and who he strives to become. He was connecting with cultural essences of Blackness through the principles of MAAT (truth, justice, order, reciprocity, harmony, and balance), the core of the African value system represented in the struggles of the Logan family against racial oppression and adversity. These connections have profound meaning for him as he works through the same dilemmas of identity, racial oppression and mature personhood for himself. This is the connected pedagogy the multicultural agenda sometimes disrupts.

It is at this deeper level of understanding that I want us to embark on developing a connected pedagogy as an alternative to multicultural education for African American children. The challenge at this deeper level is to make explicit the important qualities of an African-centered pedagogy for promoting achievement and development of African American children without succumbing to two pitfalls. The first is the pitfall of essentializing African American culture—describing the entirety of African American experience, culture, and heritage as though it comprises an essence that is separate from, and independent of, the rest of America. Although there is a distinctness and integrity to African American culture, we cannot ignore the fact that it is intertwined with the total fabric of American life.

Second, in writing this book I run the risk of creating a dichotomy between African American pedagogical practice on the one hand, and culturally mainstream traditional practice on the other hand. It is always a danger to contrast systems of ideas in this manner because of the natural tendency of human thought to create mutually exclusive categories with which to sort new information. I am opening myself to the criticism that I am advocating "a Black way of teaching that works for Black children." I worry about this over-simplification, especially when I remember the frequency with which I am asked: "Is there an urban pedagogy that is best for teaching Black children?" I always have to listen carefully for what the questioner really wants to know by asking the question—and sometimes I say "yes" and other times "no," in either case elaborating on the response that gets at what really concerns the questioner. For example, sometimes the questioner seems to want access to techniques, strategies, approaches, and activities they can appropriate to transform their practice and be successful with African American children. In that case, my answer is "no" so that I do not contribute to the persistence of "fix it" mentalities that short-circuit the deeper understandings required for accomplished practice. I do not want to perpetuate the myth of the one best system (Tyack, 1974)—that a *single* American approach to education serves all. In any event, the only appropriate, honest, and accurate answer that can be given as a single phrase is that *it depends*: It depends on what the questioners mean, understand, and who they are in that moment of questioning. Most importantly, it depends on what practitioners are *prepared to do* to transform their practice. That preparation requires a systematic detailed explanation. That explanation is the essence of this book.

The system of ideas presented in this book—an African-centered pedagogy for accelerated achievement and development of African American children—is not exclusive to African American teachers and learners. It is not a way of teaching "what works" *just* for Black children. The foundation of the pedagogy I describe in this work is a deep-seated understanding of African American experience, culture, and heritage and the ways that this understanding informs successful teaching of African American children. As you will see, it is not characterized by strategies, but rather as a system of understanding and meaning-making that all children should be exposed to and enriched by. I will not attempt a comprehensive survey of this experience, but limit it to a working system of ideas for teachers. My approach, then, will be to draw selectively upon those elements of African American cultural experience, value systems, and systems of knowing that are most relevant to schooling in America. I focus on those aspects of African American culture that are critical to formulating exemplary pedagogical practices.

A final comment about the use of the term *pedagogy*. I purposely use the term pedagogy rather than "teaching strategies" to connote teacher thought and action that are part of a deliberate attempt to promote the development of young African Americans—both in terms of the knowledge they acquire and the identities they assume. On this account, instruction and pedagogy are by no means synonymous. Pedagogy, as the term is used here, includes teachers' awareness of their own culturally mediated values and biases, as well as an understanding of how success and failure are rooted in larger societal and institutional structures. Without this awareness, teachers may develop what they think is good instruction that creates opportunities for learning, when in fact they may be merely repackaging their own worldview and cultural values. To summarize, then, pedagogy here refers to *a system of practices* that includes systematic, culturally situated, historically grounded reflection and action of the teacher regarding the lives, experiences, intellectual heritage, and cultural legacy of children, their families, and the communities from which they come.

Significant direction to a pedagogy appropriate and responsive to African American culture has been provided by the work of Geneva Gay, Gloria Ladson-Billings, Lisa Delpit, Michele Foster, Jacqueline Jordan Irvine, Joyce King, Barbara Sizemore, and Janice Hale. Although this previous body of work has not yet resulted in a unified set of public school practices that addresses the problems in the education of African American students, it has made those problems central to the debate about education in general and Black achievement in particular. This book is about instituting this important work in the practices of teaching and learning with African American children and youth.

WHY AN AFRICAN-CENTERED PEDAGOGY?

At this point you might be saying to yourself, "Okay, that example with the multicultural children's literature gave me something to think about. But if not multicultural education, *why African-centered pedagogy*?" To begin with, there is a severe disconnection between the needs of African American children and the delivery systems of public schooling in America. This is perhaps the most well established fact in contemporary educational research. Furthermore, there is a substantial research literature showing that, typically, African American students enter primary school with the same enthusiasm to learn and capacity to achieve as well as other students up until third grade. Between the third and sixth grades, all students slow in the rates of academic achievement. However, for African American students the lag is worse and they never close what is called "the achievement gap." This concern is reflected in national conversations, debates, workshops, and policy making regarding the so-called achievement gap—the persistent difference between African American students and European American students on aggregate scores on standardized achievement tests. The disparity continues to grow through middle- and high school (Hedges & Nowell, 1998; Phillips, Crouse, & Ralph, 1998).

The evidence collectively called the achievement gap should suggest to the thoughtful reader a fundamental problem with the educational process for African American children. Whatever it is that diminishes African American students' engagement with learning exists for *all* students as well. The degrading impact of these processes is clearly more pronounced in the academic achievement of African American students. The reasons for these phenomena cannot be justly or fairly laid *only* at the feet of teachers. The forces destructive to African American achievement are embedded in the way we do schooling in America. As much as we would like to believe in American public schools as the great equalizer, it is not reasonable to expect public schools to transform social injustice because they are cut from the same social fabric of American society that has generated the practices of oppression and inequality in its institutions throughout our history. In other words, as a public and as a profession, we do not really see or recognize what is doing the damage to African American children. Therefore, proposing interventions to "close the gap," especially without a pedagogy—without a theory that makes explicit core of cultural practices and social conventions—is certain to simply reproduce the long-standing unequal social, class, and racial relations that exist in America. The same core educational practices that lead to the degradation of Black achievement, if left unchallenged, will continue to educationally disenfranchise African American children in underresourced communities.

I have watched this happen repeatedly in many "start from scratch" school initiatives designed to close the achievement gap over the last two decades—including charter schools and independent public schools. As a teacher educator, I spend a lot of time in schools observing teachers' practice and all too often see Black children victimized by the mediocre practice in public school classrooms. Recently I had the occasion to observe the classroom in a newly formed independent public school. The school's head, upon hearing that I was coming to visit the school, said with an air of pride, "be sure to see Mr. R.'s classroom"—the unofficial master teacher of the school. Well I did, and had I merely read a transcript of the directed discussion he led in the sixth grade language arts classroom on the book *The Diary of Anne Frank*, I might have been quite impressed. Seeing the class, however, told a different story.

During the entire fifty-minute period while Mr. R. led a directed discussion on the book, the five African American boys who were seated in the back of the classroom were neither involved with the instruction nor paying attention. It would have been pointless to castigate the teacher, particularly since some version of this phenomena occurs in virtually every similarly organized classroom setting. The problem is more than just the pedagogical shortcomings of an individual teacher, but rather has its genesis in systems of practice that dominate our public schools. An aspect of these systems is that the disengaged, disinterested, and even disruptive behavior of African American boys is too often accepted as normal or typical in many classrooms.

As I watched in this classroom, the five African American males that were seated in the very last bank of desks were the only five in the class that were never a part of the "discussion" in the entire fifty minutes of the class. One of them talked incessantly to his neighbors; another worked on his illustration the entire time. The others alternated between talking, passing around drawings, wandering around the classroom, and putting their heads down on their desks. When I spoke with Mr. R. afterwards to get his assessment of how the class went, he remarked that he thought it was too noisy and acknowledged that there was misbehavior, but indicated no awareness of particular instances of noninvolvement of the African American students. In short, he saw what transpired as a *discipline* problem, but not as a *pedagogical* problem for the African American children. The subsequent attempts at discipline—changing seats, putting checks on the board, notes home to parents—produced no change in these students performance in class.

I share this as an example because I see some version of this state of affairs in virtually every urban classroom I visit. My point is that under our current system, one can be considered a "good teacher" and still not be effective with African American learners in urban communities. In many cases, the teachers are quite able and in many respects do fine work. In this example of Mr. R. and the previous example of Ms. L's multicultural literature program described previously, most people would see instances of conscientious practice. Yet without my *appraisal of practice*, both would have contributed to the educational disenfranchisement of their African American students.

There is a seemingly obvious but frequently overlooked point here about what constitutes successful practice—successful practice requires success outcomes for all children. For example, most people who read a transcript of the discourse in Mr. R.'s class would conclude that he was a skillful teacher. But the transcript of a rich discourse with a handful of participants did not reflect the fact that the African American males in the classroom were, at no point, participants in that discourse or connected with the learning. So it should be understood that otherwise capable, conscientious, and well-meaning teachers make choices that result in negative experiences of schooling for African American students, and that this happens all the time. Worse than this, these negative experiences go unrecognized, unseen, and unchecked only to manifest later in "behavior problems" and "achievement gap" phenomena. How do we prepare ourselves as teachers to ensure that this does not happen? Something alternative to what we currently do is called for if we are to work effectively with the young African American students.

The core of that alternative lies in a systematic understanding of the cultural and conceptual framework out of which teachers of African American children develop and grow. There are a set of core values and practices of contemporary public education, shared by culturally mainstream middle-class teachers in America, that are inimical to the education of African American children. These core values are embedded in what many of us learned to refer to as the "hidden curriculum." If I were to give you an assessment of how well we have dealt with this problem, as the collective of professional educators in the United States, I would say this: We know that there are aspects of schooling in America that are inimical to the achievement and development of African American children, but we have yet to put that knowledge into practice.

AN ECOLOGICAL PERSPECTIVE

Current and contemporary teaching practice in urban schools lacks a pedagogy that takes full account of the cultural and social dimensions of the developmental issues of African American learners on three planes. These three developmental planes are: (1) the *intrapersonal* or individual level that includes cognitive development, identity development, and character development; (2) the *interpersonal* level that includes the development of the individual's capacity to participate in social systems including the family, peer group, church, classroom, soccer team, and other social networks; and (3) the *cultural symbolic* level that incorporates the world of culturally and politically defined meanings and would include the major developmental task of forming a robust racial and cultural identity.

We have a research literature and a foundation of scholarship for each of these levels. What we do not have is a conceptual framework integrating and synthesizing what we know about development *across* these three developmental venues for the purpose of elevating the achievement of African American children and youth. The challenge I take up in these pages is that of providing the conceptual framework that synthesizes an understanding of practice at three levels of inquiry. These are: (1) a microlevel practice addressing intra-personal development of the individual learners in classroom contexts; (2) a mesolevel practice addressing interpersonal development of the relationships constituting the social, cultural, and professional fabric of the school community; and (3) the macrolevel practice addressing symbolic-cultural development of broader institutional, neighborhood, family, and support systems.

Of the three levels of development/synthesis, the individual level is most developed in educational theory, and the cultural symbolic is the least developed. More will be said later about these levels. The point here is that we need theory and practice that does not merely address these domains one at a time, but rather integrates them into a "big picture" for successfully informing teaching practice for African American children. For example, I have been critical of the learning styles and cognitive styles literature, not because it is unimportant to recognize diversity in the interpersonal development of individuals, but because this framework fails to integrate the social, cultural, political, and experiential features of development. The limitation and the danger of this level of inquiry that only recognizes difference is that it locates the issue of achievement only in the individual, failing to take full account of contextual factors and historical realities that shape human behavior and the social systems in which they operate. If we were to develop pedagogy for African American children only on the basis of learning styles and cognitive styles, we would be recreating new versions of a deficit model. This version would be based on two categories of traits—one category is the general learning style ascribed to African American children and the other ascribed to mainstream European American children.

The most basic trait in learning styles theory has to do with the basic approach to interpreting the world, which, according to the original theory, is either *relational* or *analytic* (Cohen, 1969; Witkin, 1967). Accordingly, African American children are ascribed "relational traits" and European American children are ascribed "analytical traits". Because public schooling, by and large, is organized to support the development of individuals who are more "analytic" in their cognitive/learning styles, our approach then would be to find ways to make school contexts more consonant with African-centered "relational" styles (Hale-Benson, 1986; Shade, 1982). But there are still profound virulent forces that remain invisible, even as we are able to recognize, reveal and incorporate understanding of culturally shaped cognitive styles. These have to do with the ideology of public school.

Popular cultural values are at least as important in the determination human development as individual styles. Moreover, there are popular American values that are inimical to the achievement of diverse populations of students. These values inhere in the form of popular American myths—of meritocracy, of the rugged individual (who "pull themselves up by their bootstraps"), and of the universal standard ("the one best system"). But the values also persist in the unarticulated and unexamined assumptions—such as the subtle equation of Blackness with underachievement. I think that the invisibility of Black children's plight, including Black children's progressive disengagement with schooling—is due to the tacit acceptance of this equation.

We certainly need to pay attention to the cultural features, qualities, and cognitive styles of African American children in working to elevate the quality of their schooling experience and achievement outcomes. But this attention is insufficient to improving schooling without a consistent, ongoing, deeper critical analysis that *situates our practice* in the appropriate social, cultural, and historical context. More significant than individual traits are the cultural, ideological, and political disconnections between the system of values and practices in public education and the cultural patterns of African Americans. This is addressed at length in chapters 1 and 2 to follow. For the present, it is important to note that educators have taken notice of the core American values and tacit practices that shape schooling to the detriment of effective schooling. Elmore (1996) discusses some of these as core educational practices and analyzes how they prevent school reform efforts.

Core educational practices include patterns of thought and procedures that are found in virtually every school. They are so ubiquitous and widely accepted that they rarely are recognized as anything other than the "traditional approach." Some of the perspectives include: a view of knowledge as discrete bits of information; a view of student achievement as being the degree of information acquisition as demonstrated by the quality of their recall and ability to reproduce the information they were given; and a view of teaching that assumes ability grouping is good practice. Elmore (1996) argues that our tacit adherence to these familiar and well-worn notions of schooling is what prevents school reform initiatives from taking hold. The disconnection between successful pedagogy for African American children and these core educational practices are already severe. Add then to this other "conventions of core schooling" including the silence and silencing on issues of race (Fine, 1991) and the disproportionate negative impact of high stakes standardized testing for children of color (Steele, 1997).

TOWARD AN AFRICANIST DEFINITION OF PEDAGOGY

As a profession, we are still just beginning a serious examination of the human and institutional systems that subvert academic success for African American children and youth in public schools. The tradition of American education and educational psychology is to focus on the individual, and achievement only as individual capacity without sufficient regard as to how the social and cultural environment of individuals profoundly shapes their performance. The development of the ecological perspective of Urie Bronfenbrenner (1979) was the first real acknowledgement of this idea. Though there are various articulations of, and references to, the ecological model (some of which will be discussed presently), the work of leveraging change in public schools is yet uncoordinated, disjointed, and disconnected from the knowledge of effective practice with African American children.

An African-centered pedagogy is necessary to appropriately address the social, cultural, and historical context of the schooling experience of African American children and the disconnection between African American cultural heritage and contemporary educational practice. Recent work in cultural psychology and urban educational ethnography has shown how analyses of the social, cultural, linguistic, and political situation of students of color in public schools helps explain underachievement. So we do have a research literature on the intrapersonal level of development. We know now how important it is to take all of a child's life experiences into account and that the child's academic and personal development occurs most fruitfully in settings that ally with the family and draw on community strengths.

There is a less sizeable research on the interpersonal level of human development, including the social and cultural contexts of the individual. The most useful instance of this kind of theory is called the ecological approach. Some of this theory is relevant to the African-centered pedagogy. In particular, the work of James Comer applies the ecological theory to the development of systems of practice in schools to improve the learning and development of African American children in underresourced communities. Also relevant is the work of John Ogbu and Signithia Fordham (Fordham & Ogbu, 1986), who apply ecological theory as an explanation of Black underachievement and racial identity development. Smaller still is the body of research literature that theorizes achievement on the cultural symbolic level of development and the examination of systems and institutions in the historical context of African American experience.

Though it is essential for theory to examine Black achievement in light of the social, cultural, political, and historical constitution of the contexts of schools and schooling, only a handful of theorists have done so. It is our understanding of the cultural symbolic level of development and our critical examination of schooling in historical context that is essential for refashioning successful schooling for African American children. Exemplars of this approach include the recent work of Kofi Lomotey, Mwalimu Shujaa, Nah Dove, Etta Hollins, John Ogbu, and Signithia Fordham in Black achievement, and the work of Ken Zeichner, Gloria Ladson-Billings, Joyce King, and Lois Weiner who extend this work in teacher preparation.

There are other reasons, besides the insufficiency of traditional theory, why a unifying African-centered pedagogical theory is timely. First, there are contestable issues of schooling and education that need to be resolved to advance substantive school improvement. In the absence of a framework that critically interrogates the hidden but harmful instructional and curricular practices, they are certain to continue to harm African American children. The nexus of these issues can be captured by the question, "How does traditional educational pedagogy perpetuate the underachievement of students of color?" This is the question that is continuously asked in an African-centered pedagogy, but that rarely surfaces in contemporary educational practice.

A case in point is the standardized testing movement. With the fervor over closing the achievement gap, too few interrogate the ways in which high stakes testing regularly undercuts accomplished practice. I witnessed the gradual but complete demise of an African-centered school, whose failure to critically interrogate the high-stakes standardized testing movement destroyed the best qualities of its African-centered pedagogy. The school, which had been chartered on a program of responsive pedagogy and achievement for African American children, embraced a program of "teaching to the test" in relation to the recently mandated statewide test of achievement that is supposed to assess student achievement progress on statewide content curriculum standards. In an effort to elevate test scores and align the curriculum with the statewide standardized achievement test, the curriculum, along with overall student performance took a nosedive because the practices that really helped students were scarified to the mandates of teaching to the frameworks.

The fervor over high-stakes testing attests to the second reason why a unifying African-centered pedagogy is timely. It concerns the failure of public education to critically examine the ideologies and cultural values of American education that work against the interests of children of color (see Darder,

1991, pp. 1–22 for an excellent discussion of these ideologies). Large-scale initiatives driving educational reform (i.e., the standards movement and the professionalization of teaching) unfortunately fail on this account. Despite the undisputed value that the ecological or holistic perspective has had on recent efforts to improve the quality of urban teaching, its insufficiency persists because it still focuses on systems of schooling as opposed to systems of education. This distinction between schooling and education has always been a powerful defining emblem in the collective experience of Africans in America (Shujaa, 1992; 1994), as you will see in chapter 2.

The African-centered pedagogy in these pages is designed to bridge the chasm between the needs of African American children's performance on the one hand, and current teaching practices on the other hand. The aim is to link the heritage of cultural practices and learning practices in the African American experience with the immediate school experiences of African American students in ways that promote their development as well as achievement. If we take the ethical and moral purposes of education seriously, we will look much more carefully at the assumptions, as well as the practices and policies, that are inimical to Black achievement. The tasks of educating African American children are especially difficult in the context of "traditional" American cultural folkways, because the oppression and degradation of Black people are embedded in the social fabric of American life, culture, and ideology. The popular American ideologies that will need to be critically examined include, for example: *rugged individualism* ("pull yourself up by your bootstraps"); *childhood determinism* (your adult potential is determined by the quality of your childhood experience); *innate ability* (your ability is determined by your genetic inheritance); *environmental determinism* (i.e., Black children do not achieve because their social environments are inferior); and *merit by competition* ("only the best students deserve the best opportunities"). These implicit beliefs underlie much of educational theorizing and policy, and support White supremacist logics that fuel the oppression and degradation of people of color. Recognizing that racism is an everyday fact of American life, and has everyday impacts that are made everyday, is the first step to systematically interrogating ideologies of repression, which is the goal of African-centered pedagogy.

The African-centered pedagogy in these pages develops *systems of practice* that promote development and achievement for all children, but are focused on the needs, lives, and culture of African American children. To understand the social-cultural context of schools in relation to the achievement of African American children is to understand the human systems that make up school practices. A successful pedagogy interprets the school-community dynamic as an ecosocial system constrained by psychological need (intrapersonal), social demands (interpersonal) and bureaucratic constraints (cultural symbolic). In order to understand the patterns of values, beliefs and traditions that are central to the operation of a school-community, an analysis of culture at both the individual and collective level is necessary.

I deliberately use the term *pedagogy* to denote the unity of teaching and learning as it is grounded in human experience and history and to contradict the traditional view of pedagogy as the application of the latest educational theory, techniques, or research findings. The unity of reflection and activity is a way of thinking about pedagogy and particularly important for effective instruction with African American children. This way of thinking contests contemporary educational thought and the tendency teachers sometimes have of viewing their instructional activity and students' learning achievement as independent of one another. This way of thinking also contests teachers' tendency to view diversity from a lens that assumes their own culture to be universal. Although in contemporary practice teaching and learning are talked about as though they were *independent*, I argue that effective practice requires that they be understood as *unitary*. This is an expression of a disposition held by Africanist educators and critical theorists, and is the anchoring principle of the African-centered pedagogy in this book.

This theory views teaching and learning as a unitary activity and adopts an interactionist conception of teacher and learner engagement. The theory views teaching and learning as a joint activity where teacher and learner have mutual participation but different roles. The teacher's actions and the students' actions are interdependent, codependent and jointly determine the learning achievements of students as well as the pedagogical acumen of the teacher. On this account, teaching consists of those actions on the part of the teacher that resulted in students' learning. If nothing of the teacher's activity resulted in some advance in the development or learning achievement of the students, then that teacher has not yet taught.

Why is this perspective on pedagogy—*teaching and learning as unitary*—so important to the African-centered pedagogy developed in these pages? To believe otherwise—that one can have taught without students having learned something—is the first step to a "blame the victim" mentality. The teacher who laments "I did my best teaching, but they didn't learn anything!" has taken another step down this road. Currently, the epistemological frame underlying practices in public schooling in America makes it very easy to take these steps because there is no unification of teaching and learning, particularly in underresourced urban schools. The history of urban public education for African American children and other children of color might well be characterized by the lament, "I taught them but they didn't (or won't) learn."

From the perspective of the Africanist tradition, as well as from that of critical theory (a pedagogical perspective developed by Paulo Freire, Henry

Giroux, and others) there could not possibly have been teaching if there was no learning achievement. True teaching always results in demonstrable outcomes. The evidence of teaching is in students' development and achievement as learners, and their agency and consciousness as citizens. Invariably, teachers respond to my question, "What are your students learning these days?" by describing what *they* "covered" or "lectured on" or "talked about." I often repeat the question, prefaced by saying, "You answered a different question—I didn't ask what you did in an effort to teach, I asked what your students are learning." This need to rephrase the focus on achievement outcomes illustrates how the conventional understanding of teaching is disconnected from learning results. It will take a connected pedagogy—a system of thought to change this subtle and unconscious mindset that separates the activity of teaching from learning activity and outcomes. African-centered pedagogy is a connected pedagogy that happens to focus on African American children in public school.

In the next three chapters it will become apparent why the timing for the development of an African-centered connected pedagogy is opportune. Recent paradigm shifts in academic disciplines of sociology, cognitive and cultural psychology, anthropology, linguistics, and critical theory, offer an opportunity to develop a connected pedagogy. These shifts in the traditional paradigms of these academic disciplines offer a new perspective and rich theory fully addressing the largely unacknowledged challenges to Black achievement. These paradigm shifts provide the basis for new ways of understanding the social, historical, cultural, and contextualized nature of learning, thinking, and practice that emerge from human activity (Wenger, 1998). The common strand is *situated learning theory* that focuses on the socially and culturally contextualized nature of learning, thinking, teaching, and achievement. The operating assumption is that social practice is the fundamental process by which we learn and become who we are. The importance of this approach to African-centered pedagogy is that the premise of situated learning theory is also the central premise of the pedagogy: namely, that human learning is a social activity, not just an individual one. More specifically, they share the premise that knowledge accrues through the lived practices of a people and that *inter*personal learning is as essential as *intra*personal learning.

Several other key principles flow from the convergence of situated activity theory and African-centered pedagogical theory, and these were described earlier in the Preface. To reiterate, the first principle is that good teachers create the cultural and intellectual environment for the development of knowledge, character, identity, and consciousness in their classrooms. This is an awesome responsibility and an incredible investment of power. If you doubt the power that we have as teachers to indelibly shape young people, think of all of the ordinary experiences that stand out in your memory as extraordinary moments of learning, and how you never forgot those teachers who made these moments happen.

For African American students and from an African-centered perspective, being a teacher implies a much deeper role and function than most people attribute to the classroom teacher. A Kiswahili term for this complete teacher is *mwalimu*; the term I have coined elsewhere (Murrell, 2001) and will use here is *community teacher*. From the perspective of my theory, community teachers are those who bring moments of clarity to children as they struggle to make sense of the world as they experience school. The community teacher is as mindful of children's development as human beings, as cultural beings, and critical thinkers as he or she is about their school lessons. African-centered pedagogy consist, in part, of building a community that systematically introduces these moments of profound change and discovery, rich with new meanings and interpretations of the world that contest and contradict those based in their experience outside of the school context. This idea will be developed further as the notion of the *community of practice* in chapters 2, 3 and 4.

The second principle is that the experience of schooling, put simply, must be educational. That is to say, schools ought to promote the development of young people and steward them into capable, caring, and character-rich adulthood. In any routinized, bureaucratically controlled process (namely, public schooling), it is easy to lose sight of the purpose and meaning of daily activity (namely, education). Schools are no exception. In order to prefigure the intellectual life of your classroom to promote a world of learning, inquiry and achievement, you will need to understand the deep structure of African American culture, history, language, and life well enough to appropriate it in the structuring of the classroom intellectual environment. It is within this community of our own making that we, as teachers, organize the challenges that promote academic achievement and personal development.

We know from developmental psychology that negotiating meaning and confronting challenges are important to young people's development. The disequilibrium created by this contestation and conflict of world views, and the subsequent meaning-making, is an essential process for cognitive development (Piaget and Vygotsky), social growth (E. Erickson and A. Wilson) and robust identity formation (Darder, 1991; Garrod, et al., 1999). Therefore, a program for successful teaching and learning—connected pedagogy—has to be more than a matter of strategies and teaching techniques. For African American children and other children of color, the connected pedagogy must effectively challenge the hidden curriculum and expose the ways in which the African American experience is tacitly degraded in schools. W. E. B. DuBois, Carter Woodson, Mary McCleod Bethune, and Fredrick Douglass all affirmed the idea that connected pedagogy for African American children must be (as it has been for centuries) a fundamentally subversive activity with respect to the cultural values of education mainstream America. This subversion is not merely contestation; it is the creation of a *figured world* based on the intellectual and cultural heritage of African Americans.

Accomplished teachers of African American children understand education viewed as a broader process than schooling—as a total process of promoting the intellectual, spiritual, ethical, and social development of young people, and the stewarding them into capable, caring, and character-rich adults. Accomplished teachers of African American children also are critical consumers of contemporary curriculum, educational policy, and instructional practice, and interrogate them as a matter of daily practice by asking, "How does this practice or policy perpetuate the underachievement of African American learners?" The daily practice of the accomplished teacher must involve deconstructing the ways that traditional pedagogy and current instructional paradigms perpetuate underachievement of children of color.

TWO PHASES TO CONNECTED AFRICAN-CENTERED PEDAGOGY

There are at least two phases for developing a system of successful teaching and learning for African American learners. Phase one is developing responsiveness to the children in front of us by inviting them into a figured world of inquiry. That is, we want the social world of our classroom to be culturally inviting and intellectually vibrant to all of our students, but the task of providing this for African American students in today's society requires specific reconceptualization of our pedagogy. More will be said in a moment in the discussion of culturally responsive teaching. Phase two is the ongoing work of building the community of inquiry that will contest the hidden barriers and build the supports for learning and achievement.

How to enact each of these two phases is what this book is about. The central idea of this book is that work on behalf of African American students is more than simply challenging *what is*, but prefiguring *what should be* in the intellectual, social, and cultural lives of children. Hence, merely responding or being responsive to the learning styles and issues of African American children is only half of the battle. The other half of the battle is creating the figured world of African American culture and intellectual life that invites the participation, development, and achievement of African American children. Aspects of culture that need to be a part of this equation need to be brought to children, their families, and communities.

The framework known as culturally responsive teaching mentioned briefly above (which also referred to as culturally relevant, culturally synchronous, and culturally compatible teaching) is important as a foundation for developing a connected pedagogy for African American children, but does not take us far enough. The insufficiency is not with the idea, but in the *application* of the idea in development of practice for the majority of teachers who are not African American. For most teachers, the difficulty in applying the framework is twofold. First, as mentioned above, developing culturally responsive practice is difficult when you are at the beginning stages of understanding the historical struggle for quality education for African American children. Secondly, for many teachers it is too difficult to avoid dichotomization of "mainstream" versus "African American" cultural experience. Having said that, I hasten to point out that some dichotomization has been necessary for descriptive purposes in simply articulating the framework.

Some of the most important earlier work on effective pedagogy for African American children describes, defines, and characterizes culturally responsive pedagogy in contrast with mainstream pedagogy. For example, the work of Gloria Ladson-Billings distinguishes culturally responsive education practice from what African American students currently experience in more traditional settings. With this foundation, we can move to phase two—creating a figured world of African American culture and intellectual life. In other words, we can now articulate a system of pedagogy for effective work with African American children that stands on its own, in order to avoid the destructive counterpositioning of "Blackness" to "academic achievement." With an African-centered pedagogy, we can deal with the unfortunate counterpositioning of "Blackness" to "excellence," as for example, when Ladson-Billings writes:

> The primary aim of culturally relevant teaching is to assist in the development of a "relevant black personality" that allows African American children to choose academic excellence yet still identify with African and African American culture. (1994, p. 17)

If we do phase two right we will have obviated the need for such a choice, because intellectual life and cultural traditions of African Americans will be the context for young people's educational experience.

SUMMARY OVERVIEW

We have gone as far as we can go by repeatedly asking questions that only center on the *qualities* of the individual teacher, without examining *practices* in the actual contexts and settings involving work with African American children. We know what they are—for example, teachers need to "know their stuff," be connected with the students, and center learning with the needs, interests, and current proficiencies of learners. But we cannot predicate our effort to elevate academic achievement and the quality of education for African American children on lists of qualities such as these. Without contextualizing these qualities in systems of practice, we will continue the same mistakes made by the overly technist, Western-oriented epistemologies that dichotomize theory and practice and divorce knowledge skills and dispositions from the contexts in which teachers draw on them to promote learning. Our focus now needs to be, not just on teacher knowledge, but on knowledge-in-practice. Coaching is a powerful analogy to teaching; a teacher is someone who knows how to improve a batter's swing or how to improve a diver's form. That coach is the teacher who focuses on practice—not on things unrelated to the actions of hitting and diving.

Identifying the characteristics of successful practice of teachers of African American children is, and will continue to be, critically important. Everyone needs to know about, and be reminded of, the qualities of successful practice. However, specifying teacher qualities alone is insufficient and incomplete as a means of developing connected pedagogy for African American children. There is a far cry between knowing the qualities of successful teachers, and knowing how to incorporate them in one's own practice.

It is not of much use to talk about the knowledge, skills, and dispositions necessary for successful work with children, African American children in particular, unless they are instituted in practice. Neither is it much use to talk about this sort of teacher ability apart from the social situation and the cultural context in which they are deployed. Evaluation of a teacher's pedagogical knowledge, instructional design, or teacher-student interaction have little meaning unless they can be interpreted from all of the frames that matter—the cultural, historical, and social context of the teaching and learning activity.

In this vein, the African-centered pedagogy presented in the following pages moves past listing characteristics of the practice of effective Black teachers and toward constructing a system of practice. But without embedding the principles of culturally responsive teaching in a system of practice—such as African-centered pedagogy—they remain prescriptive lists. We need more than lists of the qualities of accomplished practice, and move to an understanding of accomplished practice itself. To do that, we have to understand situated knowledge in practice.

Marilyn Cochran-Smith (1996) asks what it means to teach in ways that are culturally responsive, linguistically appropriate, and academically rigorous. She synthesizes five general features or qualities of practice:

1. Enabling significant work within communities of learners who share responsibility for learning but [providing learners] with strong adult leadership.
2. Building on what students bring to school with them—knowledge and interests, as well as cultural and linguistic resources.
3. Making activism, power, and inequity, explicit parts of the curriculum. That is, making them discussible in schools and demonstrated in teacher lives professional and personal.
4. Teaching skills and bridging gaps [in the academic proficiencies of students]. That is, helping students connect the known to the unknown, [and] current skills to new ones in order to enable them [the learners] to negotiate the power structure and the codes of the system, but also to learn to critique the system itself.
5. Working with, not against, individuals, families, and communities—or drawing family and community resources, demonstrating respect and consciously avoiding becoming a wedge between students and their families.

This synthesis of five qualities of practice is useful for articulating an African-centered pedagogy—a theory of teaching practice—because they provide a foundation for articulating the system of theory and practice for successful work with African American children. So we have ultimately and finally realized that the development of effective practices are locally situated, culturally contextualized, and historically rooted. But, again, it is a summary—a synthesis of qualities that need to be realized in a system of practice. To this list, I added three principles of practice that specify the agenda for an African-centered pedagogy. These were as follows:

- Accomplished teachers of African American children create the context, environment, and cultural community in their classrooms that provide the social and intellectual worlds for learners where rich moments of discovery, learning and development take place.
- Accomplished teachers of African American children understand the distinction between education and schooling, which Shujaa makes in an excellent essay (1994, pp. 13–37): Education is a broader process than schooling—and it is education that African American children really need. Education is understood as a total process of promoting the intellectual, spiritual, ethical and social development of young people, and the stewarding them into capable, caring, and character-rich adulthood.

- To be able to create the appropriate context and cultural community, the figured world of learning and achievement, the teacher must access and understand the deep structure of African American culture, history, language, and life.

The remainder of this book is to develop an African-centered pedagogy as a system of practice according to these principles. Let me conceptualize the pedagogy as two levels of depth—I called them *phase one* and *phase two*. Level one pedagogy is constituted by methodology. The competent phase one teacher is proficient at designing lessons, running a classroom, and has mastered the organization and structure of teaching practice. An excellent example of a phase one pedagogical system is the teaching for understanding framework (Wiggins & McTighe, 1998; Wiske, 1998). Currently, teacher preparation programs focus exclusively pedagogy at phase one. This is not a bad thing, only insufficient for children of color because deeper analysis and preparation is needed.

But there is a deeper phase of practice, phase two, characterized by a deeper structural understanding of teaching practice and instructional process in institutional, cultural, historical, and political context. It requires a deep understanding of the social, political, and historical context of education. Excellent examples of phase two pedagogy include culturally relevant pedagogy (e.g., Irvine, 1990; Ladson-Billings, 1994) and critical pedagogy (Darder, 1991; McLaren, 1989). African-centered pedagogy developed in these pages is both a phase one and phase two pedagogy.

PART I

Framing the Work

CHAPTER ONE

THE WRONG FRAMES FOR THE RIGHT PROBLEM

> What manner of education will provide African-Americans with the voice to sing the scared liturgy of their own culture? What manner of education will mold the African personality to thrive in a culture that demeaned its character, denied its existence and coordinated in its destruction? How shall we sing our sacred song in a strange land? This is the fundamental contradiction that stands before African-centered pedagogy in the United States.
>
> —Carol D. Lee, *African-Centered Pedagogy: Complexities and Possibilities*

> Schooling is a process intended to perpetuate and maintain the society's existing power relations and the institutional structures that support those arrangements. Education, in contrast to schooling, is the process of transmitting from one generation to the next knowledge of the values, aesthetics, spiritual beliefs, and all things that give a particular cultural orientation its uniqueness.
>
> —Mwalimu Shujaa

Writing this book has been, in a sense, a journey home. It has been a process of coming to a deep sense of quality education from a belated (but intentional) rediscovery of African American intellectual and cultural traditions. Who I am as an educator is a reflection of the wisdom and educational experience of my mother and father. Who I am as an educator is, therefore, also a reflection of the struggles of my parents to get an education. My mother grew up and attended public school in the urban north in Pittsburgh, Pennsylvania. My father grew up and attended public school in Glasgow, Kentucky. Both came up in the era of segregation and their respective experiences epitomize the two metaphors of Black achievement in a northern industrial setting and a southern, small town segregated setting. The contrast of experiences in a Jim Crow southern town and a larger northern industrial city is key in the construction of who I am as an educator.

It is a coming of age as an African American educator—first as a high school teacher, then as a community college instructor, and finally as a university professor—that I experienced a gradual rekindling of a truly Africanist conception of Black education. Preparing this book was the realization of a sojourn away from a northern, culturally mainstream education with no cultural Black presence—indeed, no Black people for the most part (I did not have a Black teacher until graduate school). That sojourn was toward truly African-centered educational practice through the cultural ways of African Americans as represented in the southern roots of my parents and kin. The sojourn is one of coming to cultural ways of African Americans as the progeny of a northern school system entering the figured world of southern Black educational traditions.

My first inklings that there was a rich cultural integrity to African American perspective on education was in an African American Baptist Church and the experience of learning in Sunday School and the comparisons to public school. The congregation, probably the oldest in Milwaukee at that time, was constituted almost entirely of recent émigrés from Arkansas, Mississippi, and other southern states. The Sunday school teachers were not professionally trained teachers. Their approach to teaching the "text of the day" would probably elicit criticism from professional educators regarding ways of improving their "delivery of the content." Despite whatever they lacked in formal teacher training, the experience of the "lesson" from these Sunday school teachers was noticeably richer than anything I experienced in the public school. At the time I really noticed the this richness of meaning—I really thought about the text and its meaning—something I did much less well in school.

The public school I attended was all White. My sister and I were the first African American children to attend the school. I started in kindergarten and my sister in third grade. I noticed, even at this young age, the contrast in my Sunday school experience to the then highly regarded elementary school. The school was bright and well-resourced with the best teachers. The rooms were spacious, the books new, and the materials plentiful. In contrast, the church basement was dark and smelled of mildew in the damp corners serving as the storage areas. It seemed decidedly unlike school: The set up was a series of metal folding chairs in one of four partitions in the basement, rudely cordoned off with old blackboards. The "classrooms" of Sunday school were made thus.

In place of new books there were pamphlets containing the day's lesson that we often had to share with a partner. The pamphlets contained a parable for us to read, discuss, and link to scripture.

Despite the stark physical differences, I had a sense that the more powerful learning experience was taking place in the Black Baptist Church. Despite my child's preference for the bright, spacious classroom of my public school, I was powerfully drawn to the literacy learning experience in Sunday school. Even at that young age, I understood that the difference was not a matter of teaching expertise, per se. One experience seemed real and the other did not. By real, I mean *in the world*—a glimpse of the panorama of human conditions, such as it was in Milwaukee in the 1950s and 1960s. Most importantly, keenly aware as I was of race, it seemed more real in that it was context of Black doings—activity on learning, development, spiritual renewal, and communion. My daily experience in public school, by contrast, was characterized by an implacable negotiation of place—a safe place unassailed by the constant indignities of racism. Both seemed to me microcosms of the "real world" beyond the home and family. Both seemed to hold out challenges to me for belonging and becoming. But only one seemed real in the authenticity of human values and human struggle toward those values. Only one seemed like the home to which I had never been.

Two major themes of the Black cultural experience that are central to education—double vision/consciousness and resistance through which achievement is realized. In my two figured worlds (see Holland, Lachicotte, Skinner, & Cain, 1998, pp. 41–42)—the African American Sunday School and the racially homogeneous public school—these themes were transfigured in different ways. The African American figured world was a context that aided the resolution of my identity conflicts, and gave greater meaning to the struggle. The white, public school figured world did just the reverse: it shut down any expectations I had that it would ever deal with what mattered to me and my people. The irony though, is that the contrast between the two worlds helped resolve the dual-consciousness dilemma enough to achieve academically. It was the contrast that proved to be an important stimulus to my growth and development, and much of it had to do with finding an identity I could live with. As the only Black student in your cohort, you get to be the exception. You get to be the "credit to your race" and forever labor under the responsibility of being a good representative for Black people—to be a model and emissary to white people who otherwise had not had exposure to anyone unlike themselves.

Let me pose a couple of questions to readers at this point to focus your reflection on the significance of this experience. Have you ever had to be an emissary for your race? Have you ever been given cause to even think about your race in the context of school? What is it like for children who labor under an emissary identity (for an excellent treatment of these questions, see Garrod, Ward, Robinson, & Kilkenny, 1999). For me, the resolution of the two central themes in African American educational experience—resistance to assaults on my African American identity and the dilemma of belonging due to the double-consciousness DuBois described—was through academic achievement. This was the perfect adaptation for an African American student in all-White school situations. Knowing that the full and authentic membership among groups of white, working-class German and Polish children was unlikely, it was a source of comfort to have a position to occupy on the periphery as "one of the good ones"—position legitimated by the "good Negro syndrome."

Academic achievement allowed me to occupy the role of "the exception" in the face of virulent racism. I found relative safety in the role of the "credit to my race" but labored under the responsibility of being a "good representative for Black people"—the model and emissary to white people who otherwise had not exposure to Black people. In my first year of teaching in an all-Black junior-senior high school, I began taking graduate courses in educational psychology, counseling psychology, school psychology, and anything that would provide me a greater understanding and expertise. I placed my faith in the educational system despite my growing skepticism that it simply did not work for African Americans as a whole people. I remember thinking that if I could just find the right course that would put it all together, my faith in education as the great equalizer could be restored.

I entered graduate school in school psychology right around the time of the famous *Wilson Riles v. the State of California*, a court case in which the use of IQ tests to place African American children in special education classes was contested by a class action lawsuit. Upon understanding more profoundly the role of school psychologists in the proliferation of the American system of sort-and-select, I changed programs and entered counseling psychology. Here again was a litany of courses that seemed to provide studies and theories and frameworks that merely supported the obvious, but addressed not at all the persistent underachievement of African American students in public schools.

Gradually I found that the most significant lessons that supported my success as a teacher did not come from schooling, but from an understanding of African American people, culture, and history. Gradually I understood that effective work with the people public schooling serves least well is absolutely the right problem. My educational career since my early days of teaching has been, in various forms, battling with the wrong frames and approaches to that problem.

What system of practices is needed for African American children and youth that will enrich learning and development in urban public schools?

That is the question the African-centered pedagogy addresses in this volume. I need to say at the outset that this a difficult undertaking. We are talking here about developing a system of practice that cuts against the grain of contemporary thinking on teaching, learning, schooling, and Black achievement. The history of African Americans and their struggle for history is an important background for this thinking because, in a profound sense, the heritage of African Americans already cuts against this grain of the contemporary educational schooling practices in America that have failed its populations of African American children in urban communities. This is the reason that there has to be the foundation of a successful connected pedagogy for African American children.

A careful read of American history shows how closely tied restricted access to quality education is to the social control of African populations in this hemisphere, particularly African Americans, as we will see in chapter 2. The idea of questioning the ontological assumptions of our institutions of education ought to be a foundational given as we examine how tasks associated with Black achievement get framed in the public and educational discourse. Although there are a number of social, political, cultural, and historical factors to Black achievement, the nexus of all these factors is located in the professional practices of a teacher, which is where we will focus our attention.

A SYSTEM OF SCHOOLS IN CRISIS

Currently, urban public school systems are still failing African American children in epidemic proportions. Nationwide, African American students are disproportionately expelled, suspended, and referred to special education programs in urban public schools. African American students lag behind Euro-American students in high school completion and employment. The statistics belie the fact that huge numbers of African American students are not even in this test-taking picture. Significant numbers of African American students, and other students of color, drop out of school—as much as one-half to two-thirds in some city districts. Fewer than ten percent of African American men go to college, yet they constitute 76 percent of the nation's prison population. More African American young people drop out of high school than graduate. This number will only increase with recent passing of a federal education bill that calls for the use of standardized tests for determining whether students can complete school.

The current national response to this state of affairs is an agenda to close what is called the "achievement gap." Generally speaking, this refers to the persistent and predictable difference in the aggregated average test score performance of African Americans as compared to European Americans on standardized measure of achievement. African Americans and Hispanics make up a disproportionately large percentage of lowest-performing students and a disproportionately small percentage of those achieving at the highest levels. The gap is most pronounced among test takers of higher socioeconomic status. For example, according to the recently released report of the College Board's National Task Force on Minority Student Achievement, the 1994 NEAP reading test for twelfth graders, African American students whose parents graduated from college had an average score of thirty points below whites with college-educated parents. The gap between whites and blacks with less formal education, by contrast, ranged from sixteen to twenty-five points. As I noted earlier, this gap between "minority" and White achievement starts in the first grade, widens significantly by the third, and remains stubborn throughout college and graduate school. Even those African Americans who get good grades in high school show a drop-off in grade point average once in college.

In my own community of Boston, African American students and Hispanic students fare particularly poorly. One of the primary standardized tests administered by the Boston Public Schools to determine achievement performance is the Stanford 9. Achievement performance is scored on a one to four point scale. A performance level 1 is Below Basic (below grade level) whereas performance level 4 is Advanced Student, or a student that exceeds required standards. Statistics released by the district as of this writing reveal that African American eleventh graders comprise only 2 percent of those who performed *above* the lowest level 1. Results are identical for Hispanics.

Thoughtful urban educators who have been working to improve the quality of education for these children have long argued that the crisis in urban schools requires a more sophisticated response than that of "tooling up teachers" and "raising the bar" for students. It is beyond dispute that the standardized testing industry is part of the mechanism of social inequality. Any system that participates in the sorting and selecting of children and their opportunities based upon some ostensibly "objective measure" of ability is, without question, a system that perpetuates inequality. The reason why these practices of standardized testing persist is because they are integral to the social and political fabric of America, and deeply woven into the same fabric in which the strands of institutional racism and white supremacy are interlaced.

Under conventional practice, it is too often the case that the children who are successful academically are merely the ones who are best equipped to endure the socialization and to suspend their expectations that learning is sensible, meaningful, or purposeful. From a body of ethnographic educational research, we know that children socialized in a culturally mainstream and middle class context are better adapted to this school setting than African

American children. The fact is that too many children adapt to schooling as an experience of routine without meaning, and activity without manifest purpose. The lower the quality of schools, the more prevalent this is (Goodlad, 1984; Oakes, 1985).

Too many children experience schooling as a litany of episodes where they are required to perform a number of tasks that they are led to believe are "good for them." Under conventional practices, the successful children are those who learn to steel themselves for this existence—to comply with, and perhaps become adept at meeting, the litany of demands, but have given up expecting it all to make sense. (I discover these children in instances where an "accelerated classroom" accelerates further when given the opportunity to engage in purposeful, meaningful, and valuable learning experience which they have a part in constructing, and for which they see the connections to their contemporary experience.)

It is for this reason that the recent innovative models and approaches (e.g., teaching for understanding, teaching for meaning, constructivist teaching, "Total Quality Management," responsive teaching, etc.) are likely to merely dance around the edges of effective practice with African American children in urban schools. Frameworks such as these do not offer critical perspectives on power and community development, racial, and cultural identity development and meaningful education. In an increasingly racist society, connecting with contemporary problems of violence, drugs, and fear those approaches that do not place the intellectual, social, and political life of the child at the center of pedagogical thinking will be woefully insufficient for quality education for African American children.

FROM PERSONAL NARRATIVE TO CONNECTED PEDAGOGY

The point of sharing this personal history in the context of laying out the problem has to do with the deep structural aims of pedagogy of African-centered pedagogy. The elements of those aims emerged from a reflection on my educational and personal experience. In particular, it was primarily through my association with African American people, not with the public school teachers, that set me on the path of truly powerful pedagogy. It set me on a path that has served me well as a thinker, educator, researcher, and agent of change for social justice.

The African American community teachers in the church afforded me the environment that provided me with the cultural and intellectual tools to learn and achieve in the mainstream, often hostile, schooling contexts of my later experience. Mind you, the church was a setting that was not particularly intellectual nor was it explicitly cultural in the practices of developing young people. They nonetheless did afford me a figured world of learning, inquiry and achievement—something that the public schools never provided. The critical foundation of the deep structure of African American culture, history, language, and struggle was already a part of the social and cultural fabric of the African American church community. There was already the implicit understanding of the distinction between schooling and education, that education was the broader process of promoting the intellectual, spiritual, ethical, and social development of young people.

These realizations are significant to the project of developing an African-centered pedagogy. Despite having limited access to the community teachers in the African American community, that context influenced my thinking and development in far more profound ways than the public school experience. Moreover, it was the contrast between these two settings (the African American community teachers and the settings of public school) that triggered my development in exactly the sense that W. E. B. DuBois (1903/1989) described as identity formation through a "dual consciousness." This educational experience helped to inoculate me against that which fractures the development and educational futures of so many African American boys and girls in the public schools. It is this experience, that Paulo Freire (1970) called "conscientization"—the growth to critical consciousness—that I propose we replicate for African American children in public schools as an essential part of their educational experience. However, there are significant theoretical foundations of this project as well that constitute the "right frames" to the problem of Black underachievement. The remainder of this chapter will examine those foundations.

MOVEMENT TO SOLUTION: CULTURAL DEFICITS TO ECOLOGICAL PERSPECTIVE

In the last decade researchers and scholars concerned with the specific needs of urban teaching and achievement of African American children have further delineated teaching expertise for successful work in culturally, linguistically and ethnically diverse contexts. A number of scholars (Comer, 1997; Fordham, 1988; Foster, 1989; Kunjufu, 1985; Ladson-Billings, 1984) have examined the nature of this growing disparity in the educational outcomes between African American children and their white mainstream counterparts. What these studies have shown is that culturally mainstream White school settings pose social, cultural, political, and developmental challenges for African American children that go unrecognized by school teachers and personnel, but that nonetheless have significant adverse impacts on students' adjustment to school life.

Let me provide just a brief history as to why this recent turn in educational research is significant. The research literature in the 1960s and 1970s fostered a cultural deprivation model that assumed pathology of family, home, and community as the explanation for achievement of African American children. This model promotes the idea that African American students are culturally and financially deprived, deficient, and deviant in some way (Ladson-Billings, 1994). In the last decade or so there has been some change in thinking regarding the preparation of teachers for successful work with African American learners in urban schools (see Weiner, 1993; 1999). But because research paradigms are embedded in a social and historical context, we can expect this deficit-model thinking to resurface as the political landscape changes around issues of education.

Decades of the deficit model in the 1960s and 1970s were followed by another decade of research focusing on teacher qualities and school effectiveness in the 1980s. The 1990s ushered in a perspective the ecological model, rooted in the work of Urie Brofennbrenner, the work of James Comer and educational anthropological work of John Ogbu. This approach emphasized the importance of a systematic account of social context and the interaction of the human, cultural, and political systems involved in teaching and learning. It is an important idea for examining schooling experience of African American children at a structural or sociological level (e.g., Ogbu, 1986), the role of ethnic and racial identity development in that experience (e.g., Sheets & Hollins, 1999), development of knowledge (e.g., Murrell, 1998), and the preparation of teachers (e.g., Weiner, 1993; Murrell, 2001).

James Comer, developer of the School Development Plan, terms the system of intervention *ecological* because it analyzes the behavior of teachers, students, and parents at both a social-collective (environment) level and an individual-personal level. (My entry point is to account for the interactive dynamic of the individual and social environment in instructional practices. I will, in the next section introduce this idea as the mesolevel of analysis that refers to the organization of social systems within the school context.) Comer's system articulates four environments that are seen as affecting teaching and learning in school: (1) the child's home; (2) the family's social network; (3) school environment; and (4) the larger social world. His system attempts to weave together all of these registers of influence in his explanation for the failure of poor, "minority" children in urban schools.

I provide this detail about Comer's system to suggest to you that we are now in a position to move past deficiency explanations of Black achievement, and ready to develop *systems* (both human and material) and *practices* for successful academic progress and personal achievement. I should note two other important recommendations for the preparation of teachers for successful work with urban African American learners that come from Comer's work. First, that teacher candidates need to understand academic achievement and in-school learning as a product of overall child development—a requirement that asks teachers to be concerned with the development of the whole child as opposed to only being concerned with his or her scholastic progress.

The second recommendation for teacher preparation is the requirement that teacher candidates develop the collaborative abilities and "know how" to create social climates in their classrooms that promote development and learning. This means that accomplished teachers must be able to work collaboratively with support staff, colleagues, parents and others in ways that create systems of development and achievement for children. Weiner's (1993) distinguishes the "ecological model" from a "service delivery" model in the preparation of urban teachers. The central assumption regarding efforts guided by the ecological model is that efforts to improve practices, policies, and pedagogy of urban schools cannot be divorced from a careful examination of the school climate and sociocultural organization of schools, especially as this examination draws on participation of parents and community. Now let us look briefly at how the ecological model relates to teaching.

SOCIAL CONTEXT, CULTURAL CONGRUITY, AND CULTURALLY RESPONSIVE TEACHING

One application of the ecological model involves the idea of cultural congruence or compatibility. There has been a growing consensus among educational researchers and practitioners that learning is enhanced when it occurs in contexts that are socioculturally, cognitively, and linguistically meaningful to the learner.

Culturally responsive teaching is viewed in the literature as the leading approach to address questions of "teaching to diversity" and working successfully with African American children. Culturally responsive teaching is also referred to as "culturally relevant" teaching (e.g., Ladson-Billings, 1994), "culturally compatible" teaching, "culturally responsive" (Gay, 2000) teaching, and "culturally synchronous" teaching (e.g., Irvine, 1990). Culturally responsive pedagogy is an approach to effective instruction in diverse settings. The essence of this idea that what we think and what we feel is culturally situated and shaped. Moreover, what we think and feel about certain activities and practices is socialized by how significant others feel and think about those practices and activities. For example, a student directed to write something in a journal may experience an intrinsic reward despite being asked to perform the task, whereas another student may feel none of the intrinsic reward and feel frustrated and burdened. The difference is in how the activity of journal writing is construed in the student's culture and represented to them in the situational context.

There are, however, some troubling limitations to the idea of cultural compatibility or cultural congruity. To begin with, when people talk about the cultural incongruity in reference to the experience of African American children in culturally mainstream American public school, there is little sense of "culture" beyond a static category of membership. It is difficult to avoid thinking in terms of "Black culture" as being incompatible with, or incongruous to, "White mainstream culture." This is not a very useful paradigm, nor is it a notion of culture we want to promote. If we continued on this tack, our task as educators would seem to be to reduce the "incongruity" or "incompatibility"—making the cultural pattern of "the other" (minority students) match the pattern of the American mainstream. This reductionism makes the practices of "incongruity reduction" identical to those of the "reducing cultural deficits" because the burden of change is always placed upon the "minority" group. This direction threatens to return us to the previous era of a deficit model of urban education.

The value of the body of work on cultural incongruity theory (e.g., Ogbu, 1989, 1992) was to force an account of how the differences in achievement between African American learners and their Euro-American counterparts inhered in the social and cultural fabric of their educational experiences. Where Ogbu comes up short is the hypothesis of an oppositional identity as a factor in the underachievement of African American children. The issues of how young Black people experience and adapt to school cannot simply be attributed to an oppositional identity.

The hypothesis that students who are "involuntary minorities" (to use Ogbu's term) bring to schooling an oppositional social identity and oppositional cultural frame of reference in response to racism is too simplistic. We African Americans are complete people, and therefore do not conform our cultural identities in response to the ubiquitous institution of racism to any greater degree than White people conform their cultural identities as *participants* in racism. The fact that racism does play a role underscores the urgency for an African-centered pedagogy. But the reifying "oppositional social identity" and "oppositional cultural frames" is the worst sort of essentializing with regard to culture, reducing African American cultural identity to an oppositional response to racism. How does one respond to an institution? One doesn't. One responds to specific situations, practices, and events—things that happen and actions people take as expressions of the institution. Understanding this complex mixture is more difficult, but not impossible and quite essential if we are to develop effective pedagogy for African American children.

The contribution of the educational ethnography in regard to the notion of cultural incongruity or cultural incompatibility is that it forced the following recognitions:

1. The differential outcomes for children of color in culturally mainstream school settings are complex, and not simply a matter of improving the "delivery system";
2. The most powerful factors influencing differential impacts inhere in the social and cultural fabric of their daily experience of the curriculum and the classroom as a community;
3. Professional teachers and caregivers are most successful when they are able to maintain the continuity of experience from children's interactions with their first teachers and caregivers;
4. All children develop social, linguistic, and intellectual tools for learning prior to school, but these cognitive and intellectual tools are frequently misunderstood, unrecognized, and undervalued for African American children.

Ladson-Billings (1994) develops the notion of culturally relevant pedagogy to move beyond difference in language and cultural styles to include this broader array of concerns that go into creating a responsive school context.

Within contemporary educational theory and practice, the body of work on culturally responsive practice, unfortunately, is reinforcing the marginalized status of African American learners in public schools. The focus on the "culture" of underachieving African American learners has created an unfortunate diversion from the larger political and social dynamics that create and fortify differential outcomes for African American children. The presumption of difference in cultural capital (Bourdieu & Passerson, 1997) offers nothing for improving the schooling experiences of African American children without a systematic examination of the cultural, political and social contexts in which those experiences unfold. The approach of narrowing the incongruence by itself is insufficient as an educational approach because, in the absence of a pedagogical theory, it is simply a program of cultural assimilation.

The problem that cultural congruity as a framework creates for designing effective pedagogy for African American children is that it merely repositions the African American experience as "the other"—something "out of synch" with the universalized mainstream cultural experience represented by school. It implies a process of closing the gaps and making connections, without interrogating the deep-rooted cultural values that are antithetical to the African American conceptions of education, development, and struggle.

Closing the gaps in the aggregate performance on standardized achievement tests does not constitute a strategy for addressing Black underachievement. Neither is it an approach by which pedagogy for successful work with African American learners can be examined and improved. The cultural incongruity notion presupposes an understanding of both a school culture and collective culture of African American children that does not exist. Neither culture is well enough understood for assimilation to be a viable approach for improving teaching and learning in culturally and linguistically diverse classrooms. Without first providing a means of making "commonly sensible" the important elements of culture with respect to schooling in both locations, there is really no foundation on which to build a pedagogy of culturally relevant teaching and learning.

This book looks at pedagogy holistically as a system of practices. This book develops an African-centered pedagogy as a holistic system of practices building directly on the concept of *culturally relevant pedagogy* as it is articulated by Ladson-Billings (1994, p. 17). She distinguishes the culturally relevant pedagogy in precisely the way we need to think of pedagogy: as incorporating more than language and communicative style, more than interactional competence, to include a critical and reflective regard of the social, historical, and cultural positionings of teachers and students in the conjoint actions that constitute teaching and learning. In this way the concept is important to examining and leveraging the teaching proficiencies required of teachers to provide quality education for African American children.

This book continues the foundational work of Ladson-Billings and others in the task of articulating and developing teacher proficiency with respect to African American children, but with an important difference. The point of departure for this book is in the location and articulation teacher proficiency, not in the characteristics of the individual teacher, but in systems of practice in which the teacher plays the pivotal role. This permits the specification of culturally relevant practice not just in terms of individual teachers' thoughts, values, and actions, but also in terms of human systems of productive interaction where positive student outcomes are manifest in their performance over time.

My approach triangulates (a) teacher action, both planful and in-the-moment; (b) purposeful learning and development goals for students; and (c) student achievement and development performance (see Figure 1 and Figure 2). The unit of analysis in this approach is not the individual teacher, but the activity setting in which that teacher interacts with students and organizes the milieu of productive interaction and development. In this formulation, there is a triangulating system of these three elements in dynamic tension with one another—teacher action, purposeful goals, and performance outcomes.

I discovered the necessity for developing this system of practice idea when I discovered the disconnect between what teachers valued and what they actually did. Let me tell you about one instance in which the disconnect became abundantly clear. The week before I was to visit my classroom of the supervising K–12 teacher where my student teachers were placed, we had a discussion in a meeting of the school action team in which we worked through the Table 3 found in chapter 3. In that conversation, everyone in the group was convinced, including myself, that the teacher was "culturally relevant" in his practice according to our discussion of those features. All other indications I had—samples of work from students in the classroom, the intern's journal entries of the classroom, and discussion with both the teacher and the intern individually—suggested that the teacher was an exemplar of culturally relevant teaching. The teacher in question was none other than Mr. R., teaching a lesson on *The Diary of Anne Frank*, the same I described in the earlier example.

So here was my first sense of the disconnect between a teacher exhibiting the qualities of culturally relevant practice on one hand, and what actually happens for African American children on the other hand. Here, for me, was the difference between a culturally relevant pedagogy as the characteristics of a teacher and culturally relevant teaching as a system of practices that actually produces achievement outcomes for African American children.

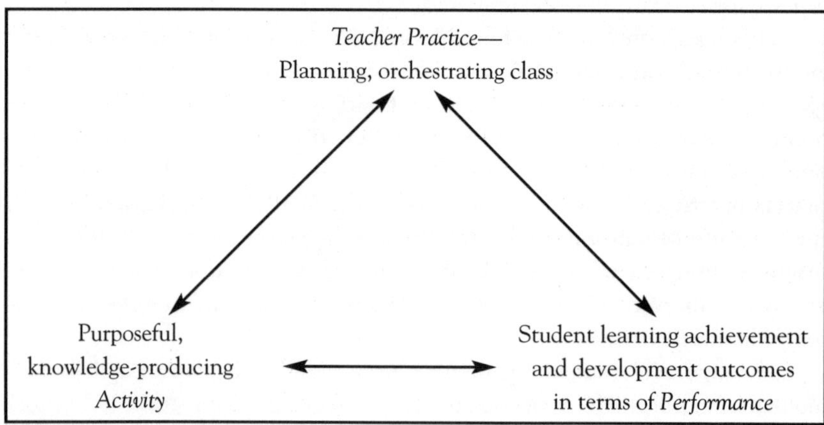

Figure 1. Activity setting—Unit of analysis triangulating teacher practice, learning activity, and student performance.

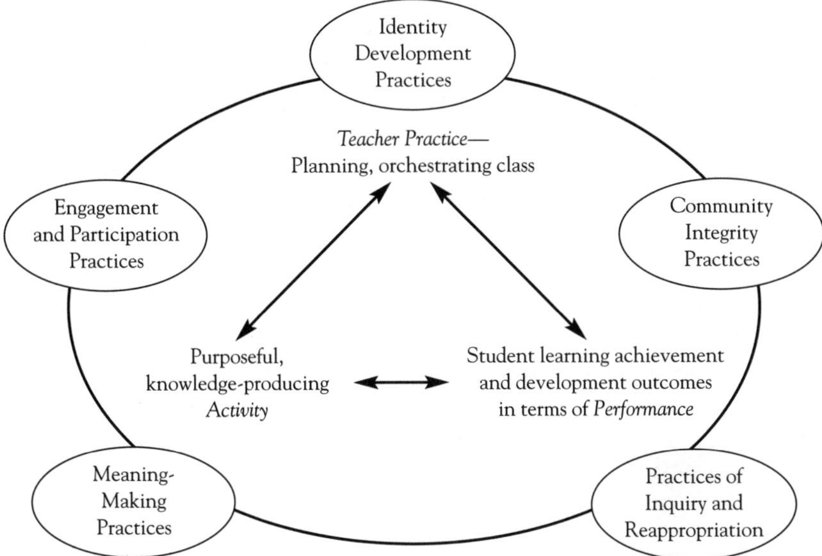

Figure 2. The basic components of the African-centered pedagogy.

SUMMARY AND CONCLUSIONS

Even though the national concern over the "achievement gap" rightly focuses attention on Black achievement (the right problem), it is the wrong response to pursue ways of "closing the gap" as long as achievement principally regarded as aggregate performance on high stakes standardized achievement tests. The real site of the problem is the quality of teaching and learning in real schools and with real learners. There is a cultural integrity to African American educational experience that is missing in contemporary public schooling. So the answer to elevating African American achievement can never simply be a matter of being responsive to *what is*; there must be a critical reconfiguring of *what should be* in the educational experience of African American children. This chapter introduced approaches that appropriately contextualize African American achievement in social, cultural, and historical context—culturally relevant pedagogy and a practice/performance based African-centered pedagogy. Culturally relevant pedagogy is important for the second type of pedagogical depth—being educationally responsive and accountable for *what is*. An African-centered pedagogy address phase one and phase two in depth of pedagogy—constructing African American achievement by drawing on the full cultural and intellectual heritage of African Americans. The entire theoretical framework is depicted in Figure 2.

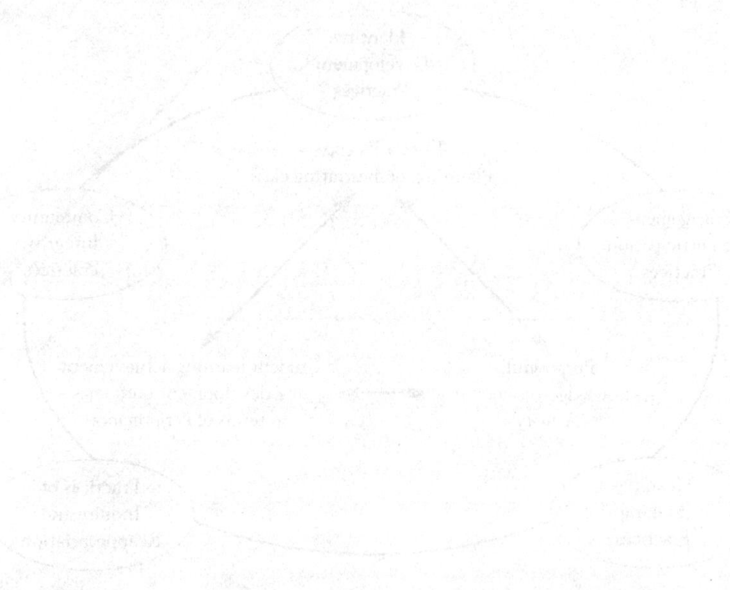

CHAPTER TWO

Traditions of African American Education—A Historical Perspective

> Regardless of the poignancy of the crimes against black Americans our oppression is, after all, only a part of a much larger malignancy. The American structure of slavery was a consequence of the economy of the New World, its roots in Europe, not Africa. Mass oppression for mass production is part of the Western psyche. Therefore the problems experienced by blacks in America have to be seen as part of that larger malady. It is impossible to extricate the black experience in America from the larger American experience.
>
> —Walter Mosley, *Workin' on the Chain Gang*

There is a cultural integrity in the way that African American families and communities construe quality education, exemplary teachers, and academic achievement. African Americans have a collective history and a collective memory that circumscribe a significant and tangible cultural heritage. In this cultural heritage, views on school achievement are not necessarily consistent with the "standard model" of traditional education. Therefore, building a successful community of practice in a school populated predominantly by African American children calls for a critical redefinition of good teaching and successful learning. It requires a critical interrogation of those individual proficiencies and abilities required for school success. In short, the task of building a community of achievement requires a new pedagogy—an African-centered pedagogy.

My task in this chapter is to make clear what I mean about historical grounding and why it is important to envisioning pedagogy for successful work with African American children. I want to make three points in this discussion regarding the meaning of an African-centered historical grounding with respect to the task. First, there is a definitive cultural and intellectual heritage that has emerged from the collective experiences of African Americans and that it has an important relationship to what education truly means in the collective memory of descendants of Africans in America. Second, without a grounding in the collective experience and collective heritage of African Americans, the ideologies of oppression that have evolved in the United States will continue to shape educational practices inimical to Black achievement.

The third point I will make as a challenge to the following statement: The system of public education in American generally works, but works much less well for African American learners. A more truthful rendering of this statement is as follows: The system of public education in America generally works well for a select segment of the population, *principally because* it fails a disproportionate percentage of American students. In other words, if we understand American history and the ideology that drives American public education, we have to acknowledge that public schooling is doing absolutely what it was designed to do—to sort and select learners in a way that ascribes their prerogatives and opportunity. These three points are essential to building the system of practices and will help students make connections with their racial, cultural, and national identities.

I start this discussion of the historically grounded aspect of pedagogy with a set of African-centered assumptions and understandings that clarify the political and cultural realities of the schooling of Black children in White America. Scholars in a variety of disciplines have traced and studied the origins and linkages of African American culture in the regions of the Ivory Coast and the Gold Coast around the Niger River delta. It is fairly well established that western African societies and nations were the predominant groups that fell victim to the slave trade, so most African Americans originated from that region. (Of the some 20 million people kidnapped in this slave trading, only half would survive the trek to the coast.) What is of interest in this scholarship are the cultural features and qualities of western African societies that have persisted, sometimes in transmuted forms that are distinct, recognizable, and significant in the organization of Black life to this day. It is important to trace the ways in which the cultural forms of Africans in America powerfully shaped the emerging cultural forms of America as a whole. The complete story of American history, the deep structure of the American culture and society, lies in the symbiotic relationship between American institutions and African culture. Historian George Rawick (1972) details the history of African Americans as they persisted through slavery, drawing on the wealth of slave narratives from the Federal Writers Project of the Works Progress Administration to show the resiliency and the re-creation of African culture in ways that became uniquely African American. He writes:

> Human society is a cumulative process in which the past is never totally obliterated. Even revolutions do not destroy the past. Indeed, at their best, they liberate that which is alive from that which stifles human progress, growth, and development. Culture is a historical reality, not an ahistorical, static abstraction. Thus, the process whereby the African in the New World changed in order to meet his new environment was dependent on his African culture. (p. 6)

I am not taking the position African American pedagogy is merely based on the cultural features of western African culture—the knowledge systems, epistemologies, and ways of being—although there are those that have convincingly made this connection (e.g., Hale-Benson, 1986; Boykin, 1986; Nobles, 1998). The point here is that understanding the deep structure of American culture involves understanding the transformation of African culture in the contestation of oppression throughout the era of slavery and after. Rawick writes:

> Rather than becoming "deculturalized," slaves used what they brought with them from Africa to meet the new conditions; they created new social forms and behavior patterns which syncretized African and New World elements under the particular conditions of slave life in the United State. (Rawick, 1972, p. xix)

So the implication for my first point regarding historical grounding is the recovery of African American historical experience must be a part of a pedagogy that envisions education of the highest quality for African American children and youth. The act of recovery is to go back and get the pieces of history you missed. If you received (as I did) a traditional education regarding American history, you probably have missed over half of the American story. Why more than half? Well, consider that you may have received the "approved" version. You know the one—the one that skirted over examination of slavery as an unfortunate national lapse of morality that was "corrected" by the Civil War. But then, you were missing at least two more pieces. One of these is the history that was "lost, stolen or strayed" (*props* to Bill Cosby). The biggest missing pieces were the resistance, struggle, and conflict created by the institution of slavery and the widespread practices of oppression; out of the crucible of this clash was forged our national character.

I will put my second point in the form of the following assertion: The system of public education as it evolved in the United States functions to perpetuate the nation-state, its current configuration of power, and the underlying core of cultural forms that spawned them. This I take as a given and is beyond dispute. We will have more to say about this later as we look at the nature of the critical inquiry necessary for the foundation of the pedagogy. The critical point here is that core assumptions and values that are fundamental to the dominant culture in a nation-state will be embodied in pedagogy, in part to maintain and perpetuate that national culture in a position of dominance. So the cultural reproduction (to draw on the work of Michael Apple, Pierre Bourdieu, Maxine Green, Kevin Harris, bell hooks, Paulo Freire, and others) of the dominant culture occurs not just in the hidden curriculum but in how we conceptualize pedagogy. The way we think about cognitive learning and development in contemporary educational practice is influenced by theory that is neither historically grounded nor culturally situated. Jean Lave, in arguing to challenge this state of affairs, writes:

> In my view, one of the hazards facing researchers on cognition, learning, and education is densely interwoven history and contemporary relations among schooling, cognitive theory, the educational establishment, and the lives of school alumni. They share underlying beliefs about life, learning, and the pursuit of life-after-school. The everyday character of schooling, its social situatedness, and historical integration with academic theories of cognition and learning are mainly treated as if they did not exist, or worse, did not matter. (1997, p. 20)

As I have said, there is a cultural integrity in the way that African American families and communities construe quality education, exemplary teachers, and academic achievement. This integrity coheres in a cultural value system and worldview of African Americans. It is this integrity that is threatened by contemporary educational practice in America because of the cultural values that contradict African American cultural values. Hale (1994, p. 135) sees the values of African American culture as derived through both traditional African religion and American Christianity. She argues that the uniqueness of the American slavery experience, resistance to slavery and oppression, and the challenge of living through America's structured inequality thereafter has created a distinctive African American folklore that has been the crucible for the development and transmission of African American cultural values. These values have been transmitted intergenerationally through the oral tradition, a tradition emanating from West African life and culture. For this reason, Hale (1994) argues that the study of cultural values of African American ought to include the core values of the African American religious tradition and the common perspective on faith, the oral tradition and other representations of the African worldview. These, in turn, can only be fully interpreted through their genesis and transmutation in the context (and aftermath) of slavery.

In this chapter I want to convey to you a picture of the *cultural patterns* and *interpretive frameworks* that define African American values regarding education. African American cultural patterns and interpretive frameworks must be made explicit in the education of African American children for two reasons. First, teachers need to know how to connect with the lives and experiences of their African American students. Second, and just as important, teachers need to know how to prepare their students to resist those American cultural values that are inimical to their achievement and character development. As I have mentioned earlier, this discussion runs the risk of broad-brush description that might seem to overgeneralize Black epistemology. What I hope to show is enough of the African American educational heritage that is distinct from how education is conventionally construed in America.

The two institutions that Africans in America have built with their own hands from the ground up are schools and churches. In these two institutions the cultural integrity of the African American experience is manifested and indelibly marked. It will be important to examine the cultural patterns of African Americans as they relate to education to lay the foundation for a connected African-centered pedagogy. There are two strands of the African American heritage with regard to education—the struggle for literacy and literacy for liberation.

LITERACY FOR FREEDOM— THE COLONIAL TO PRE-CIVIL WAR PERIOD

One strand of this cultural integrity is the struggle for literacy, embodied in a legacy in which Africans in America regard literacy and the value of education as the means to liberation. From the beginning, literacy and the quest for freedom are struggles that were inextricably linked for Africans in America. Many who suffered as slaves risked their lives in attempts to learn to read and write. Fearing more of the hundreds of slave insurrections in the early nineteenth century, legislatures in the slaveholding southern states passed laws against teaching Africans to read and write. Slaves and freedmen alike participated in teaching themselves and others to read in defiance of severe consequences. Many slaves secretly learned to read in spite of these laws (Manguel, 1996). Ex-slaves and free African Americans contributed their own money and labor to build and maintain schools for African Americans.

It is this strand—the twin struggle for literacy and freedom—which will be described in some detail in this chapter. A second strand of this cultural integrity—literacy as the means to liberation—will be examined in greater depth in chapter 9. It is the cultural pattern of critical literacy in relation to the liberation struggle of African Americans, articulated by Carter Woodson in *The Mis-Education of the Negro* (1933). This strand confronts the ideological warfare waged on African Americans through distortions, omissions, and misrepresentations of Black thought and experience in literature, history, and the popular media. Woodson's work urged that African Americans take charge of curriculum to contest white supremacist ideology. Contemporary writers such as Hilliard (1996), Kunjufu (1985), Madhubuti and Madhubuti (1991), Shujaa (1994) and others urge this as well, and have developed curriculum and literacy programs that do just that.

In the panorama of American history, literacy and access to literacy, has been inextricably linked with struggle for full participation as citizens. From the beginning, universal literacy was a cultural value in the development of American ideology—but not for African Americans. The population of white America moved gradually and steadily toward universal literacy. The proportion of Black Americans, on the other hand, gradually decreased during this period. As the number of slaves in the United States dramatically increased, so did the movement to deny literacy to African Americans, both free and slave. In a number of states it was illegal to teach African American slaves to read and write. Literacy for African Americans, freedman and slave, was always contested and a continuous struggle.

The era between 1820 and 1860 was one of dramatic change in the fledgling confederation. Urbanization and industrialization ended the dominant role of the family as the economic center in American society. Where the sons and daughters of rural America had once learned their trades, fulfilled their apprenticeships, or labored with the family unit, children of the emerging urban America increasingly worked in factories. The primary educational institutions in colonial America were the family and church, but with industrialization and the rising populations in the cities, the need for public school was voiced. Public schooling filled a void. Historian Stanley Schultz (as cited in Fraser, Allen, & Barnes 1979, p. 30) states that the role of: "The public school was to be a classroom, a family room, a church house—all things to all children."

Historian James Fraser documents the thinking of the era that favored the institution of public schools for making future citizens. Horace Mann, Secretary of Massachusetts' Board of Education from 1837 to 1848, was among the more prominent advocates for the "common school"—public school as the institution that would make loyal citizens and full participants in the emerging nation. But as Fraser et al. (1979) point out:

> When Mann talked about a common school, he did not mean a school for the common people; he meant a school that would be common to all people—the upper class, the working class, and the middle

> class. All would have a common experience, which would build a united society in America. (p. 31)

What is noteworthy about this democratic vision was how completely at odds it was with the actual experiences of Africans in American—both in the North and the South. The vision of creating a new democratic institution of the public school was completely at odds with the already established institutions of the fledgling nation—most notably slavery, and other laws and codes of systematic exclusion of African Americans from public life. It is safe to say that, during this era, few counted African Americans among "the common people."

As the historian James Anderson points out, this contradiction between the drive for universal literacy for the common man and the denial of literacy for African Americans sharply defined the legacy of *literacy for freedom, and freedom for literacy* among African Americans. If the framers of the Constitution had not explicitly articulated the diffusion of literacy among the populace as a condition of democratic participation, the significance of literacy to the struggle for freedom would not have been as great. We would not have seen the reverence for education and the struggle to acquire literacy as a powerful fixture in the cultural heritage of African Americans.

The Declaration of Independence, and its Lockian philosophy of natural rights accorded to citizens in order to realize a true democracy, implied that an educated populace is important to those collective aims. Thomas Jefferson, and later Horace Mann, John D. Pierce and others, argued that education was among those inalienable rights that should be accorded American citizens. Of course, we know from the historical record, that this was meant to include white, landowning males and certainly did not apply to African Americans, who were not considered citizens even if they were not slaves. Nevertheless, the question of citizenship would not have had such a critical bearing on African American access to literacy if it were not for this philosophical foundation of the "founding fathers."

As a matter of historical record, the federal government did not formally define the status of African Americans as noncitizens until the Dred Scott decision in 1857. It is clear however, that states built into their constitutions a number of specific codes that restricted the suffrage of Blacks. In 1811, for example, the territorial legislature of Indiana passed legislation preventing free Blacks from testifying in court against Whites. As another example, the Ohio legislature in 1807, excluded African Americans from residence in the state unless they posted a $500 bond for good behavior (Anderson, 1995, p. 21). Michigan, Iowa, and Wisconsin all denied African Americans the right to vote shortly thereafter.

In the America of the 1840s, Horace Mann and John D. Pierce advocated for the "common school" which would do more than merely tool-up children with reading, writing, and 'rithmatic—it would prepare them for democratic public life. During this time when these champions of the common school advocated for schooling that nurtured public life and democratic action, both schooling and citizenship were denied African Americans. Vito Perrone (1998), in his brief history of the ideas underlying teaching for understanding, writes of how the common school movement with its principle origins in the 1840s, began with hopes for powerful education for all children. He writes:

> The three "R's" of reading, writing and arithmetic were clearly seen as critical, but according to the early common school evangelists—Horace Mann, Henry Barnard, and John D. Pierce—more was expected. The nurturance of democratic life was a particularly important purpose, the implication being that schools and democratic action were closely linked. (p.15)

While Horace Mann was supporting a new and progressive movement of education, Horace Greeley declared his sentiment that "the settlement of the Midwest shall be reserved for the benefit of the white Caucasian race." Perrone writes:

> Although the common schools hardly became the enlightened educational settings Mann, Barnard and Pierce envisioned, they were quickly incorporated into the universal fabric of American society. Schools proliferated much more quickly than Mann could ever have envisioned, especially after the Civil War. (p. 17)

But as public schools in the 1840s and 1850s proliferated, in Horace Mann's golden age of the "common school" movement, the restrictions on African American education and literacy dramatically increased. On March 31, 1850, the Massachusetts Supreme Court rejected the argument of Charles Sumner in the Boston school integration suit and established the "separate but equal" precedent. This precedent prefigured the *Plessy v. Ferguson* ruling that continued the doctrine until its overturn one hundred years later with the *Brown v. Board of Education* ruling in 1954. There were also severe civil restrictions that dramatically influenced African Americans access to education.

The racial restrictiveness of the state legislatures of the states and territories of the Midwest became models for similar practices in new territories further westward. For example, in 1849, a year after Wisconsin formally became a state, delegates at the constitutional convention in California voted, without debate, to adopt constitutional restrictions on free persons of color. In 1857, Oregon was admitted as the only free state with constitutional restrictions against African Americans—demanding that all free people of color leave the state under penalty of periodic floggings until they left.

In Bleeding Kansas—so called because it became a battleground of proslavery and antislavery battles in the determination of its statehood—three out of four of the antislavery advocates were also anti-Black White supremacists. The interest was in keeping African Americans out of Kansas by opposing the slave interests. Anderson concludes that the antislavery movement embraced anti-Black sentiments and white supremacist doctrine. Antislavery triumphed over slavery interests in the Midwest and West in the name of white supremacy, as they argued pointedly, deliberately, and quite openly that these states should be reserved for White people and exclude African Americans—whether slave or freedman. The antislavery heroes were leaders in their state legislatures for the restriction of the rights and well-being of African Americans.

In the East, most of the states had abolished slavery before 1840 in their legislatures, but the anti-Black sentiment among the citizenry was no less virulent. According to Forrest Wood, as the nation prepared for war in 1861, most state constitutions refused to grant citizenship and equality to African Americans (as cited in Anderson, 1995, p. 29). State and federal officials repeatedly rebuffed the attempts of freedmen to join the Union army. At the end of the war, every state in the Midwest denied African Americans the right to vote and barred them from the militia (as cited in Anderson, 1995, p. 29).

The Dred Scott decision of 1857 was the culminating event in continuous drift away from the natural rights philosophy that had seemed so "self-evident" in the Declaration of Independence. When the U. S. Supreme Court held that "no black man had rights that a white man was bound to respect," African American noncitizenship became the law of the land. As Anderson (1995) shows, the abandonment of African American citizenship on the part of federal and state governments also meant the abandonment of access to literacy. He writes:

> As local and state governments faced the question of African American education in the late 18th century to the Civil War, they rejected the idea that African Americans had an inalienable right to knowledge. Rather, state and local governments maintained that it was the status of citizenship that entitled one to public education. (p. 25)

Not surprisingly, the locus of concern regarding African Americans following the Civil War shifted to the South, as the vast majority of Blacks still lived in that region following the emancipation of over four million slaves. According to Anderson, more than 90 percent of African Americans lived in former slave states, which meant that more than 90 percent of them were illiterate by 1865.

LITERACY FOR FREEDOM— POST CIVIL WAR TO THE GREAT DEPRESSION

James Anderson (1988) offers in his educational historiography a narrative of the consistent struggles of African Americans for literacy and the remarkable drive to become a literate population in the era following the Civil War to the Great Depression, 1865 to 1930. He documented the vast panorama of battles to secure funding to operate schools, as well as fights to determine the ideological foundations of education for African American children. These battles and fights took many forms—civil actions, boycotts, and community movements to wrestle control of already segregated and underresourced schools from government and White power structures intent on maintaining a system of cultural and ideological enslavement (Woodson, 1933).

According to Anderson (1988, 1995), African Americans had, by the turn of the century, achieved amazingly high levels of literacy. The postbellum rates of illiteracy among southern Blacks declined more rapidly than among Whites—a remarkable phenomenon given the severe retrenchment of the gains made during reconstruction and the systematic disenfranchisement of Blacks during the last two decades of the nineteenth century. Anderson (1995) writes that "At the dawn of the 20th century Black southerners seemed poised to achieve universal literacy and to increase their overall levels of educational attainment, particularly at the secondary and higher education levels" (p. 31). All that was needed, was a decent system of public education in order to attain these higher levels of achievement. But this is precisely what was denied.

If you knew nothing about the experience of Africans in America at the beginning of the twentieth century, you would likely view the era as a golden age of American education. This was the period of the progressive education movement. John Dewey stressed the need for a "new pedagogy" that called upon teachers to integrate the content of education and locate the practices of schooling in the activities of daily life. The progressive education movement emphasized the democratic possibilities in public education. But what was actually happening to African American learners during the unfolding of the progressive education movement?

Anderson draws on the scholarship of Horace Mann Bond (as cited in Anderson, 1995, p. 32), an African American educator whose essay in the inaugural issue of the *Journal of Negro Education* was among the first to document the dramatic shift in educational quality: The relative equality of Black public education in the late nineteenth century gave way to the gross inequality in the dawn of the so-called Progressive Era of the early twentieth century. Dramatic differences in expenditures for Black southern schools and White southern schools began to appear. For example, in 1890, Black Mississippians received approximately 35 percent of the state's school fund, but only 19 percent of that fund went to Blacks at the turn of the century, even though Blacks comprised 60 percent of the school-aged population (Anderson, 1995, p. 32).

The dominant white power structure of the south mounted a massive campaign of resistance to the educational progress of Black southerners. For example, in 1890, the Mississippi Constitutional Convention signaled the beginning of systematic exclusion of Blacks from political life in the South. The Mississippi Plan (literacy and "understanding tests") was later adopted with embellishments by other states: South Carolina (1895), Louisiana (1898), North Carolina (1900), Alabama (1901), Virginia (1901), Georgia (1908), and Oklahoma (1910). Southern states later used "White primaries" and other devices to exclude Black voters.

Other state action reduced the Black-to-White ratio of per-pupil expenditures which declined in every state between 1890 and 1919 (Anderson, 1995, p. 33). Similarly, African Americans were excluded from the southern transformation of public secondary education. According to Anderson, in 1890 less than four-tenths of a percent of the African American children of high school age were enrolled in high school (Anderson, 1995). By the early 1930s, children of rural Whites, working-class Whites, and the children of recent Europeans were systematically brought into public high school; African American children as a class were deliberately excluded (Anderson, 1988, pp. 187–200). State legislatures in the South had, in tandem with Jim Crow laws, disproportionately diverted what meager public resources there were to the public education of White children at the expense of Black children.

Perrone, in his brief history of education relevant to the "teaching for understanding" framework writes:

> Progressivism suffered in the 1930s from the difficulties of the Great Depression and the overwhelming demands of World War II that drew public attention away from the schools. (1998, p. 20)

Clearly, African American communities had difficulties and demands of their own. In 1940, roughly half of all Black common schools in Mississippi still met in structures that were not public school buildings—tenant cabins, lodges, churches, and stores. The pattern of second-class citizenship and third-class schooling continued. African Americans struggled against outright denial of literacy and education throughout America's history.

LITERACY FOR FREEDOM—HISTORICALLY AND CULTURALLY SITUATED PEDAGOGY

In glimpsing the panorama of the educational oppression of Africans in America, we are talking here, in very concrete terms, of what it means to be culturally situated and historically grounded. The cultural patterns of a collective experience of a people—in this case the struggle, through the pursuit of literacy, for basic humanity and for equal protection under the law—persist among African Americans in the present day. Africans in America continue to struggle against institutionalized inequality, which makes our heritage of literacy very different than that of mainstream American culture. The cultural integrity of African Americans is, at many points, contradictory to the core common culture of mainstream America. The common heritage as promulgated by Benjamin Bloom through his campaign of "cultural literacy," for example, is not the heritage of African Americans, and it belies, distorts, and hides the truths about how America became what it is. The fact that we may share common, uniquely American cultural values should not lead us to assume the existence of a universal American experience. Let us not assume, as "cultural literacy" advocates would have us believe, that the American cultural patterns are the same for all of us or that cultural differences do not matter. The difference can be deep and profound, particularly when it comes to the institutions of education.

As an instance of this historical grounding and a reflection focus, you might ask yourself as a White teacher where you might be now if your ancestors had been denied access to education, or barred from entering a commonwealth, and denied citizenship and basic rights by the government? Where might you be if your ancestors were publicly flogged every thirty days until they left the state (as they did in Oregon in 1857) or denied citizenship by the United States Supreme Court, stating that they had not rights that either persons or governments were bound to respect? Or you might ask where you would be if your grandparents attended schools in a region of the country where state governments preferred to have no quality public schools rather than have quality public schools that served you, your family, and your kin?

With this brief historical framing, it should be clear that a system of practices to enhance the quality of education for African American children cannot be an approach that takes no account of history and cultural heritage "bridging the gap" between the cultural experiences of mainstream America and the African American cultural heritage. Yet, this is what most applications of multicultural education attempt to do—but not just for African American culture, but for the culture of every geopolitical and ethnic group represented in the school. The approach regards the African American experience as just another "equal" version of American experience—as if the collective experience of Africans in America was independent of the rest of the fabric of American experience.

What are the African American cultural values that make it necessary to construct a pedagogy in the collective experience and heritage of African Americans? Out of this continuous historical struggle for full citizenship and literacy, comes a heritage, a set of enduring cultural patterns in the African American community. To begin with, one value is the recognition that there *is* a collective history and a collective memory of African Americans that circumscribes a significant and tangible cultural heritage. In this cultural heritage, views on school achievement are not necessarily consistent with the "standard model" of contemporary educational practice. For example, out of a history of disenfranchisement and denial of access to education, the Africanist cultural value emerged—literacy as the practice of emancipation. This value merged with another cultural feature traceable back to precolonial western African societies that were brought to the New World on slave ships—the inseparability of education from all other aspects of social and cultural life.

In the societies of western Africa, children were educated through direct participation in the political and cultural life of the community. Education, especially as literacy, was, and is, something to be put into practice in the art of living productively and generatively. Later, when these cultural perspectives were transported to the New World through the infamous Middle Passage, they were transformed into the freedom struggle. Slaves who could read and write had control over their comings and goings—being able to read "your papers" or even forge them meant greater freedom. Education, especially literacy, is something that developed and improved the lot of the community, improved as a collective of people with common heritage, struggles, and culture.

These perspectives on education survived transport through the Middle Passage and the MAAFA. The MAAFA is a Kiswahili term for "Disaster" or "Terrible Occurrence." The term is used to refer to the African Holocaust—the more than five hundred years of suffering of people of African descent through slavery, imperialism, colonialism, and exploitation. Education was viewed as the result of guided participation in the doings of the community by elders—more capable adults who would assist and intervene in a young person's actions as necessary to support the development of capacities that they would need to deal in the world. Viewed from the present day perspective in time, education is the process of becoming a capable and full participant in the intellectual, cultural, spiritual, and political life of the community. It is to this perspective, I argue, that we must return. It is beyond the scope of this book to detail the entirety of the Africanist worldview. See the edited work of Mwalimu Shujaa (1994) for a perspective on the African-centered worldview in education. The focus here is to make explicit the cultural and intellectual heritage of African Americans with respect to achievement.

To say there is a cultural integrity to African American experience is not to say that that you will find exactly the same core of practices among all Black people. But there is certainly a common core of cultural patterns that has shaped the collective experience of all Americans, but particularly African Americans in ways that make an African-centered pedagogy essential for education. Cultural integrity exists in the collective memory, literature, and experience of African Americans, but in the historical record as well—for those who care to find it and read it.

Two other aspects of this integrity should be mentioned at this juncture. One significant aspect of this cultural integrity of the African American experience with respect to education is that of intergenerational communication and teaching. The dialogical relationship between the younger, less experienced members of the community with the elder, wiser members is the embeddedness of education in the culture of African Americans. In present day schooling dynamics, this is reflected in African American parents and teachers who reveal interpretative traditions of what constitutes the effective teacher of African American children (see Foster, 1989; 1990; 1992; 1997; 2001).

The other aspect of this cultural integrity of the African American heritage is the relationship of the familial structure with the enterprise of educating the young. Among precolonial African people, there was intergenerational communication—recreated in the New World through an oral literary tradition that included folktales, legend, myths, proverbs, and story telling, as well as secret societies and religious practices. Education interrogates power.

A popular term in the educational literature is "learning community" or "communities of learning" by which is usually meant a social, cultural, and intellectual environment that is most conducive to student learning and development. In this volume, this idea is developed through the notion of a community of practice (Lave, 1988; 1997; Wenger, 1998). What would it take to build a culturally and historically grounded community of practice for African American children? Building a successful community of practice in a school populated predominantly by African American children calls for a critical redefinition of what the educational establishment deems good teaching and successful learning according to the cultural values described above. Such a community of practice would also be historically grounded.

Building a successful community of practice for a successful African-centered school also involves production of activities that are conceptually and culturally rich, deeply meaningful with respect to the commonality of African American heritage and experience in America. It would require, as many educators now argue, that the pedagogy of a people ought to build on their cultural patterns, language, and worldview. A very simple example is discourse practices—forms of talk that embody one's cultural patterns and interpretative frameworks.

A common discourse practice is the use of the "inclusive we" in referring to the United States in discussions about American history. An example is saying "*We* then made Puerto Rico a protectorate instead of a state." Another example is from an occasion in which I was observing in a U.S. history classroom. The discussion was on Trail of Tears, when Andrew Jackson, American hero, lead a forced march of the defeated American Indians and African Americans from their promised reservation land to the less desirable territory in Oklahoma. As a consequence of the Treaty of 1834, signed by a minority of Indians involved, 17,000 Cherokee Indians, who had resisted relocation by four years of nonviolent disobedience, were rounded up and imprisoned. On the forced march westward Indians began dying of disease, exposure, and thirst. It is estimated that more than 4,000 Cherokees died in the stockades and on the march. The teacher I was observing said, "This is something of a shameful period in our history. We did not treat the Native Americans very well." An African American student, retorted with some disdain, "We?! We?! Don't include me in that 'we' bit. My ancestors were slaves, so I ain't in that 'we.'" Now the student's angry response was only triggered by the teacher's use of the inclusive "we." Clearly the student maintained a position as a nonparticipant in governmental policy toward the American Indians by virtue of his being African American and knowing history from that perspective.

The point is not that we want to edit our discourse to avoid eliciting this kind of response from African American students. The point is that the pedagogy of the teacher should draw on or at least respect the historical and cultural awareness of the student. The teacher must be an expert cultural learner, so that important expressions of students' identity and positionality register. A pedagogy for successful learning and development of African American children requires a critical interrogation of students' interests and understandings.

Why a pedagogy grounded in the history, traditions and cultural heritage of African Americans? It is because the level of cultural analysis in organizing effective instructional practices must be deeper than the traditional and conventional approaches to understanding school culture. In my approach, cultural theory will be analyzed as a composite of folk explanation (common sense from the perspective of that geopolitical group) and the appropriate of academic/educational theory. Readers who are interested in reading further on the notion of cultural model should refer to Holland and Quinn (1987), Ani (1994), John Ogbu (1989), Wade Boykin (1986) and more recently, James Gee (1997) and Jabari Mahari (1998). Gee uses the term *cultural model* (1997, pp. 245–257) in the sense that I use the term *cultural pattern.* I prefer the term cultural pattern or more simply, cultural practice, to connote activity as well as systems of values and ideas. In the present formulation, educational theory is examined as culturally situated in the degraded experiences of African Americans in contemporary social and educational practices.

For success with African American children teachers need a theory of practice and a practice of theory that take account of the cultural patterns and educational heritages of Africans in America. As I indicated in the Preface, theory is by no means the opposite of practice. A feature that characterizes an Africanist worldview is that theory and practice are not seen as dichotomous, the way they are in contemporary mainstream American value systems and discourse. Without a theory of instruction, the common sense practices, the core practices that Elmore talks about, snap into place as by default.

From this perspective of an African-centered pedagogy, the goal of education is not to prepare children to fit within the system, but to revolutionize the system toward fulfilling the promise of democracy articulated in the documents (but not the deeds) of this country's founding fathers. The core of social studies—history—is a "whole truth" perspective with agency. African-centered social studies would examine the lightening rod incidents in this nation's history that forced a confrontation of its basic contradictions of liberty and equality. Racism is an ideology that positions White people as superior and non-White people as inferior. The pedagogy developed for African American children must confront this ideology if we wish to avoid them internalizing the ideology of White supremacy and White superiority.

The incompleteness of American education is in two critical respects that are contradistinctive to African pedagogy: (1) deep thought as both the process and the aim of education for liberation, self-agency, and self-determination; and (2) community participation in deep thought that furthers and develops those ends. This level of consciousness and critique is difficult to come by for those socialized in the cultural mainstream of America. So the task of teachers who wish to be successful with African American children is to confront this theoretical tradition into which they may have been socialized.

DIFFERENT RESPONSE TO BUILDING LEARNING COMMUNITIES

It is one thing to recognize the shortcomings of education reform agendas to take account of the new conceptualizations of cultural diversity and human development (as does Williams, 1996), and quite another to synthesize these concerns in a connected pedagogy to which children respond. Contemporary systems of education still interpret their failure to educate African American children as individual and cultural remediation, especially through a massive bureacraticization of special needs. In short, too much contemporary theory on achievement is embedded in the functionalist theory and transmission model of education.

The undeniable trend of public education in its handling of academic difficulty of African American children is to make pedagogical problems clinical ones (i.e., special needs). This is the single most prominent distinction between contemporary educational practice and African-centered pedagogy. Both accept the social and emotional adjustment of the student as essential considerations determining appropriate educational practice. The difference lies in the fact that this adjustment is simply a normal part of the African-centered pedagogy. In contrast to African American cultural models, the Western (European) mindset is to view educational activity as centered in the manipulation and mastery of symbol systems. In the African cultural system the disposition is to view symbols as the means of communication, and educational activity as the creation of meaning and discovery of truth. This idea will be developed further with the discussion of the five essential cultural practices for an African-centered pedagogy. These essential cultural practices reflect the cultural values and intellectual heritage of Africans and African Americans as they apply to teaching and learning.

SUMMARY AND CONCLUSIONS

The purpose of the historical grounding of this chapter is to institute a sharper interpretative lens on teaching of the social studies in the African-centered pedagogy. The missing lens concerns the set of contradictions in American ideas and values, born of their unique and fascinating development in American history. When an understanding of these contradictions is left out of the educational experience of African American learners it distorts both our sense of self as a people and the possibility for a complete working understanding of American history and its institutions.

It is not at all difficult to see the contradiction of values and its roots. The contradiction of the lofty ideas of individual freedom together with the growing institutions of human bondage and servitude are the essence of understanding American history, as well as America's political and social institutions. The "terrible transformation" (Johnson & Smith, 1998) occurred in this country's inception as a confederation of colonies. The terrible transformation is from a society that could have extended the ideals of "life, liberty, and the pursuit of happiness" to all its inhabitants, to a dual system of justice that enslaved an entire people, basing its political economy on slavery. The American colonies have, law by law, built a social system and a political economy based upon human bondage—and the form of human bondage was racial slavery. Here we have America emerging from this fledgling new commonwealth of colonies, this gem of the British Empire, that began living this contradictory system of values throughout history.

This legacy of the terrible transformation shaped the cultural heritage of African American education. There is a cultural integrity to the African American intellectual heritage of literacy for freedom. Unlike the Progressive ideal that suggests that literacy is important to democratic participation, from the African American historical and cultural perspective literacy is inseparable from the struggle for freedom. In the educational experience of most African Americans, whether in an urban northern (segregated) setting or southern rural (Jim Crow) setting there was no time to push for or insist upon progressive education or anything like "cooperative learning" or "teaching for understanding." No such option existed. As an African American you took what meager educational resources were available and made the most of what you had, which, unfortunately, was not much. Second, as an African American learner, there was little room to question whether something was rote learning or learning for understanding. Whatever was expected of you to learn, you learned because you understood that your very survival might depend on it.

Yet, there are certain essential practices of powerful pedagogy that emerge from the African American experience. Educator Asa Hilliard often points how such practices get "rediscovered" and appropriated by the European American academic community from Africanist educational precepts—including the notions of cooperative learning, multiple intelligences, "character education," and "community of caring." But these are ideas that will be *re*-appropriated, as you will see, in the African-centered pedagogy.

CHAPTER THREE

Culture, Cognition, and the Community of Achievement

What should we be doing? The answers, I believe, lie not in a proliferation of new reform programs but in some basic understandings of who we are and how we are connected to and disconnect from one another.

—Lisa Delpit, *Other People's Children: Cultural Conflicts in the Classroom*

An African-centered pedagogy is concerned with the acquisition of self-determination and self-sufficiency for African people. It is ultimately concerned with truth and the "Afrocentric mission to humanize the universe."

—Agyei Akoto, *Nation Building: Theory and Practice in Afrikan-Centered Education*

Almost every teacher has heard the phrase "community of learners." By that is meant viewing one's classroom as a collective dedicated to learning and development in all of its rich and variegated forms. It is a charming vision and an engaging metaphor for one's classroom. What would a community of learners be like if it were specifically designed to promote the achievement and academic development of African American learners? That is the question taken up next as I explain the theoretical framework in this chapter and the next.

I refer the reader once again to the diagram, Figure 2 depicting the basic components of the African-centered pedagogy. The reader will notice that there are five outer circles surrounding a larger inner circle. For the time being, I would like you to think about the larger inner circle as an African-centered community of learners. This circle represents the social, cultural, and historically situated system of practices that bind teacher(s) and learners together in the joint activity of learning achievement. I devote this chapter to developing a deeper understanding of the "inner circle" representing the community of learners. In the next chapter, I discuss in greater detail the outer circles of the diagram, representing the five essential cultural practices of an African-centered pedagogy. Their connection to the larger circle is meant to signify a system of practices that draw their meaning and relevance from the fact that they emerge from an African-centric community of learning.

So imagine a community of learning that has as its list of features those qualities of culturally relevant pedagogy articulated by Ladson-Billings—including a teacher who is connected to the children, to their lives and cultures, and to the wider community from which they come. Imagine these as the classrooms of the exemplary teachers of African American children described by Ladson-Billings, Foster, Irvine, and others. How do we make a community of learners, say in your classroom, a community of achievement for those African American students in the group?

We have said that a connected pedagogy for African American learners is grounded in the collective cultural legacy of Africans in America. The following depiction of a community of achievement for African American children begins with an articulation of the African-centered set of assumptions and understandings that clarify the political and cultural realities of schooling for Black children in White America. How should we think about "culture" and "achievement" in ways that incorporate political and cultural realities of the schooling of Black children in White America? What do we need to know to create a community of achievement for African American children? How do we create the "village" that is organized as a culture of learning, a climate of caring, and domain of development for African American children? We have the general outline—namely, appraising instructional practice form an African-centered foundation. But the specifics have yet to be filled in. We consider those knowledge foundations next.

BRIEF FOUNDATIONS HISTORY

It might be helpful to look first at several earlier attempts at addressing the achievement of African American students. The key to doing this has been to look critically and analytically at the social and cultural contexts of their educational experience. These prior frameworks include the so-called *ecological model* for explaining school success and failure, and the notion of culturally responsive teaching.

The social and behavioral sciences have not been the handmaidens to the profession of teaching that the physical and biological sciences have been to the profession of medicine. The disciplines of cognitive, developmental, and educational psychology and sociology, which have traditionally provided the knowledge base for education, are undergoing significant paradigm shifts. This is a good thing for developing connected pedagogy for African American children. Inquiry in any field is healthy when the epistemological assumptions are brought into the open, freely discussed, critiqued, and countered by others in the same community of practice. A field is healthier still if the bases of the critique are informed by authentic practice. This is one of the conditions we should seek to recreate in the inner circle of the African-centered community of achievement.

Out of a healthy state of confusion in developmental and educational psychology come paradigm shifts that more closely resemble the epistemology of African American culture. In the academic world, postmodern influences have served to shake the hold of many automatic assumptions of knowledge, power, and where it resides (Lave, 1988; 1997; Wenger, 1998). In addition to this, the growing influence of Piagetian cognitive theory, Vygotskian sociocultural theory and critical theory have shattered the behaviorist and functionalist foundations of educational theory. The result of some of these paradigm shifts has been the emergence of a learning theory—including situativity theory and sociocultural theory—that respects the cultural and experiential groundedness we require for an African-centered pedagogy. How are situativity theory and sociocultural theory useful frameworks for developing cultural psychology of African-centered pedagogy?

These two theoretical foundations have emerged from a convergence of work in a number of disciplines—cultural and cognitive psychology, semiotics, anthropology, critical theory, and cognitive anthropology. Situated cognition theory developed, in part, from the sociohistorical school of thought of Lev Vygotsky and his collaborators (e.g., Leont'ev) and followers (e.g., Wertsch, 1985; Bruner, 1997). It is school of thought known as "situated cognition" or "situated cognition theory" that pushes the discipline of psychology outward from the individual psyche, and pushes the discipline of sociology and anthropology inward from the social collective and cultural *socii*. This perspective of simultaneously theorizing the individual self and social-cultural self, along with the sociohistorical approach, provide theoretical foundations for developing the underlying cultural psychology of African-centered pedagogy.

As Kirshner and Whitson (1997, p. 6) note, both of these theoretical foundations break away from the individualistic, technist orientation of Western psychology. This is exactly the type of theoretical foundation needed for theorizing Black achievement—one that carries little of the cultural baggage of Euro-Western biases and value systems. The sociocultural perspective has already been worked into a pedagogical system of teaching by assisted performance (see

Tharp & Gallimore, 1991). The system theorizes the relationship between an individual and a caregiver or more capable person. Sociocultural theory also focuses on the structures and interrelations within activity systems—such as a family, nursery enclave, kindergarten, or day care in contemporary social settings. In similar fashion, situated cognition theorizes a community of practice as a way of examining learning from the lens of a broader social and political analysis.

What does this mean for you? It means that there is an opportunity to revise the way you have been thinking about human learning, cognitive development, and achievement. There are new opportunities for you to think about your role and your positionality in organizing the inner circle of your community of learning. There are examples of building a new community of practice that honor the knowledge traditions, cultural patterns, and sociocultural models of the African American heritage in America. Michele Foster (1997) has begun to document African American pedagogy in her portraiture of exemplary African American teachers in segregated settings throughout the South. Gloria Ladson-Billings (1994) and Jabari Mahiri (1998) have provided multiple examples of the qualities of accomplished practice with African American children. Foster and Ladson-Billings, by providing a rich descriptions of accomplished teaching practice of individual teachers in the African American tradition, lay the foundation for how to characterize the nature of the community of practice that develops other teachers in that same tradition. Their research provides conceptions of accomplished practice as a teacher of African American children looks like in the individual, so that we have the means to build it into the universe of activity in a school community. Jabari Mahiri (1998) has begun the work of enculturating a responsive learning environment by drawing on and incorporating the visages of youth culture into school contexts.

Recently I received in the mail a publication from the Association of Supervision and Curriculum Development (ASCD). It was a special volume on the topic of connected practice. Particularly telling was to find that a book on connected practice would have no reference whatsoever to the most trenchant of failures in American education especially with respect to African American children. It is interesting that in a recent ASCD publication on the new best practices, not one chapter was devoted to the learning achievement of African American children.

What is the lesson in this? You cannot have universal best practices for African American children nor can you have best practices predicated on epistemology that constructs African Americans as educationally less able. An African-centered theory is necessary to help teachers think through how to connect with African American children's lived experiences, without falling into the trap of thinking that they need to first learn their culture for the purpose of improving their "cultural synchrony with the mainstream." Despite the impossibility of learning a culture for this purpose, we implicitly (and sometimes explicitly) expect teachers to do just that to improve the success of African American children. As was discussed earlier, this is the problem with multicultural education with respect to elevating achievement—only it is not just Black culture that is expected to be "learned about," but all represented cultures of children constituting the school community.

From this perspective, a multicultural approach is of limited value in developing a perspective on culture for the inner circle. The practices of multicultural education essentialize culture. That is to say, the practice of multicultural education in public schools serves to turn culture into categories of membership—to be "embraced" and "celebrated." Critical theorists call this act of treating a process or abstract construction as though it was thing "reification." Culture is reified when people attempt to practice multicultural education, because the "culture" comes to be understood as little more than a marker or signifier of difference. The outcome, however, for members of the "celebrated and embraced" culture is that they are still othered. In practice, the culture of "othered" children is summarized and abbreviated in the interest of incorporating them into the curriculum. Simply being included in the "faces, facts, and festivals" approach to multicultural education turns out to be a fancier way of marginalizing children of color.

Connected pedagogy for African American children requires that you, as the teacher, become an expert cultural learner. In other words, you must become a student of human activity systems and human sign systems—particularly those systems the local culture provides in socializing children. Those human activity and value systems of African American culture differ from, and sometimes contradict, the system of values in play in the American cultural mainstream embodied in public schools. The importance of activity systems, sign systems, and value systems to the practices of achievement will be further developed in the next chapter, as part of the theoretical foundations of connected pedagogy for African American children. The point here is that this is where our focus of energy and understanding must be developed. This is where the severe crisis of knowledge dwells in American education in policy making and pedagogy development.

Nowhere is the crisis of knowledge more pronounced than in the literacy instruction of African American children. The public furor over what has been termed the Ebonics debate of few years ago (see the Perry & Delpit, 1998) has revealed how little teachers, educators, and policymakers actually know about linguistics or applied linguistics, and language. In particular, educators know very little about the components of language, the process of language acquisition, how children acquire their mother tongue, about TESOL methodologies, linguistics and literacy, language and culture, or language policy and planning. It is startling how many primary school teachers of African American children actually think of themselves as teaching them their own language. Foster (2001), remarking on teacher knowledge in professional development, detailed this crisis of knowledge by noting how too few teachers possess:

1. An understanding of human language, including such basic ideas like the fact that human language is intrinsic and can create an infinite number of sentences (too few teachers know what a dialect is, why it is important in literacy instruction, or how it relates to the varieties of English spoken by their students);
2. A working understanding of the components of language—syntax, morphology, lexicon, and pragmatics—where they could at least distinguish between the components and articulate their relation the literacy development of their students;
3. An awareness of the different varieties of English, particularly African American English;
4. A knowledge of language and literacy such that they know the difference between becoming literate and learning to read, and the difference between the processes of learning to speak and learning to write;
5. A sense of the importance of a coherent language policy and coherent curriculum plan to promote ongoing literacy development in their schools.

A pedagogical theory is necessary for teachers who are not African American to develop positionality—a stance in relation to the historicity and culture of African American experience required for effective work as a teacher. This is the foundation of effective teaching for African American children. Mahiri (1998), who has developed an African-centered pedagogy for literacy and technology, puts it this way:

> In order to be effective, teachers will need to become more aware of their own positionality in American culture, even as they increase their awareness of and sensitivity to diverse backgrounds, orientations, and interests of their students. (p. 4)

According to the framework of the African-centered pedagogy, positionality is the context of identity experienced and negotiated at the mesolevel—at the "meeting place of the individual with society." That is, positionality is identity that is shaped by power, status, rank, and sense of privilege in a given social context. Holland, Lachicotte, Skinner, and Cain (1998) indicate that positionality:

> has to do with more than division, the "hereness" and "thereness" of people; it is inextricably linked to power, status, and rank. Social position has to do with entitlement to social and material resources and so to the higher deference, respect, and legitimacy accorded those genders, races, ethnic groups, castes, and sexualities privilege by society. (p. 271)

For example, by the nature of classrooms, the positionality of the teacher is one of authority and power. However, the identity may be deployed in different ways such as authoritarian by display of power and force of will, versus authoritative by qualities of intellectual leadership.

ARGUING FOR THE CONSTRUCT OF PRACTICES

The life force of pedagogy is not determined by policy or principles, but by *practices*. It matters not that the faculty of an under-performing urban school decides to be "multicultural" or "antiracist" as a matter of principle or policy. It matters what the practices are. Those are not easily changed, and they are never changed for the better if they are not examined, especially if those practices go against the grain of what in is conventional practice in mainstream America.

School people almost never examine the premise as to why inequality exists. From the previous brief historical framing, we understand why, historically, local control of education has occurred so universally. Yet I remember a recent occasion where I showed a video of the 1989 Public Broadcasting System airing of a special entitled *Learning in America* to a group of teachers in a professional development activity, hoping the irony of facing the identical issues twelve years later would register without specific mention. This episode explored the issue of educational equity and explored the question of why education was so localized and so unequally resourced with so little federal oversight. The piece opened with the recognition that schools have always been a matter of local control, and not a federally mandated right guaranteed by the constitution. The treatment of the topic, however, leads the viewer to think of this phenomenon as an accident of history. One teacher commented: "Gee, I wonder why schools are always locally funded? I wonder why a right to education is not a given like the Bill of Rights?"

To recognize this as part of pedagogy, teachers working with African American students would not only have to be open to the practices of critical interrogation, but they would have to interrogate routinely their racial privilege and their participation in a political and economic system of oppression. Teachers do not routinely do this as a part of their practice. To recognize, for example, that local funding and administration of public schools has a history in America's system of exclusion of African Americans from education and disenfranchisement, you would need to begin your practice with a critical pedagogy from the perspective of Africans in America. Rarely do teachers, whether European American or African American, have the opportunity, inclination, or support to do this in public schools.

AFRICAN-CENTERED PEDAGOGY NEEDED FOR CONTINUOUS INTERROGATION

To maintain a level of critical awareness, teachers would need a system of practice—a pedagogy—that would not let this piece of critical understanding go by. This, once again, is the reason we need an African-centered connected pedagogy. The framework of culturally responsive teaching (e.g., Ladson-Billings, 1994), and variations of it (e.g., Cochran-Smith, 1996) need to be combined with a system of practice in order to elevate Black achievement. Without a system of practice, we fall prey to a phenomenon I call the "ritual of resolve."

The ritual often begins when teachers working in diverse urban public schools, whether European- or African American, decide to respond to their ongoing uneasy feelings that they need to change their teaching practices in order to be more effective with African American children. They assuage their uneasiness by finding out what books they should buy, what workshops they should attend, and what materials they should request, all in the attempt to improve their practice. But we all know that good intentions do not pave the way to effective practice. Regardless of the number of good ideas, important insights, and cultural realizations gained by this professional activity, they all mean little unless applied in the real practices of teaching and learning—and produce results.

Academic types have their own version of the ritual of resolve. The seduction of something sounding good at a paper presentation or symposium is our draw into the ritual of resolve. Too often we academicians attend a meeting and hear something that momentarily charges us up about the need to take into account serious concerns about racism and educational access. After acquiring that charge, we academic types too often feel better, as if our agreement with the new understanding or perspective has already made a difference—even though we have not yet done anything with it. I can remember many specific occasions in which the ritual of resolve becomes a surrogate for actual practice.

I have experienced and seen this illusion of practice play out in countless paper sessions and symposia at national meetings of the American Educational

Research Association (AERA). I see colleagues attending because of their genuine interest and concern about successful education of African American children and diverse populations of students in urban communities. Too often they leave with the feeling that they had actually done something about the conditions of African American children because they have resolved to make a change in their practice based on what they heard. But what change? Change does not occur unless the resolve is translated into practice.

There are powerful practices, and then there are rituals, masquerading as practices that divert us from effective work. The *ritual of resolve* is one of such ritual, and one of the reasons for developing the African-centered pedagogy. Pick up an educational foundations textbook and turn to the section that explains the purposes of education, and you are likely to find cultural transmission among those functions of education listed—and they are not referring to anything but the dominant culture.

The need to transmit cultural knowledge for developing all children—the function of *education* and not *schooling*, is illustrated by the variety of Saturday schools, after school programs, rites-of-passage programs, Black independent schools, African-centered public schools, and study groups. Culturally, historically, and politically, African Americans have already made the strategic distinction between schooling and education. Many important African American educators consider the work of African-centered pedagogy a cultural imperative (e.g., Shujaa, 1994, p. 28).

DEVELOPING THE THEORY—PREMISES AND PRACTICES

The African-centered pedagogical theory will be described as a set of seven *premises* and five *practices*. This section will explain the seven premises encompasses the theory underpinning an African-centered pedagogy. The next section will explain the practices.

The pedagogy is based upon the situated cognition perspective (situated learning theory) and activity theory that assumes that cognition is a social and situated activity, and not merely a matter of individuals acquiring knowledge that is abstract and independent of the setting. This basic idea—that human cognition and cognitive development is social and situated—is significantly modified by this project by incorporating a deep analysis of culture. The following premsises summarize my instructional application over the years of theoretical traditions of *activity theory* (Leontiev, 1981; Chaiklin, Hedegaard, & Jensen, 1999), *situated cognition and social context of cognition* (Brown, Collins, & Duguid, 1989; Lave 1988, 1991, 1997; Lemke, 1997; Minick, Stone, & Forman, 1993; Rogoff, 1990; Rogoff, 1995; Rogoff & Lave, 1984; Tharp & Gallimore, 1991),

Table 2
PREMISES OF THE AFRICAN-CENTERED PEDAGOGICAL THEORY

Premise one:	human cognition and intellectual development are socially and culturally situated in human activity.
Premise two:	the core of learning is meaningful and purposeful activity, which is embodied in practices and represented by a system of signs to communicate understanding and create a common system of meaning making.
Premise three:	meaning making is the principal motive for learning, and not merely reinforcement for the acquisition of information or new knowledge.
Premise four:	the most important form of learning is the appropriation of signs and practices of worthwhile adult activity.
Premise five:	community and symbolic culture are significant to the learning of individuals—children grow into the cognitive life of those around them.
Premise six:	the development of children's capacity to think, reason, communicate, and perform academically is a matter of practice—a matter of knowledge-in-use that is enacted in socially situated and culturally contextualized settings.
Premise seven:	Black achievement is linked to conditions of schooling that reduce racial vulnerability.

and the *semiotic, cultural, and discursive formulations of mind* (Bruner, 1990, 1996; Harre & Gillett, 1994; Resnick, Säljö, Pontecarvo, Burge, 1991; Resnick, Levine, & Teasley, 1991; Scribner & Cole, 1981; Shore, 1996; Vygotsky, 1962, 1978; Wertsch, 1985; Wittgenstein, 1953).

The first foundational premise of African-centered pedagogy is that human cognition and intellectual development are socially and culturally situated in human activity. You cannot teach children cooperative behavior without situating them in the activity of cooperative behavior; you cannot *teach* systematic inquiry without *doing* systematic inquiry. This perspective, more than any of the others, supports the cultural psychology of African-centered pedagogy. This means that achievement depends on the teacher's skill in situating children in activity contexts that promote desired developmental and intellectual achievements. Achievement is a function of both the individual's developmental history and the social and cultural support structures for that individual's accomplishments. In the African-centered pedagogy, the teacher is responsible for designing the appropriate cultural and social support structures for learners. Some will recognize this as central tenet of the sociocultural theory of Vygotsky and the notion of a zone of proximal development.

The aims of sociocultural theorists are the same as ours in developing the African-centered pedagogy. According to Kirshner and Whitson (1997), the research agenda of sociocultural theorists is to determine what constitutes appropriate of knowledge within the zone of proximal development (ZPD) of learners. Determining acquisition of knowledge in the ZPD is also the focus of African-centered pedagogy. This knowledge is viewed in both psychological terms, such as the acquisition of language proficiency and higher-order cognitive processes, and sociocultural terms, such as rules of turn taking in conversation or conventions of greeting elders. In any case, the important idea is that our inquiry of knowledge acquisition ought to be guided by an understanding of the social-cultural context —that development proceeds in a context of social interaction and cultural embeddedness. Therefore, we look at student achievement performance and cognitive development as the product of the individual's developmental history (progress), as well as the support structures created by other people and cultural tools in the setting.

The implication of this premise—that learning and intellectual development are socially and culturally situated—is that we as teachers should look at learning achievement as more than just a product of individual effort and activity, but the product of the quality of the activity setting as well. Our unit for analyzing learning performance shifts from focusing not only on what the individual does, but on the activity of the individual within a context of social relationships and richness of the intellectual environment. If you can recall your reading of Lev Vygotsky, this idea that we employ a dialectical unit of analysis (a unit that incorporates individual activity and the context of activity) is the major contribution of his work to education. Put simply, children's learning and development is conceived as a trajectory, as a direction toward some developmental accomplishment, in which individual effort, individual capacity, and social supports from more capable others contribute to the development or achievement. This dialectical unit of analysis is central to the African-centered pedagogical theory, as it is the foundation for the interactive system of learning and teaching.

The second premise is that the core of learning is meaningful and purposeful activity, which is embodied in practices and represented by a system of signs to communicate understanding and a system of meaning making. A complete pedagogy, an action theory of teaching and learning, must account for construction of meaning and understanding on two planes—the internal mental life and cognitive world of the individual as well as the external social life or cultural world in which the individual interacts. The African-centered pedagogy views knowledge acquisition as process involving interaction of these two planes. Therefore, to understand how a child constructs meaning, it is necessary to understand the presentation of signs and symbols in the learning environment, as well as how that child construes the system of signs in their attempts to make meaning. The second premise underscores the importance of human activity as the external representation of signs, sign systems, and cultural symbols that are internalized as meaning when the child attempts to make use of these signs and symbols. I recall here Wittgenstein's (1953) dictum that meaning is the use to which we put our signs. The second premise of my theory adds this dictum: Many of our signs (visible representations) are human activities, not just words, symbols, or gestures.

If you accept these two ideas—that meaning is made by our use of signs and that many signs are actually activities—then it follows that participation in activity is a form of meaning-making. Moreover, we might say that thinking is the activity of operating with signs—whether "inside the head" or as a collective activity of several people.

The external representation of meaning inheres in human activity and in human sign systems. The internal act of constructing meaning, according to my theory, is partly a process of participating in purposeful activity with others. Both the appropriation of signs as cultural symbols and the participation in cultural life through activity are significant components of learning in the African-centered pedagogy, and will be examined at greater depth in the following chapters. But for the present, the reader may be able to connect with this notion through either the "learning by doing" perspective of John Dewey, the social perspective on learning of Lev Vygotsky, or both.

Even though I ground African-centered pedagogy on the social-cultural perspective on learning, I do not mean to imply that learning is principally done *only* in interaction with others. Rather, I want to emphasize that, whether we intend it or not, rich learning experience, including deep understanding about the world, occurs in the company of others. However, we also want to build young people's capacity to learn independently. Wenger (1998) expresses the social perspective this way:

> The difference between mere doing and learning, or between entertainment and learning, is not a difference in kind of activity. It is not that one is mindless and the other thoughtful, that one is hard and the other easy, or that one is fun and the other arduous. It is that learning—whatever form it takes—changes who we are by changing our ability to participate, to belong, to negotiate meaning. And this ability is configured socially with respect to practices, communities, and economies of meaning where it shapes our identities. (p. 326)

The third premise of African-centered pedagogy is that meaning-making is the principal motive for learning, not merely acquisition of information or new knowledge. Despite what educational theory has told us in our teacher preparation coursework, learners do not learn primarily because of reinforcements and rewards, or even intrinsic interest and curiosity. They mobilize themselves to make sense of their social world and acquire the cognitive tools to more successfully negotiate it. The best example of this is language acquisition. People do not learn to speak through reinforcements, but through a drive to acquire a human capacity that dramatically amplifies the power with which they can participate in the world. This drive does not end with acquiring a language. Language then becomes the primary culturally acquired tool by which humans continue acquiring knowledge that enables their participation in the world. In the precursor to situated cognition theory, sociocultural theory, much is made of the notion of appropriation (Bahktin, 1981). Appropriation, the use of new signs for one's own ends, continues throughout the developmental trajectory of human beings.

As Kirshner and Whitson (1997) point out, the idea of appropriation of cultural tools (e.g., language, symbol systems, material tools) is an important alternative to the intrapsychological preoccupation that psychology has had with the mind of the individual. As you have seen in premises one and two so far, the African-centered theory cannot be limited to an "inside-the-head" psychology if we are to take full account of how the child learns and develops through support from, and interaction with, their cultural and social environments. The notion of appropriation forces an inquiry into human learning to consider both the internal intrapsychological (inside the individual) world of the learner and the external (cultural) interpsychological (between individuals) relations that the learner has with people, customs, and tools (both physical and linguistic).

This leads to the fourth premise of the African-centered pedagogy that the most important form of learning is the appropriation of signs and practices of worthwhile adult activity. The reader has no doubt learned in developmental psychology or educational psychology courses that human beings always learn new information in terms of what they already know. The importance of this principle—that prior knowledge is essential to learning—is expressed in every tradition and type of learning theory you are likely to experience. The notion of appropriation gives this principle action and honors the reality that human beings are more than mere information processors or information accumulators. People are capable of learning complex abilities and are motivated to acquire those abilities. Children learn, not because they are merely curious or adults expect them to, but because they seek participation in the world.

The fifth premise is that community and symbolic culture are significant to the learning of individuals—children grow into the cognitive life of those around them. A social-cultural community is where children negotiate meaning. Negotiated meaning in general, is the fabric of social interaction and learning in any social scene. It is how people experience the world and engage in what we find as meaningful. Children understand the complex abilities of reading, writing, and thinking to have value and importance, because the community of social beings that surrounds them do.

The sixth premise is that the development of children's capacity to think, reason, communicate and perform academically is a matter of practice—a matter of knowledge-in-use that is enacted in socially situated and culturally contextualized settings. Much will be said about the activity settings appropriate for successful achievement of African American children. On this account, what makes exemplary teachers is not so much the wealth of knowledge and expertise they bring, but rather their ability to enable the development of knowledge and expertise of others by orchestrating practice-rich activity settings in his or her classroom.

The seventh premise is that Black achievement is linked to conditions of schooling that reduce racial vulnerability (to use Steele's [1997] term). The flip side of this premise is that African American students under racial vulnerability experience degradation of their academic performance as measured by tests.

ESSENTIAL PRACTICES OF THE AFRICAN-CENTERED PEDAGOGY

As I noted in the Preface, this book uses a specific meaning of the term *practice* that differs from the conventional usage of the term. The idea of practice is central to the African-centered pedagogy, because accomplished practice and cultural practices are the essence of the pedagogy, to be described shortly. I want to refresh your memory of how practice is used in this theory. What most people mean by a practice is an activity, a strategy, or an approach. In the African-centered theory, practice entails more than action or activity. It also entails viewing the activity as a performance, and understanding that performance as something that must be appraised according to whether results were produced for the student. A practice is recognized as a pattern of professional activity or professional performance. The pattern is recognized by three things: (1) the design and enactment of professional activity; (2) the situational and cultural context of the activity; and (3) the consequential outcomes for the client.

This practice orientation is an extension of the well-known notion of the reflective practitioner (Dewey, 1933; Schon, 1984). "Practice oriented" incorporates action and reflection, and specifies a particular quality of reflection that I have discussed elsewhere as the *appraisal of practice* (Murrell, 2001). Every good reflective practitioner assesses his or her activity in light of the outcomes for learners or clients—that is, they appraise their own practice. For teachers, this means appraising their own teaching performance in accordance with the success or quality of student achievement performance. The following are the practices that constitute the second part of the African-centered pedagogical theory (see Table 3):

Engagement and participation practices
Identity development practices
Community integrity practices
Practices of inquiry
Meaning-making practices

To ask "What is African-centered pedagogy?" is to ask what teaching and learning are like when they are centered in African American cultural heritage. There are five distinct essential practices of teaching and learning when centered and contextualized in African American cultural heritage. These five essential practices form the foundations of my African-centered pedagogical theory. They are listed in Table 3 and depicted in Figure 3. These practices are designed to develop Identity, Community, Engagement and Participation, Practice and Meaning-Making from an African-American cultural perspective.

These five essential practices are appropriated from Wenger's (1998) discussion of social learning theory. As I explained earlier, I have grounded the African-centered pedagogy in social learning theory as articulated by Wenger and other situated cognition theorists who locate learning in the fabric of human enterprise and the context of human relationships and activity. These theorists advocate a perspective on learning that places learning in our lived experience in the world and participation with human activity. But I extend this framework to the African American experience, first by adding Engagement and Participation (or Mobilization) to the four components of social learning Wenger discusses (1998, p. 5), and then, most importantly, by developing the pedagogy as a set of African-centered practices.

Learning, according to the epistemology of African American cultural heritage, is not an individual activity, but an inherently social activity. That is, from the perspective of the African American heritage, learning is what results from the learner's facilitating interactions with caregivers and more

Table 3

ESSENTIAL CULTURAL PRACTICES IN AN AFRICAN-CENTERED PEDAGOGY

Engagement and participation practices

On the part of the teacher, these are actions and arrangements that encourage and promote the interest, engagement, and participation of students—with each other and with the learning activity. These practices aim to provide *sustained effort and commitment* with respect to the learning activity, *and sustained interpersonal engagement* with the community of learners. On the part of the learner, these are strategies and other means by which the learner mobilizes himself or herself to engage, put forth effort, and participate in the activities of learning.

Identity development practices

On the part of the teacher, these are actions and arrangements that encourage and elicit productive *self-exploration* and *self-definition* in the context of meaningful rich inquiry about the world. Literature selections and topic selections related to social justice and the students' backgrounds are particularly important for the teacher. On the part of the learner, these are actions that involve trying out different roles, representations and expressions of self by discourse, stance, dress, and particularly, language. In general, learner practices of identity development include all means of self-definition and re-definition.

Community integrity practices

On the part of the teacher, these are activities and arrangements for *organizing the intellectual and social life of a community of learners*. They require the teacher to incorporate cultural features (e.g., fictive kinship, communicative styles) and knowledge traditions of the African American heritage. These practices also identify and support students' initiative in building community integrity. On the part of the learner, these practices involve the actions of making and maintaining membership in a community. The learner participates in community integrity practices by joining, belonging, supporting other members in whatever the core activities of the group are.

(*continued next page*)

capable adults in the cultural fabric of a significant activity. This perspective contrasts with the mainstream cultural view of learning as an individual enterprise. The predominant metaphor of learning in both American popular culture and educational thought is that learning results from individual mental effort and ability. Contemporary thought among American educators has,

Table 3 (*continued*)
ESSENTIAL CULTURAL PRACTICES IN AN AFRICAN-CENTERED PEDAGOGY

Meaning-making practices	
	On the part of the teacher, these are activities and arrangements for making explicit cultural models (especially sign and symbol structures) and cultural patterns to amplify the interpretative frameworks of learners. These practices are particularly important for discourse practices and for engaging students in what Freire calls "reading the world." On the part of the learner, these are practices of inquiry that involve appropriation (taking for their own use), interpretation and consumption of cultural forms, signs, symbols, and other forms of symbolic representation. The aim is for learners to develop deep skills in analysis and interpretation of information and ideas, as well developing a critical regard of how and for what purposes they were produced.
Practices of inquiry	
	On the part of the teacher, these are activities and arrangements for critically interrogating the use and consumption of signs, symbols, and other symbolic representations. Learner practices of inquiry are conceived as various forms of recursive reappropriation—they take on and use (or sample) the phrases, signs, and images of others for use in their own expressive repertoire. This involves making students aware of their appropriation of symbols, signs, and other representations of meaning in the act of expressing and creating new meaning. The aim for learners is that they develop the critical capacities to analyze, reflect, critique, and act to transform the conditions under which they live.

in the last few decades come closer to recognizing the African-centered perspective—as evidenced by the now trite and overused articulation of the African proverb "It takes a village to raise a child." By and large, however, this perspective is not at all reflected in the core practices of public schooling in America.

The contrast is in the historical experience of African Americans to what have become the core practices of schooling in the United States. Where learning to read might mean winning one's freedom, helping others to escape slavery, and uplift the community as a whole, learning has come to be measured by a numerical score generated by an individual's success on manipulating a symbol system on some paper and pencil test. In contemporary American culture, the common view of learning is that it is something that mainly happens in school, brought about by systematic actions and practices at the direction of a

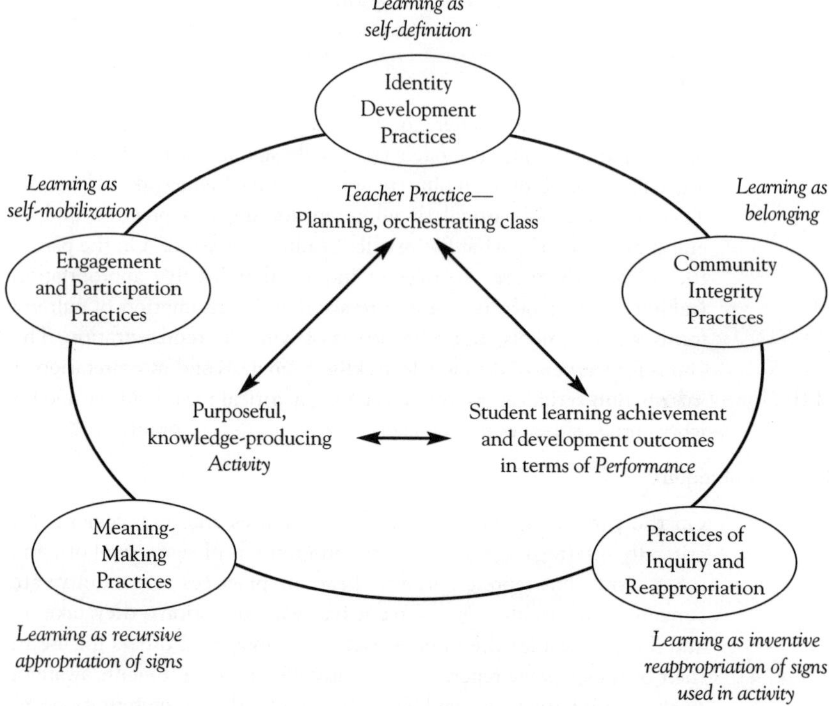

Figure 3. All components of the African-centered pedagogy.

teacher. In the African American cultural heritage, learning has never been simply equated to schooling and school performance.

Participation in adult life, according to the African-centered tradition, is when young people progressively increase their acquisition of, and involvement in, the practices of the immediate community, and construct identities with respect to these practices in the process. This sense of "participation" coincides with that of the situated cognition theorists, who view participation both as an action and a form of belonging in a community of practice (a concept to be discussed later). The situatedness of African Americans in a cultural heritage means a deeper sense of learning of individuals-in-communities. On this account, learning for individuals is an issue of engaging in, and contributing to, the practices of their communities. For communities, learning is an issue of refining practices to enable young people and ensure progress and prosperity for them in the future (this is also a part of the situated activity theory thinking, see Wenger, 1998, p. 7).

SUMMARY AND CONCLUSION

A pedagogy is more than just set of strategies and approaches—it entails a philosophy of education. A pedagogy engenders answers to the implicit question: What should be the function and purpose of public education in contemporary society? A pedagogy works well when it addresses this question appropriately for the children, family, and communities being served. Historically, the functions and purposes of education have played out differently from White mainstream America, and the pedagogical theory offered in this book responded to the African American experience. A pedagogy always engenders a direction and a purpose for learning, whether it is a formal one like the African-centered pedagogy presented in these pages, or a personal one incorporating some or all of the many educational frameworks discussed earlier.

The pedagogy is a set a seven premises (Table 2) and five practices (Table 3) that will help you as a teacher of African American children become an expert cultural learner. The premises explain the theoretical precepts and the practices articulate the way that teachers need to incorporate cultural learning into their professional repertoire to be effective with African American children. Cultural learning for a better world is valued in our educational debates and discussion, but rarely articulated. People are content with the form, but not the substance of multicultural education. Unless we are willing to fully engage what it means to know the world through a widening understanding and read of human systems and cultures, the default approach of multiculturalism will continue to be a boutique look at cultural differences.

PART II

Pedagogical Theory for Building a Community of African American Achievement

CHAPTER FOUR

Overview of the Pedagogical Theory

> In sum, there is a theoretical tradition, part of Western history, institutionalized in Western schooling, in which teaching/transmission is considered to be primary and prior to learning/internalizing culture. What is transmitted is assumed to be received in an unproblematic fashion, while processes of instruction and learning are assumed to be general and independent of what is to be learned. Let's call this a functionalist theory and note that it offers explanations of how school works and of what is the matter when it doesn't work, and that it is embedded in a theory about relations between society and the individuals who pass through and are socialized into it.
>
> —Jean Lave, "The culture of acquisition and the practice of understanding"

This chapter lays out the remaining conceptual framework and the theoretical underpinnings of the African-centered success pedagogy. This discussion will entail explanation of several key ideas in the internal circle of the theoretical model depicted in Figure 3—activity setting, practice, accomplished practice and community of practice. This chapter introduces the key theoretical formulations from cultural psychology, human development, and the social sciences and reinterprets them as they are manifested in the African American epistemologies and cultural pedagogies.

PEDAGOGY AS THEORY

A pedagogy is an instructional theory of that is realized as a system of practice. It is a theory of teaching-in-practice. By this I mean to say that a pedagogy is both an interpretive and generative framework. That is, it is a theory that informs how you make sense of activities, behaviors and all manner of human expression in your classroom. On this account the theory is interpretive in that it is a system of ideas that permits the teacher to make good sense of the classroom scene and what transpires in the activity of learning. But on the other side of the coin, it is also a system that is generative, because the teacher applies that good sense in the generation of effective teaching practices, such as the orchestration of classroom life and the design of instruction to bring about real learning achievement and personal development of the students.

A pedagogy is an interpretive framework and generative framework. The interpretive framework of the African-centered pedagogy helps the teacher to incorporate the cultural patterns of African American children and construct learning experiences that provide developmental scaffolding for them. The generative framework of the African-centered pedagogy will help the teacher ensure that he or she organizes learners' experience in a familiar and supporting cultural and social fabric. I have presented five component practices (Table 3) of African-centered pedagogy by which you can recreate your classrooms with cultural fabric familiar to your African American students so that you can draw on their lives, experiences, and culture to generate an enabling learning environment.

PEDAGOGY AS KNOWLEDGE-IN-PRACTICE

In the previous chapters, I have defined pedagogy as a holistic, active-reflective theory of teaching and learning. But now I want to add the idea of pedagogy as knowledge that is put to use in systems of activity that constitute accomplished practice. Accordingly, a pedagogy is not merely a blueprint or map for educational practice—but more like a script for accomplished practice that leads to the development and achievement of children—intellectually, socially, and spiritually. At this juncture, these are the working descriptors of the notion of pedagogy:

- An active-reflective theory of teaching and learning;
- Knowledge-in-practice;
- A system of organizing human systems, instructional materials, and human resources that promotes the learning and development of children;
- A rich cultural content—in this case the literature, recovered narratives, and cultural works of African Americans;
- A socioculturally, linguistically, and historically grounded system of teaching.

The African-centered pedagogy consists of five essential practices, which form the basis of a teaching system. The remainder of this chapter will explain and illustrate this system.

AFRICAN-CENTERED PEDAGOGY AS WORKING THE SYSTEM OF ESSENTIAL PRACTICES

Developing one's pedagogy involves grappling with a trio of concerns for effective teaching—human nature, human institutions, and human values. I have presented these concerns as a challenge—how to find the right content and right mix of these qualities of human experiences in the constitution of your classrooms and your schools. Later, I will address how the five essential principles form the pedagogical basis for meeting this challenge. The point I want to make here is that it is important to keep at the forefront this notion of knowledge-in-practice as we struggle for balance in this trio of concerns.

The African-centered pedagogy, as the five principles, offers a way of seeking a balance between the often conflicting systems of values, institutional demands, and developmental tasks. If we understand pedagogy as knowledge-in-practice, it becomes easier to think of the requirements of effective pedagogy for African American children. To begin with, it makes explicit the fact that teaching knowledge does not make good teaching practice unless it is applied and results in student achievement. By substituting "knowledge-in-practice" we have the phrase that becomes *African-centered knowledge-in-practice*. This more accurately conveys the purpose of this book, particularly to those who are used to thinking of pedagogy as a strategies or methods.

African-centered knowledge in practice conveys exactly the meaning of pedagogy undergirding this book. The other implicit meaning in the phrase African-centered knowledge-in-practice is the emphasis on the notion of a community of practice as the framework for understanding the appropriate mix of the cultural, familial, and social foundations of a child's education. Moreover, this sense of pedagogy means that we educators must be systematic, deliberate, and insightful as to how to organize the experience of school in ways that maximize the contribution of these foundations of children's development.

Using the pedagogy successfully is a matter of using the five practices (Table 3) as a single system of practice. There is an artistry of synthesis at the core of successful African-centered pedagogy. "Working the system" of essential practices means that the accomplished teacher does not work on one aim at a time, but rather all five aims all of the time. For instance, the way to further the aim of increased student engagement and participation is to organize an instructional activity setting that offers something that is interesting to the learner in a way that furthers understanding about the world (meaning-making) and self (identity formation), which incorporates three of the five aims in the pedagogy. The means by which the teacher makes some topic or theme interesting might be to create discourse events such as dyads, debates, focus groups, or critical forums that build a community of inquiry—thus incorporating two more of the five aims, community engagement and inquiry. Working the African-centered pedagogy as a system of practices in this case is a matter of working on all five "channels" in a way that practices syncretize into one script of accomplished practice. Now that we have examined the five essential practices and the seven premises in the last chapter, let me now explain how they come together to form a system of practice.

ACTIVITY SETTINGS—INSTRUCTIONAL ACTIVITY SYSTEM

Recall that, according to the theory, our unit of analysis for examining teaching practice incorporates both teacher and learner performance. I am using the term *activity setting* as the way we will refer to the "units" of teaching and learning. It is the foundation of African-centered pedagogy because it is the critical first step in accomplished instruction. In this pedagogy, the important first step in teaching is a conceptualization of the setting in which learning activity is to take place. Before you plan anything else, you need to know such things as the actions you will take as the teacher, what performances you *expect* of your students, what performances you *will not accept* from your students, and their readiness for the activity (both intellectually and dispositionally). Doing this thinking is preparing your instructional activity setting. The visual schematic for this system is depicted in Figure 4.

This way of conceptualizing the structure of teaching and learning events in your classroom contrasts with conventional notion of a lesson plan. Planning your instructional activity setting is both more detailed and expansive than doing a lesson plan, although both refer to the organization and structure of instructional activity. Though both refer to the structured situation in which you enact instruction, most lesson plans specify primarily what you do as the teacher and what is expected from students as a consequence. By contrast, an instructional activity setting not only specifies the desired outcome, but also specifies the experience of learning as a joint enterprise between you and your students. When you describe your instructional activity setting, you are specifying the totally of interaction of learners with each other and with you. Of course, some activity settings are very common and familiar. A reading group is an activity setting. Show-and-tell is an activity setting.

The use of this terminology—*activity setting* and *activity system*—is not meant to be a technical exercise in theory building, but rather to provide a vocabulary for extending our thinking about teaching and learning as a structured situation that considers more than just learning goals, materials, and time limits for phases of the "lesson." It is a vocabulary for thinking about the architecture of a learning event or experience that connects intellectually,

Curriculum Unit Big Idea:

Grade Level and Subject Matter Focus:

Lesson Concept(s):

Describe here the **conceptual content** of the lesson – **Be specific** about what concepts, information, and procedures children are to learn.

(Even if you are used to writing lesson **Goals** here, you still must specify the ideas/information children are to learn or the skills/abilities children are to acquire as a consequence of the lesson.)

1

Understanding Performance:

Describe here what students will do to demonstrate understanding as a result of the **learning activities** of the lesson. Tell **what the children will do** to demonstrate that their **learning achievement** has "gone beyond" merely knowing the concepts, information, and procedures.

(The better job you do in coming up with a **generative task**, the easier it will be to specify the understanding performance for the lesson.)

2

Learning Goals:

Describe here what knowledge, skills, and dispositions students will acquire or practice in the course of the learning activity in a **List of Learning Goals**.

(Even if you are used to writing **Objectives**, you still must be sure to specify the learning expectations that **students are supposed to achieve**, and **NOT** in terms of what the teacher wants to accomplish.)

3

Performance Assessment:

Describe here the means by which you will determine whether **every student** has achieved each of the learning goals for the lesson. Please include a **List of Criteria** by which you'll judge whether each student has achieved what they were expected to, as stated in the **Learning Goals**.

4

Activity Setting:

Describe (attach additional sheet as needed) a (1) **List of Materials Required**: (2) a rough **Time Sequence Breakdown** for the length of the instructional period you're planning for (this could be 40 minutes, or three class periods); (3) the **Discourse Practice/Pattern** for each set in the sequence (e.g., whole group instruction, cooperative learning groups, individual seat work, dyadic inquiry); and (4) the **"Wrap up"** (with what student product, performance, demonstration, or exhibition of learning will the lesson conclude?).

5

Figure 4. Instructional Activity System

socially, culturally, and even spiritually with your students in ways that promote their intellectual, social, and spiritual growth. Activity on this account includes social interaction and relationship building, as well as what teachers are used to thinking of being "on task." On Figure 3, it is the structure of any given setting in the inner circle.

The idea of *activity setting* is also meant to invoke understanding of teaching and learning as a scene in which teachers and learners are coparticipants and coproducers of learning achievements. Most of us were not trained to think of teaching as a conjoint enterprise—even though this is a principle idea in Vygotsky's theory and his familiar notion of the zone of proximal development. We are used to seeing ourselves as the primary actors and students as those who respond to what we do. As a result, we analyze our teaching practice, our pedagogy, in terms of what we do as teachers, instead of as the dynamic of interaction among you, your students, and the learning context that produces worthwhile knowledge and promotes development. The fact that we are coparticipants in a network of actions, interactions, and activity designed to develop children as learners too often goes unnoticed.

Even when the teacher is in a totally directive mode (e.g., giving a lecture), it is important in that moment to understand the experience as one of coparticipation with your students. Even in lecture, directed discussion, or direction-giving, the teacher and learner are coparticipants. Regardless of the activity setting—whether it is instructional or simply lining up the children to got to lunch—the accomplished teacher is continuously aware of the fact that she is engaged in a joint productive activity. Every activity or action can be viewed in terms of a desired educational outcome that both learners and teachers are jointly responsible for. Sometimes the outcome (e.g., a product) is represented by a piece of student work, and sometimes it is nothing more than the successful establishment of a useful routine (a process) such as moving to the lunchroom quickly, quietly, and without incident. This latter achievement, a social practice, is no less important than the intellectual practices (or what Grant Wiggins and the Coalition for Essential Schools call "habits of mind").

The notion of activity setting helps us, in our practice as teachers, stay conscious of the fact that in-the-moment-teaching experience is always two-way, always interactive, and always negotiated with our students. Accomplished teachers are always aware of their students' experience of the instruction and curriculum context, and the fact that teacher and student both have roles. In this way, the notion of an activity setting organizes our practice as teachers and focuses awareness on the respective roles of teacher and learner. By being aware of the roles played by both teacher and learner in an episode of teaching, we can more systematically orchestrate the events that will enhance the likelihood of learning. With an ongoing awareness of roles, it is easier for us as teachers to shape what students should be doing, what we should be doing as teachers, and how we should be responding to each other in any given setting.

CULTURAL COMPETENCE IN THE CIRCLE OF PRACTICE

Hopefully, this idea of thinking of instruction in terms of a well-designed instructional activity setting, as a system of interaction organizing how you and your students are mutually engaged in the joint production of knowledge, makes sense to you. At this point you might be thinking that this is the foundation of all good teaching, and you'd be right. It is consistent with many currently popular educational ideas are already familiar with—cooperative learning, learning community, caring community, and total quality management to name a few. With this collaborative, interactive, and practice-focused way of thinking about teaching in hand, I can now be more specific about the requirements for African-centered pedagogy. It has to do with teachers' understanding about culture as they fashion their activity settings, their circles of practice. It is now time to look more closely at what makes the African-centered pedagogical model distinctive—*cultural competence*.

I begin by asking you to recall the idea of cultural congruity or cultural synchrony (Irvine, 1990) from chapter 3. In capsule, the idea posits that African American underachievement is the result of two cultures being incongruent. Specifically, the asynchrony between "culture of the mainstream school" and the "culture of the African American home" leads to misperceptions of African American children's true ability and miscommunications that generally degrade the quality of their educational experience in comparison to their European American peers. The culture of the school is recognized by the familiar activity settings that you only see in school. Many of these are familiar "cultural furniture" to most people, Black and White. If you have ever watched children "playing school" you will recognize routines, arrangements, and even teacher talk in their play that seems very familiar and conventional. I am recalling the many times I have seen little girls (and think about why *girls* always get to be the teachers) admonishing their age-mates at their "desks" to do their *own* work. In this play you might catch glimpses of core practices that almost everyone will recognize as school practices—for example, African American girls playing the strict teacher at the front directing individual seatwork. While many of the familiar, if not tired and worn, schooling practices are benign, many others are not in the context of African American children's educational development.

ACTIVITY SYSTEMS AND CULTURAL COMPETENCE

Earlier I introduced the idea of activity setting to serve as a conceptual tool for unpacking school practices that seem conventional, commonsense, and customary. As I argued earlier, regardless of how natural and normal these core schooling practices might seem, many are damaging to African American children. It therefore behooves the accomplished teacher to critically examine the conventional and the customary practices to revise them so that effective teaching with African American children can be developed.

The concept of the activity setting, besides providing a means of talking about practice, also is the means for talking about a "piece of culture"—whether it occurs in school or some other setting. For example, a common home-based literacy activity setting is the bedtime story. An activity setting is a recognizable pattern of routine activity of practice that has markers that characterize the activity commonly understood by the participants. Similarly, everyone is familiar with the activity of show-and-tell. It involves turn-taking, public talk, and representing to an audience something the current speaker finds interesting or noteworthy. The specifics of how long the activity goes, where the speaker stands, and how well and respectfully the rest of the children listen, are all aspects that the teacher shapes in the repeated occasions of this particular activity setting. Similarly, story time in kindergarten has markers such as setting, the physical locations of learners and the teacher, the pattern of discourse, and the actions taken by participants. The point is that it is the teacher who determines the culture of literacy learning events by the way he or she organizes the activity settings for reading and writing.

The main point about culturally responsive education is that the skilled teacher is able to configure the cultural world of the classroom so that there is a continuity of experience between home and school for African American children and children from other nonmainstream cultural communities. This continuity already exists for most culturally mainstream children as the activity settings of school that have recognizable markers are often the ones that children adopt when playing school. An example is the cultural familiarity of story time in school based on it similarity to the bedtime story at home. Story time places the teacher at the front and center of a circle of students sitting cross-legged on the floor. The teacher, with the book in hand, reads in an engaging, animated, story-time voice, and pauses after each page to show the entire group the picture, moving the book slowly from one side to the other so that children can see the illustration accompanying the text. These are actions similar to the bedtime story script in many households.

The African-centered pedagogy is a system of teaching designed to help you identify and incorporate those aspects of your students' cultural lives that need to be configured in their educational experience in your classroom. The pedagogy completes the task that cultural congruency frameworks have begun—namely, specifying practices that should be attended to in the creation of the activity setting that includes, engages, and connects with all children. You cannot develop effective activity systems without the appropriate cultural knowledge of the students you are teaching. The five essential practices of the African-centered pedagogy are designed to do that and we turn to that discussion following a further clarification of the idea of activity system.

ACTIVITY SETTING AND ACTIVITY SYSTEM

Now that we have a vocabulary—the term activity setting for referring to a chunk of teaching and learning as a cultural event as well as an instructional one—I want to talk next about the systems of teaching practice. To do that, I introduce the term *activity system*. An activity system is the teacher's social and cultural organization of activity settings. The activity system in your teaching is your system of settings in which you and your students interact. Your activity setting includes management or orchestration of routine events, for example how you move your class to the library or line them up to go to lunch. More important than these sorts of transitions, however, are the relationships you create between your instructional settings and the curriculum. What will your children *do* to learn?

Cultural competence is most crucial in the design of activity systems. The description of a teacher's activity system is actually a description of that teacher's classroom culture. The ways of doing things, the forms of talk, the "rules of engagement" among students, the rules and codes of conduct, are all aspects of the activity system. A good activity system gets you a lot of "achievement mileage" as you work with your students over days, weeks, and semesters. The subject of the next chapter is how to design activity systems to get a lot of "achievement mileage" with African American students in urban school settings. For the present, I mean to introduce the term activity system and foreshadow the deep analysis it will permit us in subsequent discussion.

The idea of an activity system provides an important way of dealing with your current classroom management concerns. Using the idea of activity system, I will demonstrate how classroom management is a seamless extension of one's pedagogy. Many beginning teachers (and more than a few experienced ones) think of classroom management as a skill repertoire that is distinct from the rest of their teaching. That is, they see their classroom management skills as those which allow them to do their "real teaching." Using the notion of the activity systems, I will show that management is part of the same fabric of practice involved in creating activities and designing instruction. Instructional decisions are also simultaneously management decisions, and the best teaching comes from resolving them in tandem with one another.

Let us, for the moment, consider the challenge of teaching in a fourth grade classroom with a focus on language arts. You know that periods of sustained independent reading are important to literacy development. To promote this you have instituted a period of silent reading time. You have created book-nooks in areas of the room for students to curl up with a book and read. You know that silent reading time may be an activity setting that requires that the teacher emphasize social practices of self-discipline, respectful engagement with others, and honoring space. You have designated locations in the room that are to be occupied during reading time—old sofas, bean bag chairs, lofts and other book nooks, are the physical locations of the activity. You notice that some students really prefer silent reading time (individual) to story time (collective).

There are, of course, obvious differences between the two activity settings designed to promote literacy development. The physical location of students in the silent reading time activity setting is more diffuse than the story time activity setting. But the fact that there are clear student preferences for one activity over the other in your class may be more than just mood or momentary choice. Suppose you have students who are not yet independent readers, who do not yet enjoy reading on their own, or both? Do you try to increase the occasions of independent reading increasing time on the silent independent reading activity setting? Do you find an alternative to silent independent reading for those whom you suspect are not yet proficient? How do you balance the need for experiencing literacy as a meaning-making event (such as in story time) with developing appreciation for independent reading? To answer these questions, you not only think of what activity is going to "work" but also base your decisions on what is pedagogically required for both the short term and long term. This level of thinking is what we mean by developing an activity system.

THE CONCEPT OF ACTIVITY SYSTEM IN THE RESEARCH LITERATURE

Activity systems are studied formally under the heading of learning environments (Wilson, 1996) and written about as the notion of learning community. The notion of the instructional activity setting is very much like Wilson's (1996) conception of the learning environment that incorporates four metaphors of learning: (1) of instruction as delivery system; (2) instruction as classroom setting; (3) instruction as product; and (4) instruction as process.

You need not think of activity system as these four cut and dried categories, but simply as a way of thinking simultaneously about what is taught, in what kind of setting, for what purposes and by what means.

Activity system, according to this theoretical framework, refers to the teacher's repertoire of activity settings, together with a sense of when to employ activity settings to bring about learning achievements. In specifying an activity setting there is an account of: (1) how the learner is situated in the social context of other people and relationships; (2) the setting or space wherein the learner acts using learning props, tools, and devices for collecting and interpreting information and/or interacting with others; (3) a frame—or common set of assumptions about the current setting and activity held by participants; (4) a manifest purpose or goal for the activity; and (5) an outcome or product. I have represented these components of an activity system in Figure 4.

The point in introducing the formalized, research based approaches to the activity system is to suggest to you that there are two levels of applying African-centered pedagogy. At one level, you draw on principles—for cooperative learning, assertive discipline, or for teaching for understanding. At a deeper level, you draw on a capacity for cultural inquiry. At this deeper level, organizing your activity system depends less on your understanding of learning theory or cognitive psychology than it does your ability read and appropriate aspects of African American culture.

Let us return to the literacy learning activity setting and illustrate an African-centered pedagogical set up at the two levels—considering of the instructional setting and then the activity system in general. As you consider literacy learning in your classroom, your thinking is a matter of organizing or constructing the literacy-learning activities. This involves asking yourself a series of question. For the delivery system (activity system) these might be questions like, "What do I need to ensure that students receive what they need in the way of literacy learning this year? How do I make sure that everyone gets the support they need to reach the proficiency of independent reading for understanding and content?" For classroom setting (activity setting) consideration, you might ask yourself questions like, "How do I organize on a routine basis, classroom activity that will develop children's proficiency in reading?" For consideration of the "products" of teaching and learning, you might ask yourself questions like, "What will I have to show that indicates appropriate levels of proficiency and achievement? What forms of student work are evidence of the achievement and proficiency all my students must acquire?"

Those are examples of the kind of questions you might ask yourself as you attempt to provide reading and literacy learning. Shortly we will examine how we do this more systematically in a way that addresses the needs of African American children in underresourced urban communities (depicted in Figure 4).

For the present, let me summarize our actions as teachers. When we successfully deploy activity settings and activity systems, we:

- provide a degree of student initiative and choice, wherein students are given room to explore, and determine goals and products;
- adopt an instructional role where we foster, support, and scaffold learning activity, but not in coercive or controlling ways;
- encourage student initiative so that they assume roles that develop proficiencies;
- recognize and take account of the complexity of social and cognitive requirements of student learning and development as we design instructional activity settings;
- understand that our most successful in-the-moment work as teachers is that of orchestrating purposeful learning activity, providing appropriate tools and resources, and ensuring that feedback supports trajectories of learning.

In addition to the instructional activity settings that teachers develop as part of their teaching practice, there are activity settings in which they work with other professionals in the building. These are called "professional activity settings" and will be discussed in chapter 5.

Wilson (1996) also invokes the idea of "learning communities" as being more appropriate than his notion of the learning environment so as to take account of the fact that students learn from one another at least as much as they do from the material setting. His definition of a constructivist learning environment—"a place where learners may work together and support each other as they use a variety of tools and information resources in their pursuit of learning goals and problem-solving activities"—nicely summarizes the prior conception of the learning community.

SUMMARY

This chapter elaborated on the African-centered pedagogies defining premises and practices, attempting to show how they should come together in an activity system. A schematic for teachers to organize the surface structural characteristics of their activity systems is presented as Figure 4. Also, I discussed the deeper cultural read for applying the pedagogy, and several actual practices are shown in Table 4.

Table 4
Specific Cultural Practices in an African-Centered Pedagogy

ENGAGEMENT AND PARTICIPATION PRACTICES

Create generative instructional activity settings

- Organize learning activity as *generative tasks* so that content is represented in ways that are culturally relevant and socially significant;
- Make explicit purposes of *task management* and *social engagement* in the learning enterprise so that learners develop greater agency in the task of self-definition (individual) and a sense of social justice (collective).

Develop cultural props and conceptual tools

- Incorporate culturally established knowledge traditions—e.g., narrative, the oral tradition, and Black rhetorical style;
- Construct new knowledge traditions—e.g., Bob Moses using the Boston Transit Authority "red line" as a representation of a number line (Moses & Cobb, 2001) for developing mathematics literacy; building a book community (Meier, 2001).

Employ a living curriculum—such as "movement history" where students:

- Question the assumptions of the activity, materials, or other symbols/signs—in short, answer the usual questions seen as "troublesome" in the transmission model of education;
- Address the historical struggle of African American people.

IDENTITY DEVELOPMENT PRACTICES

Select literature for identity development so that it serves to:

- Develop oralcy and create opportunity for oral performance—explanations, narratives, presentations, and other forms of public talk;
- Represent culturally familiar experiences, roles and situations—proposes credible role models in culturally recognizable and experiential significant contexts;

Create spaces for oral performance and public talk that:

- Create opportunities for inquiry practices in subject matter content;
- Encourage use of knowledge in multiple social/intellectual settings.

Encourage emergence of Indentity-in-Activity (Roles)

- Make explicit the importance of sustained interpersonal engagement so that the student shows increasing initiative in productive activity in the setting with increase in focus, energy and commitment.
- Create pathways into the instructional enterprise and activity setting—*participation structures* for enabling self-definition where students find a sense of place within the learning community.

Table 4 (*continued*)
SPECIFIC CULTURAL PRACTICES IN AN AFRICAN-CENTERED PEDAGOGY

COMMUNITY INTEGRITY PRACTICES

Evoking fictive kinship

- Develop understanding of the term—a socially recognized link between individuals, created as an expedient for creating family-like links as people cope with special circumstances. Fictive kinship bonds among African Americans have been based upon common struggle, as well as on friendship and other personal relationships outside of marriage and descent.
- Allow social activities and relationships to be organized by African American cultural heritage. For example, identifying *fundi* (Swahili term for teachers, instructors, and knowledgeable elders) for the community.

Build a sense of Harambee (the Swahili word for working together)—

- Appraise of instructional activity, the groups progress and common work as a collective effort;
- Harambee evokes the idea of collateral, community reflection, where instructional practice is appraised as a shared activity.

Use of culturally familiar discourse practices

- Intentionally use narrative, call-and-response, indirection, and other wordplay in instructional activity and informal interaction (cf. Foster, 2001);
- Focus on narrative development—African American children's spoken and written narrative knowledge.

PRACTICES OF INQUIRY

Tapping and developing the idea of collective memory

- Ensure a common understanding of collective memory as how a people experience their present in light of the past (St. Jean & Feagin, 1998);
- Select fables, folktales, proverbs, and so forth that are the repositories of African American collective memory and wisdom.

Cultural modeling

- Make explicit cultural props, symbols and knowledge systems for finding entry into a discipline;
- The best exemplar for cultural modeling in *language literacy* is the work of Carol Lee (e.g., Lee, 1995, 1995, 2001) and her Cultural Modeling Project; for *mathematics literacy* the best exemplar is the work of Robert Moses (e.g., Moses & Cobb, 2001) and his Algebra Project.

Table 4 (*continued*)
SPECIFIC CULTURAL PRACTICES IN AN AFRICAN-CENTERED PEDAGOGY

PRACTICES OF INQUIRY (*cont.*)

Structuring a trajectory for the development of learning

- Ensure that instructional activity settings focus on a clear goal performance and specify the desired achievement—learning trajectory with a beginning point (implying an initial assessment), a worthwhile achievement, and the process in between;
- An example in mathematics literacy learning: the five steps in the Algebra Project curriculum process (Moses & Cobb, 2001, pp. 120–122).

MEANING-MAKING PRACTICES

Organize literacy practices as an extended conversation and elaborated activity.

- For example this might be the enactment of stories with props (e.g., puppets, images of the characters throughout the room);
- Make explicit the differences in the epistemology of African Americans and European Americans.

Highlight inter-textuality of literature.

- Select literature that speaks to other literature, text that re-appropriates narratives and themes from other know texts—e.g., *Flossie and the Fox* (McKissack, 1996) as a re-appropriation of the story of Little Red Riding Hood.
- Re-appropriate literature and symbol systems for cultural inquiry—for using media representations of (e.g., the film *Mississippi Burning* and its misrepresentation of civil rights struggle) exposing the distortion of Blackness in entertainment media.

Make explicit cultural models.

- Look for patterns in sign systems, in the symbolic culture represented by specific events and experiences;
- Structure instructional activity so as to develop valuable capacities (e.g., narrating, analyzing, interpreting, communication of mathematical reasoning) that require thoughtful application of knowledge.

CHAPTER FIVE

From a Community of Caring to a Community of Achievement

> This is a critical juncture in African history, and every thought and action has the potential for becoming liberating or incarcerating. We can no longer be satisfied with aping the rehashed thoughts and programs of our non-African mentors and teachers. Blackening western philosophical ideas and Eurocentric discourse is far too inadequate for the task of understanding the being, becoming, and belonging of African people. African thinkers must penetrate the puzzles on African terms. We must create the context for our own growth and development. As professionals in service to our people, we must engage in a deep, profound and penetrating search, study, understanding and mastery of the illumination of the African spirit in our time and place.
>
> —Wade Nobles, (1995)

This chapter interprets the theory of African American educational achievement in terms of existing frameworks on learning communities and culturally responsive teaching—using the notion community of practice to construct an African-centered community of achievement in public schools. I should say at the outset that many such projects already exist as private schools and independent schools, and many are exemplars of African-centered school communities. One example is a network of African-centered school communities called the Council of Independent Black Institutions dedicated to the development of schools as African-centered communities of achievement. Similarly, as of this writing, there are more than 400 African-centered charter schools and over 100 independent schools, most of which are the result of an increasing activism in African American communities that have organized to redress the failures of the public school system to promote and sustain achievement for the children of those communities. Although these schools are independent public schools and private schools, they are a resource to the present project—building an African-centered community of achievement in public schools.

The purpose of African-centered pedagogy in these settings is to design education specifically for the needs of African American learners. In these settings, the goal of education is not to prepare children to fit within the present system, but to revolutionize the system toward the promise of democracy articulated in the documents (but not the deeds) that shaped America. The core of social studies, for example, is history approached with a "whole truth" perspective and with agency on behalf of African American children. Rather than being restricted to the text and a chronological march through epochs, teachers appropriate media and reactions to the media—such as the film *Amistad* or the documentary *Africans in America*—as the catalyst for instruction on a period of history. A *movement history* (McDowell & Sullivan, 1993) that critically reinterprets the "lightning rod" incidents in this nation's history help African American students not only learn the conceptual content, but also to critically contest the inherent contradictions of liberty and equality in America.

Because racism is an ideology that positions White people as superior and non-White people as inferior, the pedagogy developed for African American children specifically confronts this ideology to inoculate children from internalizing ideologies of White supremacy. The incompleteness of American education is in the lack of pedagogy to help African American students negotiate their "double-consciousness" and their sense of resistance to institutional authority that supports inequality. African-centered pedagogy seeks to address this by encouraging: (1) deep thought as both the process and the aims of education for liberation, self-agency and self-determination; and (2) community participation in deep thought that furthers and develops those ends.

WHY NOT CRITICAL PEDAGOGY?

Informed readers might wonder at this juncture about the absence of critical theory or critical pedagogy in the list of five pedagogical approaches of my theory. Critical theory is a theoretical framework and a method of analysis that carefully and systematically critique social structures, cultural institutions, and the otherwise hidden factors of social problems. The framework and method are characterized by the disposition of praxis, which means that value of theory is based upon its relevancy to human enterprises and its location in the activity of those enterprises. This notion of praxis implies an activism in the development of theory and new knowledge. It implies theory building as more than an exercise of academics, but based in the human activity of real struggles with real problems in schools. It is a human activity that is discursive, reflective collaborative, and interrogative (constantly questioning).

I have not stated either as a separate approach because a critical theoretical perspective is suffused throughout the African-centered pedagogy. For example, the pedagogy is based upon the critique of social structures and cultural institutions of America—of African Americans as well as those of the mainstream culture, which Banks (1988) has called the macroculture. Additionally, my pedagogical theory is based on praxis as both a disposition towards schooling and a method of inquiry. Finally, as discussed earlier, the understanding of theory as knowledge-in-use is a central tenant of African-centered pedagogy.

Because it incorporates these three aspects of critical theory, critical pedagogy is not stated in my pedagogy as a separate approach because African-centered pedagogy is not independent of Black culture, history and intellectual traditions. Though informed by the work of Paulo Freire and writers who have taken up his legacy (e.g., Antonia Darder, Maxine Greene, Donaldo Macedo, Peter McLaren, and Henry Giroux), the critical theory from an African-centered perspective stands on its own terms. Some of this foundation is the work of critical race theorists such as Derrick Bell, Black feminists scholars such Audre Lourde, bell hooks, and Patricia Collins. However, most of this foundation is a broader historical legacy, encompassing the intellectual traditions of Fredrick Douglass, W. E. B DuBois and Carter G. Woodson from earlier eras.

African-centered education, on this account, embraces the traditional wisdom that "children are the reward of life" and it is, therefore, an expression of our unconditional love for them. In order to serve African children our methods must reflect the best understandings that we have of how they develop and learn biologically, spiritually, and culturally. This is the where Black independent schools become an important intellectual resource to look to for models of pedagogy and curriculum. The idea that the development of the whole child is a collaborative responsibility is an organizing principle. In its statement of purpose, the Council of Black Independent schools states that African-centered education:

1. Acknowledges Afrikan spirituality as an essential aspect of our uniqueness as a people and makes it an instrument of our liberation (Richards, 1989; Clarke, 1991; Anwisye, 1993; Ani, 1994);
2. Facilitates participation in the affairs of nations and defining (or redefining) reality on our own terms, in our own time and in our own interests (Karenga, 1980);
3. Prepares Afrikans "for self-reliance, nation maintenance, and nation management in every regard" (Clarke, 1991, p. 62);

4. Emphasizes the fundamental relationship between the strength of our families and the strength of our nation;
5. Ensures that the historic role and function of the customs, traditions, rituals and ceremonies—that have protected and preserved our culture; facilitated our spiritual expression; ensured harmony in our social relations; prepared our people to meet their responsibilities as adult members of our culture; and sustained the continuity of Afrikan life over successive generations—are understood and made relevant to the challenges that confront us in our time;
6. Emphasizes that Afrikan identity is embedded in the continuity of Afrikan cultural history and that Afrikan cultural history represents a distinct reality continually evolving from the experiences of all Afrikan people wherever they are and have been on the planet across time and generations;
7. Focuses on the "knowledge and discovery of historical truths; through comparison; hypothesizing and testing through debate, trial, and application; through analysis and synthesis; through creative and critical thinking; through problem resolution processes; and through final evaluation and decision making" (Akoto, 1992, p. 116);
8. Can only be systematically facilitated by people who themselves are consciously engaged in the process of Afrikan-centered personal transformation;
9. Is a process dependent upon human perception and interpretation (Thus, it follows that a curriculum can not be Afrikan-centered independent of our capacity to perceive and interpret it in an Afrikan-centered manner [Shujaa, 1992]);

These statements identify qualities of an activity system for an African-centered pedagogy. That is, they describe the features of the figured world that the teacher takes into account in creating the cultural community of his or her classroom. Even though African-centered independent schools enjoy a much greater flexibility in the determination of its pedagogy than do most public schools in large urban districts, they offer an illustration of the communities of learning. To illustrate this point, it is useful to note the growing after-school movement that offers the potential for African-centered and other culturally supported educational programs to shape the day curriculum. Increasingly, parents and educators are organizing afterschool programs that provide the whole-child enrichment and development experiences that are often lacking in the public schools. The fact that these programs are based in the public schools, and many times involve teachers from the school hired to run these programs, suggests that the potential for influencing the culture of schools is closer than we might think.

The question continuously posed here is how to develop this rich pedagogical frame in public schools. The counterpart of African-centered independent schools in the educational literature is Nel Noddings' (1992) notion of the caring community and the notion of communities of learning. These formulations, but for the lack of a "humility of good anthropology" (Meier, 1982), come close to a conception of the "village it takes to educate the child" in the public schools. A different conception more appropriate to collaboration in successful urban schools is that of the African-centered community of practice (Lave, 1988, 1997; Wenger, 1998) is developed in reference to the contemporary formulations of the learning community.

How do we move toward implementing the African-centered pedagogical practices in successful African-centered schools to public schools that do not have the critical mass of African-American community leaders? An extension of the notion of community of practice provides the answer and becomes an important part of the pedagogy.

EXTENDING THE IDEA OF COMMUNITY OF PRACTICE

Let us turn to the notion of community of practice (Lave, 1997; Wenger, 1999) and articulate a systematic way of thinking about how to develop current activity settings (namely, current practice and afterschool programs) into coherent activity systems (namely, African-centered pedagogy) that powerfully educate African American children. In a true community of inquiry and practice, both you and your students have a role, a participation structure, if you will. Take the first of the five essential practices of the African-centered theory—engagement/participation. On the part of the teacher, these are actions and arrangements that encourage and promote the interest, engagement, and participation of students—with each other and with the learning activity. Your role in engagement/participation practices is to elicit from your students sustained effort and commitment with respect to the learning activity, and sustained interpersonal engagement among classmates. Your students have a responsibility as well. Their aim is to mobilize themselves to put forth the necessary effort and participate in the activities of learning.

Similarly, for the African-centered pedagogical practice of identity development, your activity includes providing the material and symbolic arrangements that will encourage and elicit productive self-exploration and self-definition from your students. Literature selections, forms of critical discussion, thematic topics selected, and forms of participation are in your tools for promoting identity work in your classroom. With this done, students readily take on their role, as identity clarification is a motive in child and adolescent development. Your students are naturally motivated to try out different roles and functions in the context of engaging learning activity.

I have been arguing throughout this chapter for the third of the five essential practices in the African-centered pedagogy—organizing the intellectual and social life of a community of learners. I have also argued for practices four and five that amount to critical interpretation and appropriation of cultural signs, symbols and ideas. Here, you institute these practices of inquiry among your students as your contribution in your classroom community of practice. Culturally interpreted inquiry consists of various forms of recursive reappropriation, the interpretation, internalization, and use of ideas, symbols, and meanings. Your students use the ideas, phrases, signs, and images of others for their own expressive repertoire and interpretive toolbox. Your role in the community involves making students aware that they are consumers of the material and symbolic representations of culture. I might argue that, taken together, these five practices of the African-centered pedagogy would serve well in as the framework for developing any intellectual community. But the content and combination of these five are specific to the difficult tasks of reaching cultural competency.

To put it simply, a community of practice is a group of individuals bound together in a mutual activity with mutual exchange of ideas, values, and actions toward a common purpose or set of purposes. Phase one of building this community is relatively easy—providing the structure or defining the activity setting (see Figure 4). Phase two is the more challenging task of developing the setting into a new cultural community dedicated to common aims of achievement, development, and mutual support. A good example instructionally related to cultural diversity is Uri Treisman's (1985) work with the student study tables and study groups, where he was able to demonstrate that academically underserved African American and Hispanic college mathematics students could rise to levels of achievement that were quite impressive. Treisman showed how the mathematics achievement performance of African American and Latino college students was dramatically enhanced by the activity setting known as a study group. The first phase, forming a study group was easier to arrange than the second phase of building a culture of sustained effective effort and mutual support. He was able to accomplish the latter and that is what produced the dramatic achievement results.

Whether as students or teachers, people do their best work when they are in a community—a social setting where they are valued, where what they do is valued, and where the contribution they make is to a common interest, activity, or goal. This is as true for the classroom learning situation that is proven to support the academic achievement of African American and Hispanic students as it is for building collaborative partnerships between schools and universities. Teachers do not come to school each day to form a community of practice any more than they come to form a professional culture. These structures are created out of activity, relationship, values, and shared understanding. In other words, teachers come to school to do their job, and in doing so collectively create a human system that operates with some level of efficiency and purpose. I argue that the efficiency and purpose of teachers working with African American children in underresourced communities can be dramatically enhanced with a greater consciousness about, and understanding of, the intersection of parent, teacher, and cultural communities. It is the shared urgency of the plight of African American children in public schools and the cultural legacies of education among African Americans as a people, that richly shape a community of achievement.

The concept of the community of practice offers a powerful alternative to the traditional view of teaching as a solitary activity. The traditional image of the urban teacher is that of the intrepid and dedicated individual, working tirelessly behind their closed classroom door and struggling valiantly to make a difference in the lives of the children they teach. Unfortunately, this image is propagated throughout teacher preparation, even in some systems designed to select for accomplished urban teachers. For example, even though the STAR system developed by Martin Haberman (1995) provides fifteen valuable criteria for the accomplished urban teacher, they are all intrapersonal characteristics of the individual teacher, as opposed to specifying the interpersonal systems of practice that constitute pedagogy.

In an African-centered pedagogical framework, working with others who share the same conditions is important to the enterprise of successful teaching. There is a quality of community membership with critical awareness that is missing in contemporary "rugged individualist" articulations of teaching abilities. Does this quality of "collaborative capacity" added to the others make for a community of practice? The answer is "yes" because the shared consciousness, understandings, and skills for critically negotiating institutions of schooling can only be developed through collective experience. Teachers negotiate the professional day sometimes with each other, sometimes against each other, and sometimes in each other's presence. The continuous negotiation of school life with the parade of confrontations and challenges, both in the classroom and out, are what make teaching what it is in practice and what makes the setting a community of practice.

As indicated previously, the job of teaching is too often described only in individualistic terms. In so doing, we overlook the degree to which the enterprise of teaching in a given school is not carried out in each other's presence. If we continue to take an individual's decontextualized view of teaching, we are apt to miss the most critical aspects that determine thinking, acting, decision-making, and actual practice. It is for this purpose that we approach teaching practice as a community of activity. In a different professional context—insurance adjusters—Wenger (1998) noted:

> I found that it is the collective construction of a local practice that, among other things, makes it possible to meet the demands of the institution. (p. 46)

Teachers do many of the same things. They rarely share their practices—as indeed, they rarely articulate, even to themselves, what they are doing and why. There is much more than this commonality of experience, however, that brings them together into a community of practice. They share a context, containing the same challenges, constraints, directives from administration, annoyances, sanctions, and rewards. This is the set of experiences teachers in a school deal with collectively, but not necessarily in the presence of one another.

What is a practice in this framework? Practice is what teachers have developed in order to be able to do their jobs and have a satisfying work experience. Naturally, we hope and expect that this satisfaction will be tied to the demonstrable achievement of their students. In the contemporary view of the teacher, "having tried hard" is too often sufficient as the criteria by which a teacher deems himself or herself to be a "good teacher." In the practice perspective of the African-centered pedagogy, "good teaching" is measured by "good practice" that is, in turn, determined by demonstrable achievement of the students. It is the social dimension of doing that is left out of our contemporary conceptions of pedagogy and leads us to overlook the most critical component of effective pedagogy. As Wenger (1998) states:

> The concept of *practice* connotes doing, but not just doing in and of itself. It is doing in a historical and social context that gives structure and meaning to what we do. In this sense, practice is always *social practice*. [italics added] (p. 47)

Engagement in social practice is the fundamental process by which we learn and become who we are. African-centered pedagogy views learning as a process of identity development, as cognitive development, and development of consciousness, and not just a matter of acquiring skilled competence and scholastic ability. The crisis of knowledge in pedagogy is that the second part of each case—identity and critical consciousness for intentional participation in the public life of a critical democracy—is the part that nobody seems to know how to do on a consistent basis. There needs to be human systems that promote these qualities.

I have begun promoting the evolution of the idea of practice over performance. A performance may be taken as (i.e., assessed as) an aspect of a developing practice among students. What I am moving toward is the notion of *practice* supplanting the notion of *ability*—since ability is a term that may be too hopelessly loaded and tainted with the connotation of innateness. Practice is at once an externalized activity and an embedded expression of a person's capacity. Practice is externalized ability. When we assess the quality of teaching, it is better to refer to teachers' *ability* as put to use in a way that can be publically appraised as practice. Practice is the expression of ability that manifests in the achievement success of students.

The successful African-centered school articulates the quality teaching as practices. In this case the purpose of pedagogy is viewed as teachers' internalization of quality practices. This makes conversations about the rich contexts of activity, material, and literature are most likely to bring about the internalization of quality practices possible. The engagement of teachers can be based on elevating practice throughout the school.

SITUATED CULTURAL THEORY

Why an African-centered pedagogy in a community of practice for teachers of African American children? As I have argued in the previous chapters, it is because of the level of cultural analysis required to organize effective instructional practices to deconstruct the traditional and conventional approaches to understanding school culture. In the cultural theory of the pedagogy developed in this book, teaching practice is understood both as a composite of folk explanation (common sense from the perspective of that geo-political group) and as relevant educational theory. Readers who are interested in reading further on the notion of cultural model should refer to Janice Hale (1994), Wade Boykin (1986), and James Gee (1997). Gee uses the term *cultural model* but I prefer the term *cultural patterns* or *interpretive traditions* to avoid connotations of a static structure or a cultural type that can lead to facile generalizations. Cultural patterns and interpretive traditions connote recognizable organization of human activities and practices as cultural features.

Gee's (1997) formulation of a situated cultural model (pp. 245–257) is a good reference for readers interested in the idea of situated cognition. In the present formulation, educational theory is examined as culturally situated in the degraded experiences of African American in contemporary social and educational practices. Gee (1997, p. 238) states that "cultural models allow us to relate people's everyday folk theories (i.e., shared stories that they use to explain their experiences) to more formal theories in academic disciplines." His example is the interpretive frame (cultural model) of middle-class parents who explain the new disruptive behavior of their toddlers as growth toward independence, while working class mothers interpret disruptive behavior as a need to be socialized toward cooperativeness. "Here we see patterns not in the mind [a movement away from the too-internal, too-unsituated schema theory], but actual material configurations of objects, tools, people, and activities in the world."

This is a nice, theoretically based example of the importance of being able to accurately interpret behavior by having the appropriate cultural model or cultural interpretive frame. I will continue to use the terminology of cultural pattern and interpretive frame to refer to culturally specific events and human interactions in school settings. For the purposes of the African-centered pedagogy, these also denote the academic knowledge relevant to the culturally, historically, and politically situated experience of African American children and families. The key ideas, as in Gee's (1997, p. 247) notion of a cultural model, is that there are collectively shared understandings that help people recognize settings as familiar and that organize the flow of events and experiences day-to-day. These shared understandings are patterns of relationships and signs that people recognize are what the teacher must work with in building a learning community, along with the historical heritage.

I have been arguing that the rugged individualist American cultural value is problematic for Black achievement in particular, as well as for educational reform in general on at least two counts—both of which Elmore (1996) and Weiner (1993) examine in depth. One is the cultural norm of individual merit in the American education. This is the idea that learners are successful because they deserve it, that they merit (ostensibly) it through their own effort and individual qualities. For teachers, this cultural norm results in their failure to recognize that accomplished teachers develop their ability through experience and collaboration with others. The second cultural norm is a technist or positivistic view of human psychology, especially motivation. This is exemplified in the misguided view that teachers motivate students, as if eliciting student interest and activity were merely a matter of applying the right technique, strategy, or behavioral principle. In truth, eliciting learner's sustained effective effort in learning activity is much more dependent on the teacher's skill in creating conditions under which children see activity as valuable, meaningful, and important to acquire for success in the adult world.

Educational writers recognize this in the characterization known as "learner-centered" teaching, but unfortunately tend to suggest approaches that more resemble the individualistic, technist psychology that disregard the requirements for building a culture of learning and development. Other writers have at least identified the core popular American cultural values inimical to achievement. Among these are rugged individualism ("pull yourself up by your bootstraps"), intelligence-as-innate-ability, and competition (cf. Comer, 1997, pp. 5–16). However, it is one thing to note the failure in educational reform initiatives to take account of cultural diversity in achievement (cf. Williams, 1996), and quite another to synthesize these concerns in a working pedagogy for success among African American children. That is the task before us—developing and maintaining a community of inquiry and practice.

IMPLEMENTING A COMMUNITY OF PRACTICE

How do we implement the African American community of practice framework? I would like to begin by considering the systems of assistance to teachers attempting to improve their practice. This whole notion of structured but informal assistance is a key piece of African-centered pedagogy. The task for creating a school of achievement for African American children is that of building an African American cultural and intellectual community in the classroom, and a community of practice among the adults who support learning in both the classroom and the school. In both cases, praxis—the practices requiring a mode of learning, inquiry, interrogation and deliberation that poses and solves problems situated in real activity—is required. In both cases the assistance of performance is required, as well as the maintenance of an activity system that draws upon African American cultural and intellectual heritage.

One reason why organizing these conditions for a successful African-centered pedagogy are difficult in contemporary educational practice is the way that professional development is typically set up. The standard approach to professional development is solely focused on the capacities of individual teachers, most often independent of their actual work and the systems of practice that could possibly elevate the performance of teachers and students. Though the literature on professional development schools and partnerships explicitly calls for the improvement of teaching linked to achievement outcomes of learners, this is the connection that is consistently lacking.

The operating principle for African-centered pedagogy is that improving practice is not something done in isolation, but in collaboration. If we are concentrating on a single adult regarding the assessment of or assistance with practice, we ought to do so in the context of that individual's interaction with learners and colleagues. This is important for in-the-moment activity and other instructional practices. Rather than focusing on only the teacher-child dyad, we are opting for a unit of analysis that involves teacher, learner, activity, and outcome. In short, we opt for the unit of analysis I have been calling practice. The essential cultural practices are depicted in the outer circles of Figure 3, and described in Table 3 and Table 4.

Practices are embedded in the complex organizations of schools and school life, and by having "practices" be the "take" of what is going on, we tap into the teaching and learning events in context. Minick, Stone, and Forman (1993) expresses this well:

> If Vygoksky's insights concerning the role of social interaction in psychological development are to be effectively incorporated, the links between dyadic, or small group interactions, and the broader sociocultural system must be recognized and explored. Actions are at once, and the same time, components of the life of the individual and the social systems, and will be defined and structured, in certain respects, by the broader social and cultural system. (p. 257)

Developing teachers means developing their practices and the contexts of their practice. The African-centered pedagogy offers the means for understanding these contexts as systems of practice. It is the system of practices in schools that need to be our primary focus in order to create the conditions that maximize learning and development of African American children. So taking your development as a teacher seriously, means taking seriously the knowledge traditions of human development from African American cultural communities. In turn, taking seriously the knowledge traditions that shape the intellectual world of children means taking account of the culture, history, and lived experiences of children.

Finally, taking the social-cultural context of schooling seriously means regarding the notion of the zone of proximal development as more than a psychological phenomenon we learned about as preservice teachers; we need to apply it to ourselves in conjunction with our emerging capacity to promote achievement. Both teacher and learner have learning trajectories, and we improve our abilities as teachers if we learn to see the interdependencies of these trajectories. The notion of community of practice as we have been developing it here is a theory of education that deals with both learner and teacher, experience and activity. It is a unified theoretical framework that not only accounts for activity related to the teacher-learner interaction, but also accounts, simultaneously, for the social-cultural context of that interaction.

In the ideal community of practice, professional development would consist of assisting teachers develop the cultural content of their classrooms so that children progress through a learning trajectory of worthwhile achievement. It is in the spirit of this ideal that the African-centered pedagogy is extended to teaching practice. Tharp and Gallimore's (1991) conceptions of the activity setting and triadic analysis articulate this idea and will be developed further in the next chapter. Many aspects of this idea of activity setting are already in use in educational frameworks. For example, the idea of learning centers—a science table, and mathematics table, a reading corner—is a specific use of the idea of activity setting in the organization of an elementary classroom. These settings are more than locations, because they have some direction, indicated purpose, and constraints on the learning activity that students carry out there. Other examples of activity settings are study groups.

The richest example of a structured activity setting that culturally models a community of literacy practice is the work of Carol Lee (1995). She has developed an instructional activity system in which the linguistic capital that many African American students already possess—the various forms of signifying, such as rapping, "playing the dozens" for example—is scaffolded in the development of sophisticated approaches writing and literary criticism. In other words, her instructional activity settings use students' extent usage of African American English as the foundation for scaffolding their capacity for literary response. Since signifying and other forms of verbal play involve indirection and double entendre, African American English users already have a heightened capacity to look beyond surface meanings to the more subtle intentions of the speaker. Through her graded exposure to cultural models, literature, and analyses, instruction scaffolds students to a more extensive and sophisticated use and recognition of metaphor, symbolism, satire, and irony.

PRACTICE AS THE INTEGRATION OF CONTEXT AND CULTURAL CONTENT

Activity settings are recognized by their practices. Instructional activity settings are recognized by the common practices of the teachers—lecturing, demonstrating, setting up cooperative learning groups, for example. Practices imply activities that are done on a regular, routine basis, something that has some recursiveness in the daily operations or the daily interactions of people engaged in a purposeful enterprise in learning achievement. In other words, the idea of practices provides a cultural situatedness or cultural meaning, a contextualized meaning to activity. When appraising teaching practices, we include in our analysis the cognitive components of the activity as well as the cultural ones—including the quality and nature of the discourse, interaction, and relationships in the learning community. That is to say, when appraising practices, we want to be particular in understanding the meaning and value that the participants attach to that activity and the setting in which they are participating. As Tharp and Gallimore (1991) point out, practice is the integration of content and context.

PRACTICES AS APPRAISED PERFORMANCES

Jay Lemke (1997) clarifies practices as distinguished from performances this way:

> Because practices are not just performances, not just behaviors and not just material processes or operations, but meaningful actions, actions that have relations of meaning to one another in terms of some *cultural system*, one must learn not just what and how to perform, but what the performance means in order to function and be accepted as a full member in a community of practice. (p. 43)

The practice orientation is an extension of the well-known notion of the reflective practitioner (Dewey, 1933; Schon, 1989). "Practice oriented" incorporates action and reflection, and specifies a particular quality of reflection that I have designated "appraisal of practice." Appraisal of practice is the ignition key to effective, transformative teaching in any cultural setting. *Appraisal of practice* carries a deeper meaning than performance assessment because it implies that teaching performance is evaluated, in part, on how well the teacher draws on the cultural resources of learners and their communities. Reflection is systematic self-evaluation in light of outcomes, but in the case of African-centered pedagogy, draws on the heritage of African American history and culture as well. These outcomes include the achievement instructional aims in conjunction with the production of new pedagogical knowledge and new forms of cooperative interaction that develop all participants—learners and their families, teachers, and everyone connected with the enterprise of educating the learners.

CASE ONE—SIXTH GRADE SOCIAL STUDIES

Let us turn now to the case of beginning teacher to see how the African-centered pedagogy framework applies in his practice. The teacher is completing his third year of teaching in the heart of urban Boston. He is a white male in his early thirties and came to Boston after completing his masters degree in American Studies. The middle school is predominantly Asian American, but has a significant proportion of African American children (about 40 percent). The novice teacher cares about urban schools and wants very much to be successful with all the students in the school. He was attracted to teaching by a special incentives program that the state department of education launched to entice "the best and the brightest" into teaching. The program consisted of an alternative teacher preparation route to certification, a fifteen-month intensive training, in addition to a signing bonus. As the reader will see in the following case, there are specific ways a teacher's practice can move from simply caring to actual competence in bringing about a community of achievement in the classroom. This case is fictional and is a constructed composite of real events, interactions and dialogue from middle school classroom visits accumulated during the last three years.

I enter at 8:30 A.M. on a Monday morning, and the sixth graders of a new middle school in an urban district are sitting in a U-shaped table configuration—an open rectangle with the open end facing the front board. Two Asian American girls, an African American boy, and an African American girl are seated to the teacher's right as he faces the class from the front; two African American boys and three Asian boys are seated in the middle segment, and seated on the teacher's left are an Asian American boy, an African American boy, and another Asian American boy. The three African boys at the middle and left are seated at the corner of the partial rectangle of desks. Most of the students have their notebooks out and in front of them and some of them are writing.

8:35 A.M.

Teacher: After the bad day we had yesterday, everybody has a clean slate today, so we are going to start fresh. Does everybody have their [sic] textbooks? If they are over on the shelf can you grab them.

Several students move from their desks to get their textbooks

Jabari, one of three African American boys sitting at the corner of the rectangle, is one of the focus students of my observation because he has been identified by the staff of the school as a problem child. He is clean cut, well-groomed and the tallest student in the class. He has grabbed something from the textbook shelf and is headed back toward his desk when the teacher remarks: "Jabari, not your portfolio, your textbook." On this and several prior occasions, Jabari displays a dismissive and disrespectful air toward the teacher. The teacher gives Jabari a warning verbally when he seems indifferent to the request.

Teacher: I don't want to have to break up that little corner over there.

He is talking to the trio of African American boys seated at the corner of tables to the teacher's left, Raheed, Jabari, and Martin. These three African American boys frequently sit together in their other classes.

Teacher: You don't have your notebooks out with the heading down. That's against classroom rules right there. Would anyone like to read for a bit on the section on the Code of Hammurabi?

The teacher introduced the lesson by announcing that the topic of the class will be on the Code of Hammurabi. In this first phase of the two-period class session, his usual process is to have students read a portion out of the textbook, stopping them periodically to develop the content. Raheed volunteered and began reading. Jabari got up to sharpen his pencil and lingers at the pencil sharpener. The teacher pays no notice.

Sonya: (*interrupts*) Scuse me, I got somebody else's book.

The class pauses while she exchanges with someone. Raheed resumes reading the selection until the teacher stops him.

Teacher: "Okay, what is this section about?"

Darius raises his hand and provides a correct answer and the teacher gives him a colored paper marker at his desk. Darius immediately writes his name on the marker. This is part of the teacher's token economy, where students receive markers at the discretion of the teacher for each "desirable behavior," making the markers reinforcers. Each marker a student receives as a reinforcer can be placed in a lottery jar or his desk with his or her name on it. At the end of the week there is a lottery drawing for a prize. The students understand that the more tokens they have in the jar, the greater their chance of winning something.

8:40 A.M.

Jason continues reading. He is one of the African American target students and is seated to the teacher's right.

Teacher: Alright. We're talking about the code of Hammarabi.

The teacher means this to be the signal that the class is moving into phase two of the instructional setting, transitioning into the phase where the teacher is trying to lead a directed discussion on the reading.

Teacher: Was this the first set of laws?

He waits. Some indicate "no."

Teacher: Then why are we reading about these and not earlier ones?

At this point the teacher was attempting to elicit the participation for a directed discussion. Pedagogically, he was hoping students would make the connection between our knowledge of ancient law and the fact that the code was written in stone and that we might only know about the artifact because it survived these many centuries.

According to the teaching for understanding framework, it is important to frame generative topics—topics that elicit interest because they go to the core of what is worth knowing about a subject area. As explained in the last chapter, African-centered pedagogy takes this idea of a generative topic further by deploying it through five essential practices. In this case, the practices of engagement and participation, meaning-making, and inquiry might have been furthered by posing generative questions. The teacher might have elicited vocal participation by opening inquiry to the "law written on stone" theme and by asking a generative question, such as, "Who knows what it means when someone says that something 'is not written in stone'?" To briefly illustrate the meaning making practice, I should note that this was an opportunity to have linked the colloquialism about something "written in stone" into the inquiry about Hammarabi's law.

Martin volunteers to read. Everybody seems to like Martin. He is always smiling and good spirited. However, he is regarded as hyperactive and has been identified as needing special services.

8:46 a.m.

The entire table directly opposite the teacher has not been following along in the reading. Jason is playing absent mindedly with his key chain. The rest are looking around, making a comment to one another whenever the teacher appears not to be paying attention.

Teacher: What is a code? Let's see a show of hands of who knows what a code is.

No hands go up.

The teacher wrote out the definition on the board. As he did, he reminded the class that they should be taking notes. This is the first mention, since the beginning of class, of the need to write notes from the information provided on the dry erase board. I wonder whether it is expected that students routinely write down information in their notes. The notation I make about this is to address later some of the mechanics of community integrity practices. The goal is to encourage students to regard notetaking as a learning practice, as something they do regularly whenever there is a conversation about worthwhile information.

Neither Jason nor Jabari, two of the African American boys, are writing anything down. Everyone else appears to be. Jabari has his calculator out and a pencil in the other hand. He drops it just as Jason answers the question of why there was a set of laws. The teacher appears not to notice.

8:51 a.m.

The teacher is now reading main ideas for the lesson from the teacher's guide.

Teacher: Does everybody understand this?

No response.

Noting the lack of response he gets with such a question, I resolve to talk later with this teacher about his positionality—where he stands in relationship to the task and the text. The key pedagogical question concerns whether he refers to or reads from the book whenever there was something he expected them to write in their notes. I plan to have him reflect on the symbolism of this position by asking the question, "Why would you expect students to know (by taking notes and preparing for the subsequent quizzes) information that you appear not know yourself as indicated by your reliance on the text to make points about the material? Do you think students don't notice that you are asking them to master content you haven't mastered yourself? Do you think they haven't noticed your repeated reference to the teacher's edition of the text?"

As the teacher continued with the guided discussion routine, the number and range of provocations form Raheed and Jabari increased. The teacher shortened his guided discussion to move to a writing activity—each student is to write his or her own interpretation of a civil code or law. The teacher abruptly passes out strips upon which he has typed a law from Hammarabi's code. This action is the only signal that discussion has ended and a new phase of instructional activity has begun.

Teacher: "Okay, now . . . I need everyone to focus.

Waits a few moments.

Teacher: I need to give you the instructions on what I want you to do. I want you to look at your laws and try to explain it in your own words so that your fellow classmates understand the law. And then, I would like you to explain what kind of punishment there is. And then, I want you to say whether the laws are fair or not. And finally, I would like you to say something about the value of the law.

Experienced teachers will notice right away what is problematic with this task. It is too complex to be given orally—especially since it has four parts. The conceptualization of an inexperienced teacher often fails to take into account the developmental appropriateness and difficulty of the task for his or her students. On a surface planning level, the first thing that might strike you as an experienced teacher is the complexity of the task for a sixth grader. They are asked, with no advance preparation to interpret the meaning, locate the sanctions for breaking the law, and finally, evaluate the law for fairness and explain what they would do about it. That is a lot to ask a learner, especially when the purposes for doing so do not go beyond mere compliance.

On a deeper level of meaning and purpose, there are questions relating to what sense this activity makes. For example, while it might be a good way for students to pay closer attention to the nature of laws in ancient times, the confound of punishments in ancient cultures from the perspective of students' present sensibilities does not make much sense. The central issue about the task is that it is not generative or scholastically purposeful, and seems too complex for the setting. An activity should organize and elicit student action, not inhibit it. It should also make sense, seem doable, and seem worthwhile. In this classroom, none of the children, in fact, did anything meaningful with it. The Asian

American girls on the east side of the room are trying to read their strips. They are confused and finally call the teacher over. There is a period of at least five minutes where no one is doing anything purposeful related to the task.

Notices the absence of activity.

Teacher: Oh yeah, I want you to be writing in your notebooks . . .

9:02 a.m.

Jabari is just sitting.

Teacher: Just write down some words and sentences that will help you explain . . .

Over the next seven minutes, the teacher goes around from desk to desk and appears to be giving individual guidance on what to produce. He then begins collecting the paper squares (i.e., tokens) he gave to several students during the directed discussion. He picks them up and puts them in the jar. Jabari says to the teacher (calling him by another teacher's name) saying, "Raheed says he likes you. He says he wants to marry you." The teacher hears this but does not respond. The little verbal jibes from the African American students at the corner steadily escalate over the next few minutes.

9:06 a.m.

There is a shift in activity from reporting out to reading the law written on each of the strips.

Keyshawn, an African American female reads her law. The observer could not really understand it—too long. As she reads, Martin and Shaunta are play-slapping back and forth. During the entire time of Keyshawn's reading they carry on. The teacher does not look over but continues his attentiveness to the reader. Then, after Keyshawn has finished he comes over to the corner where the African American boys are to remark:

Teacher Is there some reason why you were disrespecting Keyshawn that way?

They do not respond.

Teacher: (*threateningly*) The less we get done in class, the more we'll have to do as homework.

Keyshawn does a good job in her explanation—the code is about bearing witness. Jason offers an explanation.

Teacher: Why did Hammurabi decide to have this law? Darius?

Darius: Because he was a retard!

The teacher then calls on Jabari who proceeds to "hold the floor" when explaining his law. He is jivin' the explanation because he has not put any effort into generating consequences for the law and simply proceeds to talk. However, no consequence came from the teacher. The teacher takes the strip and provides the explanation for him.

Under different circumstances, this would not be a bad instructional plan. From the students' perspectives, why would they take the previous phase seriously? Only a few people shared, and they saw Jabari get away with a total "snow job" when he was called upon.

A note about shaping the social practices in the classroom: The teacher is drinking coffee in class. Can students drink things in class?

Note about Jabari: I asked Jabari if I could ask him a question straight up: why he did not do the worksheet. He said, "I do my work." I said "But you didn't today." No response. "Do you like the work?" And he said, "I hate it."

ANALYSIS OF ACTIVITY SETTING FOR ESSENTIAL CULTURAL PRACTICES IN THE CASE

I present this case not to single out the insufficiencies of the teacher, but to illustrate opportunities for the deployment of the African-centered pedagogical theory to improve practice. Let us first examine the activity setting of this teacher in light of the five essential cultural practices of an African-centered pedagogy. This analysis is summarized in Table 5. The principal component missing with regard to engagement and participation practices was the absence of a generative task. The idea of the generative task is the African-centered counterpart to the generative topic idea of the teaching for understanding framework (cf. Wiske, 1998). The difference is that a generative task is the focus on activity as well as rich thematic content in an instructional activity setting. It is defined as an intellectually stimulating, culturally significant, and scholastically valuable activity or series of activities that results in the achievement of learned performances we value most. Every child responds to activity that manifests as something worth doing and worth achieving. Moreover, African American children already possess many of the cultural resources for writing, speaking and oratory. Children need not be attracted to what is fun, but they do need to see activity as worth doing or participating in. This is both a conceptual task and a motivational task for the teacher—and this pedagogical creativity needs to be applied in the development of the instructional activity setting.

Generative tasks result in the production of quality exhibits and exhibitions, as well as the continuous growth and achievement of those global abilities, academic talents, and habits of mind we value most—such as critical analysis, reasoning in public talk, and writing clearly and persuasively. In an African-centered pedagogy, generative tasks:

- Engender activity that every child can perform with assistance, but that nonetheless simulates a challenging problem-solving situation or creative performance likely to be faced by an adult in the discipline or field of study;
- Involve purposeful activity that encourages more than the mere use of memory, but requires that the child make judgments about what information, procedures or strategies apply to what he or she is planning, justifying, or creating;
- Create a social context where the discourse routines and interactions among children assist in the acquisition and learning of needed abilities, skills, and knowledge;
- Are intrinsically interesting, intellectually enticing, and socially engaging to the child;
- Require a multiplicity of actions and continuous, ongoing, self-determined activity all applied toward meeting a known challenge;
- Elicit from children the requisite subject matter knowledge, skills, and attributes that become the means, rather than the ends, of scholastic achievement;
- Engender the construction of meaning, the emergence of competence, and the synthesis of understanding because it is culturally responsive and situated in an activity that children find purposeful, realistic, authentic, and valuable;
- "Ferret out potential" to use Grant Wiggins' words. In other words, generate opportunities for children to develop abilities and skills not anticipated or planned for, but are nonetheless scholastically valuable; and
- Force recognition of the "big picture"—those essential learning performances and significant abilities (e.g., district or school outcomes) representing what we want our children to be able to do, be like, and know upon completion of their education.

The teacher's instructional activity setting did require several actions that are a part of generative activity—including reading, directed discussion, presenting their own interpretation of one of the codes and writing their own codes—but this was not sufficiently engaging to students.

It might have been useful to organize these activities into a generative task—more worthwhile in terms of producing new understandings—by scripting the law-writing activity so that it had more manifest purpose. For example, the students might have been more engaged and productive if the activity were prompted by the generative question: "What codes of conduct do *all* cultures and/or civilizations have?" This might provide a level of inquiry such that the motive for participation is more than mere compliance with the teacher.

The teacher attempts several management strategies that have limited potential as community development practices. He employs a behavioral management technique where he dispenses round tokens made of colored construction paper. Students receive a yellow marker as a warning or signal of inappropriate behavior, analogous to putting the name on the board. He also employs a token economy where blue markers are reinforcements for good classroom behavior—they are opportunities to win a prize through a weekly lottery.

This system of external motivation of rewards is not sufficient or appropriate for successful work with the children in this classroom. Behavioral management by itself is working at odds to an Africanist sensibility, where the goal is for children to internalize motives for learning. With the technist system of rewards and punishments, it is extremely unlikely that children will engage because they internalize dispositions of achievement and the value of learning. What should replace the external rewards in this teacher's approach is one that elicits children's intrinsic motivation to be a part of community, to do and learn about interesting things, and to experience their sense of self. Behavior management might be useful for managing a few behaviors that are necessary for community building, but the place to begin in shaping comportment in the community is children's sense of belonging, worth, and purpose.

Activity System

The unfortunate condition that existed for this teacher was that whatever solidarity that might exists among the students is grounded in their collective opposition to the authority of the teacher and to escape from the tedium of the curriculum experience. Recall the quality referred to in the teacher preparation literature as "withitness"—the teacher's awareness of the social and

Table 5

ESSENTIAL CULTURAL PRACTICE ANALYSIS OF CASE ONE

Engagement and participation practices	The key piece missing in the teacher's practice was a generative task. The setting that required reading, directed discussion, presenting their own interpretation of one of the codes, and writing their own codes was not sufficiently engaging to students. It was not a generative task in that the purpose for doing the activity, beyond merely complying with the teacher, was not apparent to the students.
Identity development practices	There was an absence of identity work in this activity setting. It was not a setting that the learners really wanted to be a part of. They did not desire association with the social setting. If this were true, the teacher would not require the use of token reinforcements for mere participation. If the teacher had set up the learning context as a community, the learners would vie to become participants.
Community integrity practices	In a community construed and orchestrated for learning, the students themselves have a role in the construction of the group practices—for inquiry, for completing instructional tasks, for narrating, and for social engagement. Other community integrity issues prominent in this case are that a conception of worthwhile learning is missing. As indicated by Jabari's comment, children feel that they are not doing an appropriate or challenging level of work. The teacher has communicated extremely low expectations, which students see are beneath their capability. The teacher is not exercising this practice because whatever integrity of activity and relationships that exist come from him, instead of inhering in the group.
Practices of inquiry	Directed discussion on preset, rote, recitation patterns of discourse are weak forms of inquiry, if they can be considered inquiry at all. Effective practices of inquiry are animated by genuine curiosity and an authentic need to find the truth of something. This genuine curiosity and purpose is missing in this teacher's classroom. Very few activities of learning—narrating, writing, explaining, critiquing, analyzing, or researching.
Meaning-making practices	In the classroom, children are not asked to do things that advance their knowledge. Like so many classrooms, education here is the transmission model or Freire's "banking concept" where the manifest purpose is not really understanding anything, but rather accumulating factual information.

interactional dynamics of the classroom. Future success may be linked to students' perception that the teacher is "with it." Many of these issues were later successfully addressed by adopting two aspects of the African-centered pedagogy—developing an activity system (depicted in Figure 4) and developing generative tasks. There are several points to be made about the teacher's inquiry practices of an African-centered pedagogy. First, let us look at the practices of inquiry at the microlevel, the level of student learning in the classroom. There was a clear conceptual content—expressed as the topic of "The Code of Hammurabi." However, the integrity of the instructional setting was weakened by the fact that the teacher was not clear about the concepts, procedures, and information the students were to learn (Box 1, in Figure 4). For instance, what is it that students should know? Several facts emerged in the reading of the material that might have been stipulated as the content (Box 1, Figure 4):

- In a small room in the Louvre museum in Paris, France, stands a black diorite stela, or column of stone on which is inscribed, in a Semitic language, the Code of Hammurabi.
- The Code of Hammurabi is the most complete remnant of Babylonian law.
- This collection of laws has been ascribed to the reign of Hammurabi, the sixth and best-known king of Babylon's first dynasty.
- The area over which Hammurabi ruled is Iraq today. Formerly it was Mesopotamia, the land between the Tigris and Euphrates Rivers.
- The code consists of 282 case laws, or judicial decisions, collected toward the end of Hammurabi's reign. The decisions deal with such matters as family, marriage, and divorce; tariffs, trade, commerce, and prices; and criminal and civil law.
- He is credited with uniting most of this area under one extensive empire for the first time since Saigon of Akkad did so in about 2300 B.C.
- The body of Sumerian law under which city-states had lived for centuries.

This lack of specificity and clarity of the subject content made it difficult for him to articulate the learning achievement he expected as a performance (Box 2, Figure 4). None of this material is expected in the performances or assessments of the students.

The teacher has them doing potentially valuable things—reading, interpreting text, generating text—but not in form that is recognizable as achievement or understanding performance (Wiske, 1998). The teacher needs to specify what student actions, performances and/or product represents a learning achievement for the Code of Hammurabi. This is typically stated in the learning goals (Box 3, Figure 4) and these specific goals are used as the criteria for assessment of the understanding performance (Box 4, Figure 4).

For all the effort that went into creating the strips, it is unfortunate that they did not support meaningful activity. The task is therefore not a generative task. It is not generative because it is too complex and unclear for the students in the setting. An activity should organize and elicit student action, not inhibit it. Nobody did anything meaningful with the strips, even though they were given specific directions. The Asian American girls on the left-hand side of the room were trying to read their strips. They seemed confused and finally called the teacher over to get help.

Now let us turn to the mesolevel of inquiry, looking at the situatedness of the African American students in the classroom. There is a challenge for this teacher to connect with the African American students. The first order of business for this teacher to appraise his practice at this level is to interrogate what is at the root of the attitude of resistance and rebellion of Jabari, and the excessive disengagement of Raheed and Martin. The fact that Jabari does not display this attitude toward all of his teachers is an important understanding that should come from a mesolevel appraisal of practice. This is possible only in a school that operates as community of practice and where the teacher learns from other teachers how Jabari does in their classes. In an African-centered community of achievement, there would be a conjoint commitment to Jabari's success that would involve a collective recognition of where he is developmentally and dispositionally. This collaboration is more than merely a matter of teachers comparing notes on behavior, but collaborating on his progress as a matter of collective responsibility for knowing each child well enough to promote development.

There is an epistemological issue with respect to the teacher's meaning-making practices. Missing is a notion of worthwhile knowledge, concomitantly with worthwhile work. As indicated by Jabari's comment, children know when they are doing an inappropriate level of work, especially when the task is a minimal completion of information on sheets or low-expectation homework. The teacher communicated extremely low expectations about the value of the homework assignment that was treated as a threat of punishment rather than something worth doing to advance their learning.

What students are given to understand as quality work is an issue of community integrity practices. The sense that the work students are doing is worthwhile comes in large measure from the larger activity. Are they doing worksheets or organizing data? Are they finding facts or doing research? The pedagogical task facing this teacher is to organize the instructional activity with an eye to the larger performance and worthwhile learning achievement.

This system is depicted as the activity setting (Box 5, Figure 4.). The recommended starting point for improving practice based on this experience is to begin with the community integrity practices.

SUMMARY AND CONCLUSIONS

The idea of learning enterprises in the form of generative tasks is the same idea the teaching for understanding framework tries to get at with its notion of the generative topic (Wiske, 1998). My theory extends that idea to incorporate as our unit of planning and thinking, the generative topic plus the activities and the outcomes of student work on that generative task. A good generative task organizes students' learning activity. An excellent task organizes students' learning activity as well as increases opportunities for them to *organize themselves in the task* and the process of active learning.

Cultural identity might be thought of as an individual's self-portrait of him- or herself, painted in the colors of cultural symbols, values, and signs. This internal representation or cultural concept incorporates the individual's understanding of the multilayered and interdependent connections between aspects such as status, race, ethnicity, cultural values, and behaviors.

CHAPTER SIX

Teaching as Assisted Performance in the African American Tradition

> Teachers and students are working together, on real products, real problems. Activities are rich in language, with teachers developing students' capacity to speak, read, and write English, and the special languages of mathematics, science, the humanities and the arts. They teach the curriculum through meaningful activities that relate to the students' lives and family and community experiences. Teachers challenge students to think in complex ways and to apply their learning to solve meaningful problems. Teachers and students converse; the basic teaching interaction is *conversation* [italics added], not lecture. A variety of activities are in progress simultaneously—individual work; teamwork; practice and rehearsal; mentoring in side-by-side, shoulder-to-shoulder, teacher-student work. Students have opportunities to work with their classmates. They all learn and demonstrate self-control and common values: hard work, rich learning, and helpfulness to others.
>
> —Roland Tharp, *A Vision of a Transformed School*

Tharp (1997) describes a community of practice and inquiry that we currently have the know-how to create. Why then is it with so many powerful articulations of pedagogy for African American children (cf. Jackie Jordan Irvine, Janice Hale, Michele Foster, Vanessa Siddle Walker, Gloria Ladson-Billings, Carol Lee, Asa Hilliard, Mwalimu Shujaa, Kofi Lomotey) that public school educators working with African American children have not been more effective? The answer lies in the absence of a system for action and appraisal of practice. Without a system of action and appraisal of practice—a system of practice—it is too difficult to overcome the institutional, cultural and historical barriers to quality education for African American children. This chapter explains the theoretical underpinnings of an African-centered system of practice (Lave, 1988; Tharp, 1997) based on the foundational notion of teaching and learning as conjoint activity, where assisting performance is the primary teaching activity. The chapter is a description of African-centered pedagogical practices that exemplify the principle of teaching as assisting performance.

Public schools are spheres constituted by a diverse array of people, all of whom bring their unique cultural lenses. Reconstituting a school so as to become culturally relevant for all children is complex and difficult, but much more so without a community of inquiry and practice where people share goals and teaching practices. School people cannot build these communities merely by instituting or declaring a new set of policies and procedures. Community building requires meaning-making of the sort only possible if all participants share a common foundation of ideas, beliefs, discourses, and stories.

How the community of educators in a school reconstitutes itself has everything to do with the how it operates as a culture of learning and development for young people. The task of creating communities of practice in urban schools dedicated to the success of African American children is to reconcile the divergences between the African American cultural heritage and mainstream American culture. The tasks of developing responsive pedagogy for African American children and other children of color is integral to that of building enabling, healthy, and supportive social and cultural environments in the school.

ORGANIZATION OF A COMMUNITY OF PRACTICE

As demonstrated in the last section, the interconnection among people and their practices is severely underdeveloped in contemporary designs for successful school development in urban contexts. One part of the challenge is that of developing a conceptual framework that allows us to look at achievement and practice together, and at three levels of inquiry. These levels of analysis are: (1) a microlevel addressing development of the individual learners in classroom contexts; (2) a mesolevel addressing development of the relationships among institutions, learners, and practitioners constituting the social, cultural, and professional fabric of the school community; and (3) the macrolevel addressing development of broader institutional, neighborhood, family, and support systems.

The knowledge base for the microlevel of the individual has been investigated for years, and you perhaps remember the heyday of discussion on learning styles, cultural styles, and cognitive styles. There is a substantial knowledge base in this literature that links patterns of culture to behavior. Understanding the features of communication, cognition, and learning that have cultural signatures is important, but only scratches the surface of what teachers need to know. An understanding of individual behavior is important, but the social and cultural contexts of children's home and school environments must also be part of teachers' understanding.

Without situating our knowledge of learning styles in cultural context and institutional values, we might well end up working with still another form of stereotyping that merely ascribes a typology of behavior to culture groups. Accordingly, African American children are ascribed "relational traits" and European American children are ascribed "analytical traits." Public schooling is, by and large, organized to support and nurture the development of individuals who are more "analytic" in their cognitive/learning styles (Hale-Benson, 1982; Hilliard, 1976; Shade, 1982).

The knowledge base for the mesolevel of analysis, where we consider the cultural and social contexts of children's development, is less well articulated in educational writing. For this discussion I will follow the usage of Tharp and Gallimore (1991) and appropriate the term activity setting. Briefly, the term activity setting denotes the unit of analysis for understanding the social, cultural, and interactional makeup of settings in which people come together for a purpose—such as student achievement or teacher development. These two aspects—teacher development and student achievement—are yoked in the African-centered pedagogical model. The idea is that both student achievement and teacher development are worked on simultaneously and collaboratively in the daily practices of teaching and learning. The student achievement focus is examined through the idea of the instructional activity setting (as depicted in Figure 4). The focus on the teacher and essential cultural practices is examined through the professional activity setting (as depicted in Table 5).

Instructional activity settings within classrooms include such things as independent learning centers, cooperative learning groups, reading groups, and whole class instruction. Professional activity settings include such things as staff meetings, team meetings, and conferences. Teacher capacity to develop activity settings is the linchpin of developing learning communities of effective practice. Two points should be made regarding how these fit with an African-centered school of achievement. The first point is that to organize a community of practice, participants in a partnership need to be able to analyze and assess the activity settings of their professional work in conjunction with student achievement. This means analyzing the social-interactional dynamics and the purposes of collaborative activity, as well as the meaning participants attach to that activity, in order to determine appropriate policies, tasks and strategies. The second point is that the processes of organizing a learning community are most effectively done in collaboration with others—teachers, parents, and other stakeholders in the quality education of the children in the school. That is, instructional quality is improved to the degree that teachers can collaborate on and assess the effectiveness of each other's practice.

Complex issues do not exist in a vacuum. The goal of successful collaboration is to dramatically amplify the possibilities of organizing the school life of children. The activity setting has to be worked on so that rather than generating a temporary resolution, the larger issue is brought to the entire school community of the collaborative. Resolutions of difficult issues cannot and should not be accomplished in a single setting, or just among teachers. Resolutions need to be instantiated in the practices and policies of the school, as well as the cultural sensibilities of African American children and their parents.

The task of developing a school of achievement is to create an activity setting among teachers, African American parents, and community stakeholders for the purposes of improved instruction for African American children—to build a new community of practice. One of the important aspects of doing this is to enrich the tasks of professional development by creating activity settings other than conferences. Tharp and Gallimore (1991) note:

> Effective teaching does not require authority. The assistance of performance can sometimes be provided more effectively in its absence. Even authorities can assist performance only through the exercise of modeling, contingency managing, feeding back, questioning, and cognitive structuring. Rather than teaching being dependent on authority, it is more nearly the opposite; indeed, teaching is the process on which authority depends to achieve its aims. (p. 85)

The creation and orchestration of activity settings is the single most essential capacity of an educator who is a participant in a community of practice. The task of teachers who are seeking to improve their effectiveness with African American children should be to build communities of practice and activity settings that draw on African American culture, history, and intellectual heritages. There needs to be the development of knowledge of both individuals and cultural systems as they interact throughout a community of practice, and are enacted or instantiated in an activity setting.

COMMUNITY OF PRACTICE AND ACTIVITY SETTINGS FOR SCHOOL DEVELOPMENT

How do educators interact in a school of achievement? Addressing this question requires appraisal of practice at the mesolevel of inquiry. It involves extending the notion of assisted performance from classroom instructional practice to the venue of professional activities. Triadic analysis is a simple yet important idea—that any assessment, evaluation, support, assistance, or scaffolding of teaching can be done in connection with the resulting experiences and learning achievements of the students and across levels of authority or expertise. It is no secret that there are insufficient opportunities, resources, and personnel to accomplish the type of professional development activities popularly envisioned in the school reform literature. The point is that activity settings, as I have described them above, must be created at all levels in a school of achievement. This is the task of the community of practice—creating strategically designed activity settings that promote the occurrence of assistance at all levels of the school organization but still are linked to the learning achievements of the students in the school.

Schools of achievement dedicated to improving the educational quality of African American children organize themselves differently than most public schools. Most schools, including professional development schools in collaborative partnership, operate in a bureaucratic system characterized by a linear chain of command. In this sort of design, individual A (e.g., principal or director) directs and evaluates individual B (e.g., lead teacher or supervisor) who in turn directs and evaluates individual C (e.g., a classroom teacher or intern). What the triadic analysis suggests is a different sort of organization of practice in which the functions of the setting are not primarily those of directing and evaluating, but rather providing assistance in creating a new culture of practice.

This type of organization has certainly been identified often enough in the collaborative partnership literature as a desirable goal. However, what appears to be lacking is a systematic account or conceptual framework of how this is to come about in the specific work examining the school programs of African American children. The basic formulation of the conceptual framework for collaborative partnership work is threefold: (1) The function of direction, regulation, and evaluation are altered to that of assisting performance; (2) the means of assistance are to be mutual and reciprocal (bilateral) rather than hierarchical (unilateral); and (3) the lines of communication are expanded from a linear, sequential, top-down structure to an organization with multiple linkages.

An example of this last point is an organization in which individual A (e.g., director or principal) assists individual B directly, as well as others (e.g., other experienced teachers, parents, or college faculty in the partnership) who can assist individual B; and individual B (e.g., lead teacher or supervisor) assists individual C (e.g., teacher or intern) directly and by creating conditions for others (e.g., parents, colleagues) to assist C. So the function of those in administrative and authority roles shifts from regulating and directing to assisting and collaborating on the essential cultural practices of the school community. The infrastructure provided by the idea of the activity setting and the analytical framework provided by the triadic analysis is described by Tharp and Gallimore (1991, p. 84):

> Each position in the organization is restricted in its range of contacts. Most contact is with the next individual in the chain of supervision. In general then we can suggest that good work in each position consists in assisting the next position to assist the third and so forth down the chain for the ultimate benefit for the student. The good work of the superintendent lies in assisting the principal to assist the grade level chairs; their work consists of assisting in developing the children by assisting them through their zone of proximal development.

This approach of triadic analysis is dramatically different from the organization of practice extant in most urban public schools, whether or not they are collaborative partnerships. The presence of collaborative partnership partners does not change the bureaucratic structure of schools. Effective development of the essential cultural practices for quality education for African American children requires a restructuring of the lines of responsibility and assistance. The triadic model and the conceptual framework of the activity setting are the most likely and theoretically developed means by which collaborative partnerships may begin the critical work of examining the social and cultural contexts of teaching and learning—to "reinvent" the school learning community.

African-centered schools of achievement, using a triadic analysis, can enrich the working relationships in new activity settings that afford authentic and meaningful participation for parents and community stakeholders in the work that matters. The unpacking of the social-cultural context of teaching in relation to the organizational structure depends on the principles of triadic analysis and the notion of the activity setting that come from the conceptual framework I discussed above, referred to as assisted performance (a synthesis of traditions from neo-Vygotskian, Deweyian, situated cognition, and cognitive learning theory).

COMMUNITY OF PRACTICE AT THE MACROLEVEL OF INQUIRY

The most significant portions of the collaborative partnership movement are not so much what happens in professional development schools, which tend to recapitulate and fortify current practice, but in networks and larger school systems of collaborative partnerships that are able to take on the tasks of critique, reinvention of practice, and support of innovation. The goals of inquiry and reflective practice are not likely to be realized in any meaningful way at the level of individual collaborative partnership (for the reasons elaborated by Murrell and Borunda [1997]—namely the "tyranny of the mundane"). They will be realized from a community of practice that involves networks of participants from different collaborative partnerships serving similar community needs and interests.

For urban educators to make a point of respecting the wisdom of community people is not simply a political stance, it also embodies an important component in a powerful theory. What would an African-centered school of achievement look like if the school community can ensure the development of all five African-centered essential cultural practices in Table 3? Let us examine that in the following case.

CASE TWO—ELEMENTARY SCHOOL LITERACY LEARNING

THE SETTING

The residents in the area of Roxbury are classified among those neighborhoods that are classified "at risk" in Massachusetts. African American youth have been the fastest growing segment of the youth population committing suicide. Though many successful youth programs have reduced gang violence over the last five or six years, the gang activity is still higher in these neighborhoods than in any other section of Boston. These communities are particularly educationally underserved. It is estimated that between 70 and 80 percent of the sixth-graders have little or no mastery of reading or mathematics. Some have estimated that less than 50 percent of the ninth-graders should have been promoted out of middle school.

The school is the John Fitzgerald Kennedy (a pseudonym), a K–5 elementary school located in an underresourced neighborhood in the city. Prior to the last four years, the composition almost exactly mirrored the ethnic percentages of the entire school district—49 percent Black, 26 percent Latino, 15 percent White, and 10 percent other. However, over the last three years the proportion of African American children in the school grew from 50 percent to 85 percent due to the closing of some neighborhood schools and redistricting.

Ms. McCleod, the retiring principal, is an African American woman with significant stature in the African American community and neighborhoods of Lower Roxbury and Boston. She had been a longtime advocate of children and for their educational opportunity. In her final years as principal there had been some friction between three major factions in the faculty. The smallest group consisted of the most recent hires, all of whom were White and described themselves as the "progressive" group. These teachers all had been teaching five years or less. The largest group consisted of older teachers within three years of retirement. Seven of these were white, one was Puerto Rican, and one was

African American. The second largest group consisted of 7 African American teachers, all of whom had at least ten years of teaching experience and all had reputations among parents as the most accomplished teachers in the school. These teachers have been described as "black artful teachers " (Foster, 1997, 2001; Piestrup, 1973). The phrase refers to qualities of cultural responsiveness, linguistic skill, performance style, and authoritative voice, and other capacities underlying their high degree of success educating African American children in underresourced urban communities. Ms. McCleod had spent a good deal of her time dealing with parents who would vie with one another to get their children into these teachers' classrooms.

In recent years, there had been a growing perception that discipline problems were on the rise and that student achievement performance was dropping in the wake of the schools lower-than-average standing on the published reading scores of elementary schools in the district. The faculty became polarized between Black and White teachers, and between the "Young Turks" and the "old guard" who began to blame each other for the perceived tarnish on the school's once glistening reputation. Ms. McCleod was responsible for the many years of excellence in the school and was an extremely capable principal. She exhibited strong leadership qualities and had always been able to maintain group civility among the teachers. However, the internal furor over the decline in the school's reading scores became an increasingly divisive issue among the different factions of teachers. Although the change in aggregate scores was primarily due to demographic changes, including a 95 percent turnover in the last three years, several teachers wanted to attribute the decline to policy and Ms. McCleod's administration.

One of the conflicts concerned whether the school was going to contract with national curriculum consultants to deal with the new state curriculum frameworks, the accompanying high stakes test and curriculum. The African American teachers, who were suspicious and critical of the consultants' connection to a conservative foundation, and who dominated the curriculum committee of the school, led the charge to reject the offer. Their refusal to contract with these consultants was taken by some of the "old guard" teachers, and "young progressive" teachers as a refusal to "get the house in order." Among themselves, the African American committee members saw this rejection as being in the best interests of the children in the school and community. Nonetheless, bad feelings about the committee's decision were still smoldering when the new principal was hired in early summer.

Ms. Maher, a dynamic career educator in the district and a white female in her late forties, becomes the new principal of the school. She and Ms. McCleod had known each other for more than twenty-five years and had been involved in many community-based education movements with her.

MEETING WITH THE PRINCIPAL

When the new principal arrives the kindergarten teacher and the second, third, and fourth grade teachers, all from the "young progressive" faction, schedule a meeting with the principal to talk about the grade level teams. These teachers were each paired with one of the experienced Black artful African American teachers, and they were hoping that Ms. Maher would reassign the teams so that they could work with others of the "young progressives" group. In trying to make their case for different assignments based on "professional compatibility," they obliquely criticized the practice of each of the African American teachers on their grade level teams. They make it clear that they do not approve of the methods of the Black teachers. In the course of the meeting they spoke about the kindergarten teacher in a nice way, but not without digs on her failure to be "developmentally appropriate" in her classroom. Below are two samples:

Meeting Comment # 1
The "young progressive" kindergarten teacher says this:

Teacher 1: I think that there is a range of good teaching styles. But I just took this course on the "Meaning and Development of Play" and the professor was talking about how children really need to *play*. She said that an amazing amount of development occurs through play. And it just makes me feel so bad when I walk past Adrianna's room and see these little tikes hunched over working on their letters when they should be playing. I don't think Adrianna realizes how much happier her children would be . . . and her too . . . if she would just lighten up a little bit and let the activities emerge from the children. So what if they want to spend an extra ten minutes in the block area? As long as they are engaged and interacting—they're learning! I'm not talking against Adrianna, I think she would feel so much better about things if she would just loosen up a little.

Meeting Comment # 2
The "young progressive" fourth grade teacher says that about another of the Black teachers:

Teacher 2: She yells at her children. She is *too* strict. She has them toeing the line about everything. And then what happens is that

> Jill gets involved in that assessment project and is always traveling down to central office and to other schools. A then other people have to take over her class every Tuesday morning, and nobody can control those kids because Jill isn't teaching them *inner*-discipline. She isn't teaching them how to control themselves. She rules that classroom by the force of her personality. And so she creates a bad situation, not just for the people who have to take over her class, but for the kids themselves. Mr. Gregg, the gym teacher, is always complaining how her class acts in the gym. He has to speak to them a million times to get them to pay attention.

Ms. Maher listened patiently and carefully, and weighed several possibilities in her mind as to the unspoken motives. When the teachers had finished, she explained that she had intentionally assigned the teams so that the more experienced African American teachers for the kindergarten, second, third, and fourth grades could work with them to develop their practice. She explained that she had carefully considered these four teachers' "incompatibility of styles" argument, but was not persuaded. Ms. Maher concludes the meeting by saying, "I think it *is important* to have a diversity of styles, and it will be of value to us as we build relationships. The contrasts in style can inform our collective teaching knowledge of practice. That's why I made these assignments as I did. So, unless there are other factors, reasons, conflicts or issues regarding working with your assigned team partners, this meeting is over." Unwilling to push it further, the four young teachers left the principal's office.

PRECIPITATING CONFLICT

In October, the intern for the second grade has her idea for her unit to be taught in the class. The intern and the second grade teacher collaborate on the unit and they decide to try out a new curriculum on diverse families and get the enthusiastic approval from new the principal Ms. Maher. The teacher and the intern agree that they want all children to feel included and that this will be a theme in the curriculum unit. So one day the intern read *Heather Has Two Mommies* (Newman, 1989) at the morning meeting and *My Daddy's Roommate* (Willhoite, 1990) in the afternoon, both of which deal with gay and lesbian families.

Some of the Black parents were very upset when the topic of the new unit came up at the Parents' Council meeting. One of the parents had shared being asked by her second grader if she knew any people who were gay. She shared with the other parents her surprise when her daughter said they were learning about it in school. This parent called to inquire, but had not heard back yet when she called the office. There were five other parents at the meeting who had children in Ms. Damien's room. The next morning, this group of five brought their concern to the principal. They wanted to know why the teacher or the intern had not informed them of this curriculum content.

The parents stressed to Ms. Maher that it was not the content of curriculum they objected to. They wanted to be assured that they could communicate with teachers about the content, especially for topics that they would have wanted to be prepared for when their children asked them questions about what they thought. The parents also stressed that they did not want to change or prevent the unit, but were angry because they did not appreciate being caught so off guard. But they strongly felt that they, as parents, had a right to be informed in advance by the teachers about the topic of gay families.

The new principal (Ms. Maher), after only five weeks in her new position, was a bit shaken by the vocal assertiveness of the parents. As a result, she misinterprets their insistence and solidarity as a challenge to her administration, and mistakenly views the visit to her office as a challenge to academic freedom and a threat to teachers' autonomy in choosing curriculum. She promises to put their concerns on the agenda of the next "town meeting"—a new means of community talk and decision-making that the school had yet to try out. She says to the parents "We'll iron everything out then."

The town meeting the following Thursday evening quickly turns contentious. The issue of parental communication about curriculum gets lost as several teachers and parents begin to advocate for the right to introduce diverse lifestyles in the form of the unit on different kinds of families including the segment on gay families. The assembly, becoming polarized across racial lines, began arguing at cross-purposes. While some of the White parents and the young teachers advocate for the curriculum and the Black teachers and parents argue for advanced notice of curriculum issues, neither interest had been abrogated.

Throughout her career as a principal Ms. Maher had always made it a point to back up her teachers. Finally, she makes her position clear but too emphatically—stating that this was about teaching kids about bias and discrimination and that "parents don't determine the curriculum." Ms. Maher attempted to close off the complaining. She says "I am not going to have this reactionary stuff in my school. How else are children going to learn about bias and discrimination?" There is a chorus of gasps among the Black teachers and parents at this remark. One Black woman says aloud without identifying herself "Oh, so now *you* are going to teach *us* about discrimination?" Ms. Maher immediately realized her poor choice of words and tried to recover by saying, "You know what I meant." But it was too late. The African American parents who had been her allies in the meeting were allies no longer after that statement.

CASE EPILOGUE

The glaring issues in the social context of the school—determination of curriculum, racial tension, gender identity issues and institutional power—forced the school community to confront the natiure of the learning community. Out of this confrontation the opportunity to apply the five pedagogical practices. At the request of several of the parents, Ms. McCleod, Ms. Maher, and several of the teachers sat down to look at the literacy learning component of their Whole School Improvement Plan. Someone brought a quote to argue for the focus on narratives and doing oral histories.

> Everyone has a story to tell. As a matter of fact, the shaping of life experiences into stories is a universal and essential human behavior. By telling stories, we create meanings, heal traumas, and build communities. We create the understandings of our individual and collective pasts, which allow us to know who we are and shape our visions for the future. (Cohen, Roelofs, & Battat, *n.d.*, p. 1)

Narrative is the fundamental meaning-making strategy of all human beings. The afterschool staff and a few parents began to explore developing oral history projects that children worked on during the day, and could continue on in the afterschool program. The units they developed began with an exploration of what oral history is. The teachers concentrated on the ways to develop literacy skills by providing children opportunities to listen to stories and respond with stories of their own. Children are familiar with the story form, and the introductory activities promote the idea that stories can also be an occasion to learn about different people, places, and cultures. Children become familiar with stories of a variety of different genres—folktales, stories, ballads, fables, and so forth—as they prepare to create their own compositions. The outcome for the unit is that the children understand oral narrative as both a source of information and as a source of stories. They will express ideas about what they can learn about, and from, people who are different from themselves. Basing children's exploration of such topics as "community" or "family" in the narratives of oral history creates a real and authentic reason for students to listen to, analyze, and work with stories. Stories become the vehicle for purposeful investigation of significant ideas and information.

CHAPTER SEVEN

The Classroom Ecology of Culture and Language

> The culture into which an individual is born stresses the certainty of his potentialities and suppresses others, and it acts selectively, favoring the individuals who are best endowed with the potentialities preferred in the culture and discriminating against those with alien tendencies. In this way the culture standardizes the organization of the emotions of individuals.
>
> —Gregory Bateson, *Naven*

A growing ethnographic research literature has identified instances of cultural incompatibility between dominant mainstream culture and the cultural set represented by urban African American children. Although this research has provided examples of cultural incompatibilities that depress academic achievement, the conception of *cultural incompatibility* is an insufficient explanation for formulating pedagogical theory that will reverse the negative educational outcomes for African American learners. What is needed, and that has been our purpose thus far in this book, is to create a theory of pedagogy which articulates culturally-responsive, developmentally-appropriate, and pedagogically powerful teaching and learning practices for African American children situated in urban public schools.

In terms of culture and school practices, there is a question of balance that has to be resolved. That balance concerns what cultural resources from home and community can be productively incorporated with school practices to create a new culture of achievement and development. But effective practice does not lie in the bifurcation of, or balance between, African American culture versus mainstream culture. Rather, the ecology of cultural practices emerging from home, school, and heritages of people is the issue of balance to be resolved. The responsibilities and effectiveness of a teacher are defined, in part, by the pervasive influence of language and culture on classroom activities.

How should we think about culture as it applies to the education of African American youngsters? As the work of C. A. Bowers and David Flinders (1990) has shown, thinking of the classroom as an ecology of language and cultural patterns is particularly important for effective work with African American children. Cultural patterns of communication from the Africanist tradition are important foundations upon which to build learning experiences for African American children. This chapter develops the African-centered pedagogical theory further and discusses the means by which teachers can develop and draw on their capacity to read these cultural patterns, and incorporate them into their instructional practices with African American children.

In our earlier discussion of cultural values, I distinguished the Western tradition, with its valuation of a mind-body dualism, from an African-centered view of mind-body holism. Recall that the Euro-American value of dualism is the epistemological belief that a person's ideas, beliefs, and intellect are autonomous of the body and essentially disconnected from that person's lived experience, and, by default, from sociocultural context. This cultural value is the foundation upon which the traditions of both European and American education devalue lived experience of African American people. Witness the myriad of instances in education such as the "affective domain" and "cognitive" domain dichotomy in curriculum, and the division of rationality and affect in learning styles formulations and "brain research."

In this chapter I examine what it means to create a figured world of Black achievement by incorporating a new value system in a system of effective teaching that is also centered in the system of values and perspectives that already exist in school contexts. To do this, we need to recall the previously described three domains of meaning that are involved in this discussion of learning community:

1. The intrapersonal venue concerning what we see as important to the development of individuals on the microsystemic level;
2. The interpersonal realm concerning what we value for the development and sustenance of human systems (including the family, community and other social networks on the mesosystemic level;
3. The cultural symbolic venue incorporating the world of culturally and politically defined meanings of a people on the macrosystemic level.

I appropriated the notions of figured world from Holland et. al. (1998) and community of practice from Lave (1988) for thinking about how these three domains of meaning come together in the construction of an African-centered pedagogy. The notion of a community of practice is, as I have discussed earlier, a fairly specific theoretical framework proposed by Jean Lave and Etienne Wenger. The reader will recall from earlier discussion that the social learning theory and activity theory underlying the notion of community of practice is highly relevant to our present discussion of an achievement-oriented pedagogy. In appropriating the notion, from this point on I will work with the idea as community practices, with an "s" on the end.

With this modification I want to signify that what we are talking about here is not a single practice as it is used in the literature, but a multiplicity of practices. What binds a community together is not a single professional practice—like teaching, jurisprudence, dentistry, or basket weaving—but a collection of practices, including cultural ones, that emerge out of the construction of a new common culture devoted to the development of young people—particularly those least well served. That is to say, I am invoking the notion that effective teaching is a multiplicity of practices. To build an African-centered success pedagogy, it will be necessary to think in terms of a multiplicity of practices, at a multiplicity of levels, developed simultaneously and in parallel. In addition to this multiplicity, it is important to think of practices in terms of the three domains or levels of meaning listed above.

COMMUNITY OF PRACTICES IN PLACE OF MULTICULTURAL EDUCATION

In place of talking about multicultural education and the approach of "teaching to diversity," I am going to talk about how effective, responsive pedagogy emerges from the development of a community of practices. I want to talk about the idea building a learning community or community of practices as a matter of changing your dispositions and practices. Culturally responsive pedagogy in diverse settings is more than what is expressed in the mantra of what a teacher "knows and is able to do" by adding "what the teacher is disposed to do." The general disposition of importance is that of regarding the classroom of African American children as you would any other community that you value and participate in by choice.

I would like to begin this description of a community of practice with the metaphor of family or, in the African American tradition, kinship (see Rawick, 1977 for a discussion of the historical bases of kinship). If we understood the social context of our classrooms as we do our family contexts, think how much easier it would be to recognize the need for common routines, traditions, practices, celebrations, and forms of talk. Think how much more aware we might be of participants' sense of identity and place within the group. I think we move to a deeper working understanding of a community of practice that is democratic and responsive to diverse backgrounds when we think about how families attempt to achieve fairness, justice, and provide for its members a sense of place and belonging.

The notion of kinship is important, because the African American experience can be understood as a sophisticated, interclass, intergenerational kinship system. Every family has its rituals and routines. In my family, coming up, one was having dinner together and sharing the events of the day. Certain discourses were expected, predictable, and almost comforting even in their repetitive routine—like being asked by my mother what I learned in school that day. Regardless of the content of (or lack thereof) our response to the question, the routine was important as discourse that fortified human bonding and connection around the idea that learning was important. Each of us children had a place in line to talk about our day in school. These sorts of experiences are the basis of important human ties and connections, and we would like analogies of these types of connections in the classroom.

More important to this discussion is the fact that families have a common tradition and a common history. Your classroom and school should also develop common traditions and history that are recognizable and familiar to your African American students.

At a certain level, "family" is a useful metaphor for the community of practice and the figured world of inquiry we wish to establish in our classrooms. This is the same notion of a community of caring suggested by Nel Noddings' notion of a caring community. In addition to the rituals and routines that bind a group of people together, the figured world of your classroom should, like families, nurture caring relationships. This is easier to do in elementary school, but is just as valuable to middle schools and high schools. This is seen in the development of clusters, houses, and any number of terms referring to the organizing smaller groupings of students to reduce the anonymity of students and increase the connection and relationships between a core of teachers and a group of students.

Things that you share in common are part of what form the relationships you have with students in your "classroom family." Rituals—or routine practices—analogous to "What did you learn in school today?"—are important social practices that you want to develop and apply to create the "classroom family." The meaning that gets attached to this depends on a shared heritage and common traditions.

Among the social practices that I observed recently was a cleanup ritual—those last twenty minutes of the day on Friday afternoon when the board gets washed, the floor gets swept, the erasers get cleaned, and the children are engaged with their task or chore that rotates every week. Of what value is this? It is encouraging children to invest in the care and maintenance of their physical space. More importantly, it is encouraging the social practice of investing in the collective group. One White boy said cheerily to the African American boy sitting at his desk "You don't have to worry about your chores today. . . . . I already did them."

The idea of place in this sense is what educational ethnographers have described as participation structures. In a family, you would not dream of bringing home a gift for one child and not the other. Parents exercise this awareness all the time, making decisions that maintain an ecology of relationships so that one child is not privileged over the others. We need the same sensibilities in our classrooms. We are talking here about an ecology of relationships that is important to the development of identity and sense of place of each participant in the community. Maintaining a social and cultural ecology means operating as though your students are family members and you are trying to find a balance of interactions, participation and sense of place.

At another level, the metaphor of family represents the repository of commonly held cultural values and heritage. This is the critical feature missing in the education of African American children. The other metaphor is culture. The basic understanding to begin with is that for African American children, the developmental task of identity development is complicated. The cultural expression of African American heritage is often ideologically at odds with the cultural framework of mainstream America. This is why an African-centered pedagogy for Black children is essential for promoting the most significant developmental task that African American children face—namely identity development. The social and cultural components of school should support the process of self-discovery. It is interesting that none of the major textbooks used in programs of teacher preparation adequately address what might be the most significant factor in the elevating Black achievement—the formation of a robust, integrated, and empowered identity as Black person in contemporary society. When African American students attend culturally mainstream schools, the task of establishing a healthy identity is complicated by the fact that they are, in at least one sense, bicultural. The task of defining who you are is complicated when you have a foot in each of two worlds, and try to negotiate each with your own personal needs for safety, efficacy, belongingness, and achievement. The task is further complicated to the extent that the cultural expressions, representations, and demands of those two worlds often contradict one another.

One manifestation of this identity work is described by John Ogbu, an African anthropologist who studied African Americans in an urban high school together with Signithia Fordham (1986). They examined the experience of curriculum as factors relating to achievement and identity. What they found was a phenomenon they called "racelessness." Racelessness is the notion that African American students begin to deny their identity as Black people in the process of striving to achieve whenever students attribute studious behaviors to mainstream cultural norms more than Black ones.

Consider that prior to desegregation, the school communities that were virtually all Black did not have the conditions under which Ogbu and Fordham's phenomenon of racelessness could occur (for a full development of this argument, see Siddle Walker, 1996). The value of this work is to show how the ways in which students construe their school experience impacts on their identity as learners, achievers and cultural beings.

From the standpoint of my framework of African-centered pedagogy, identities are not static nor only defined by the school context. I argue, as do Holland et al. (1998), that identities are situationally and continuously constructed in different contexts that ebb and flow in the social life of the school. Holland et. al., use the term *improvisation*—identity is continuously negotiated and recreated under the constraints of privilege, status, and performance demands. Young people are able to project themselves as subjects in different contexts—to construct a "symbolic self" in a context or situation that they try out, to improvise. They write:

> Identity is a concept that figuratively combines the intimate or personal world with the collective space of cultural forms and social relations. We are interested in identities, the imaginings of self in worlds of action, as social products; indeed, we begin on the premise that identities are lived in and through activity and so must conceptualized as they develop in social practice. (1998, p. 5).

In other words, individuals in situations are always negotiating a sense of self in a location between the person and the collective—the place where the self leaves off and the rest of the world begins. Adolescents, in particular, engage in the construction of what Holland et al., call "practiced identities" in contexts that include, simultaneously, their figured world (webs of meaning of the individual's own creation) and positionality (roughly the idea of role or situatedness in a given social setting). Adolescents continuously improvise their agency in every given situation. Much of what some contemporary literature terms "oppositional identity" is merely improvisation that teachers and adults merely interpret as oppositional. More will be said about this in chapter 8.

The phenomenon of "racelessness" Ogbu and Fordham observed need never occur. They observed a particular context with features that contributed to adolescent's in-the-moment constructions of self. The good news is that we as teachers can create contexts and design experiences to promote achievement oriented identity development. In different arrangements of social and power relationships, such as in the all-Black community in the segregated schooling in the rural South that Siddle Walker (1996) describes, the phenomenon in which Black students disidentify with achievement need never occur. The phenomenon of racelessness is nonetheless interesting because it points to the broader phenomenon of the conflict presented to African American students and other students of color in school settings. What I think is valid about the idea is that it shows how being Black in America poses risks to healthy and robust identities.

What Ogbu and Fordham (1986) discovered in their study at Capitol High is that the process of identity development for those African American students was complicated by the fact that doing well in school seemed to them to represent contradictions to their identity. African American students who strove to achieve faced the peer pressure of being accused of "acting white." The adult role models in school were mostly White and middle class, and therefore were unlike the role models of African Americans in the students' family, community, and church life. The school models were not those that African American adolescents wanted to emulate. So being academically successful, in some ways, represented something undesirable.

For the Capitol High African Americans, actions like turning in your homework, participating in class, and getting good grades were seen as ways of "acting white." In short, their view was that it was not cool to be studious because you would be perceived as "acting white." This perspective can cause conflict for the African American students who want to achieve. To adapt, the Black students at Capitol High would discount their high grades, or hide the fact that they did well. A wonderful media illustration of this phenomenon was depicted in the well-known film about teaching, *Stand and Deliver*. The scene representing an instance of adapting to this conflict between current identity and school achievement involved Angel Guzman, a gang member attending Garfield High School in East Los Angeles interested in doing mathematics in Jaime Escalante's class. The young man caught up with his teacher on the way to the book storeroom, asking to be let back into class and saying he could not let his homeboys see him carrying around a mathematics book. The two "cut a deal"—an agreement in which Angel would do his homework, come to class, even offer "protection" in exchange for having three books: one for his locker, one for home, and one for class.

Whether students deny their race (racelessness) as a consequence of excelling academically, as that study suggests, is not the point I want to make here. Personally, I would not go so far as to think that this happens to any significant degree. I believe there is rarely a categorical rejection of one's race as much as it is adopting an identity that feels right. But the conflict between one's identity as an African American student in the world today and academic achievement is quite real. You more than likely have observed this yourself—instances in which students will down play their academic success. Probably a far more serious type of conflict is *stereotypic threat* (e.g., Steele, 1992, 1997) mentioned in the Introduction. Briefly, *stereotypic threat* refers a similar sort of stressor to African American students' academic performance. It refers to performance situations that degrade the achievement performances of African American students and other students of color. Stereotypic threat for African American students is being at risk of confirming, as a self-characteristic, a negative stereotype about Blacks lacking in intelligence and achievement potential (Steel & Aronson, 1995). Steele (1992), who introduced the concept, argued that although all students experience anxiety over possible failure in academic settings, individuals who are members of historically disadvantaged groups experienced an additional level of anxiety over confirming the negative stereotype of their group through their poor performance. Steele (1997) was able to show that in test situations where African American students felt their performance could reflect on the abilities of Black people, their performance was significantly worse than their performance in situations where no such stereotype vulnerability was present.

Now here is the task for African-centered pedagogy—to create a new symbolic culture in school settings so that the figured worlds that students construct as part of the identity work of adolescence do not incorporate negative images of Black achievement. In most public schools, this means taking on the triple threat created by the conflict between academic success and Black identity. What is the triple threat? Well, imagine the multiple dimensions of the quandary for you as an African American student. On one hand you have teachers who may be expecting less of you because you are Black. So you try to avoid internalizing self-talk like "This teacher doesn't think I can do it." On another hand you have a national media telling you that you are less able, as represented in the national conversation about the so-called achievement gap which presumes that if you are Black you do less well on standardized tests. So you may be fighting not to internalize self-talk "Society thinks that Black people are less able academically." Finally, you have peers who see your desire to achieve as "acting white" and a "sell-out" to a certain extent. Your struggle here may be "Do I want to keep my friends or do I want to succeed in school?"

Unless you are a person of color, you more than likely would never encounter this triple threat. It is important to note that these phenomena in Black youth culture—that it is not cool to be smart and stereotypic threat—are actually created by contemporary schooling practices. The irony is that achievement is central to the traditions of African American, particularly literacy as a means of opposition to oppression. I would go so far as to say that this irony is not merely an accident of history but evolved as part of the fabric of American life, as I alluded to in chapter 3. In any event, African American children do not need pep talks about "beating the odds" or test remediation. They need exemplary teachers who can "hook them up" with their own heritage and legacy of achievement as a definition of what it means to be African American in the United States.

An exemplary teacher of African American students must be prepared to assist students in this struggle for identity—a preparation that requires a deep knowledge of African American cultural history. African American adolescents, like all adolescents, are continuously negotiating the question "Who will I become?" As an adolescent, sooner or later you have to decide which aspects of a wide array of adult roles, behaviors, and cultural symbols you are going to incorporate into your construction of self. Those who are disconnected from a tradition, the history and heritage of their people, are at a severe disadvantage in this process. Healthy identity development requires that young people connect with the heritage and history of the people they see themselves belonging to.

Cultural knowledge is essential to building a community of learning in your classroom. As the teacher you are the chief architect of the intellectual and social life in your classroom; you must be able to interpret what is going on as African American children and youth struggle with conflicts of identity, place, and justice. In your classroom community, you decide what place certain symbols and expressive forms will have. How you make these judgments with regard to the symbols and expressive forms of Black people has everything to do with how well you connect with African American students. In turn, how you connect with African American students has everything to do with the cultural community you encourage, nurture, and develop. For a few years now, rap music has been a nexus of concern about youth—an expressive form that many have seen as dangerous, violent, and inappropriate. But anything that has meaning to people is worth discussing, worth analyzing, and worth working through.

SUMMARY AND CONCLUSION

The task of an African-centered pedagogy is to provide teachers with a framework to recreate the symbolic culture of the school setting so as to reflect the cultural world of Black achievement. In Capitol High School (Fordham, 1988), the figured world (Holland et al., 1998) of high-achieving African American students ascribed "non-Blackness" to "academic achievement." In the Caswell County Training School (Siddle Walker, 1996), the figured world of African American students certainly did not have this ascription. The question is, how do we create figured worlds of achievement that leave out the negative ascriptions and build in the many powerful ascriptions of literacy, education, and the struggle for freedom that is the heritage of African Americans? In any event, we know that there are two phenomena that we as teachers should try to counteract—disidentification ("racelessness") and race-based performance anxiety ("stereotypic threat").

CHAPTER EIGHT

Discourse Practices in a Community of Achievement

> Humans are both blessed and cursed by their dialogic nature—their tendency to encompass a number of views in virtual simultaneity and tension, regardless of their logical compatibility.
>
> —Holland, Lachicotte, Skinner, and Cain, *Identity and Agency in Cultural Worlds*

This chapter describes the social and intellectual practices that are important for successful work with African American children. As I discussed in the last chapter, classroom discourse has become an increasingly important area of research in education, and has produced useful insights as to how discourse processes mediate social, intellectual, and cultural practices of a classroom as a community of learners. In this chapter I detail aspects of discourse practices that teachers need to acquire in order to construct learning communities that meet the needs and scaffold the development of African American children. I explain the relationship between discourse practices of the teacher and the social organization, pedagogical decision-making, and cultural context created in the classroom. I also further develop this notion of practices as the basis for organizing cultures of learning—and for revising instructional practices, pedagogical decision making, and classroom interactional routines in ways that promote understanding among African American students. Finally, I further develop the notion of building a *symbolic* culture—the context in which young people are continuously improvising (Holland et al., 1998)—or negotiating what I have been calling a situated identity. In this chapter, we look specifically of African American students' identity as it is situated in literacy learning, social studies and mathematics.

To develop a rich context for teaching, an analysis of the discourse processes in the discipline communities, of mathematics, history, and language arts, is needed. By "discipline communities" I am referring not just to subjects in school, but also to enclaves of people in those disciplines such as "scientists doing science," "historians doing history" and so on. Later, in chapter 10, I will use, as an example, my own classroom to illustrate the oral and written discourse practices that help define discipline communities. The following discussion examines the relationship between the discourse routines of an academic discipline (i.e., American History) and the learning experiences of African American elementary and middle school learners. In this explanation I draw again on the research traditions I discussed earlier—situated cognition, situated learning theory, and the sociocultural perspective.

According to these perspectives, what counts as disciplinary knowledge of a particular community of practice (for example, your class "doing history as historians") is a product of two knowledge sources. One of these is the corpus of knowledge in the discipline, and the other consists of learners' constructed understandings and enacted practices of the disciplinary knowledge. In other words, knowledge consists of content such as the laws of thermodynamics and the causes of the Civil War, as well as learners' understanding and use of this content knowledge. Thus, in any classroom, the total package of knowledge must be understood as partly "constructed" and partly "received."

The part that is constructed occurs as individuals interpret the content, and build an understanding based upon their experience and prior knowledge. These are the learner practices of meaning-making and inquiry in my theory. According to my theory, learners do construct more than knowledge and their understanding of the content—they also construct themselves as users of that knowledge. That is to say, learning is a process of identity management as a learner participates in a setting. Humans naturally appropriate the discourse practices (i.e., the language and forms of talk) of the group as they participate in the group —like your class as a community of learners—who then affiliate over time and build common knowledge together.

The "received" part of the knowledge package is what teachers call "the material." This is the content specified by curriculum guides, frameworks, and content standards. Of course, not just any "American history knowledge" or "English knowledge" will do and there is a limit to the "legitimate scientific knowledge" that the community can construct, given that they are, after all, not "real" scientists, historians, or professional writers. But the point here is that learners' acquisition of both received and constructed knowledge is a social process shaped by the discourse and practices of the community in which that learning takes place. The activity and the relationships among their peers also mediate access to, and development of, these knowledges.

CULTURE, IDENTITY, AND CLASSROOM DISCOURSE

I have argued throughout this book that classroom learning is a social process requiring considerable communication, coordinated action, and common understanding. I also argued that an effective pedagogy for African American children depends upon understanding the patterns of these processes well enough to ensure the engagement, identity development, intellectual participation, and sense of belonging necessary for full academic development. The foundation of these arguments is the sociocultural perspective and situated learning theory discussed earlier. From this foundation, I reasoned that the ways in which culturally mainstream teachers organize their classrooms could adversely influence students who do not share the cultural assumptions and social backgrounds as their teachers. By the same token, if we have an African-centered, responsive pedagogy as a guide, we can organize the life and activity of the classroom to positively influence student achievement and intellectual development.

I have also established in the last chapter that "culturally Black" students in "culturally White" school settings must not only negotiate the interpersonal conflicts regarding race among their peers. They must also negotiate the intrapersonal or internal conflicts of identity as well. Many African American learners are likely to experience this internal conflict as the tension between two desires. On one hand is their desire to avoid the appearance of selling out their blackness or being otherwise "uncool" by appearing to "act White" by their studious behaviors in school. On the other hand is their desire to achieve academic success that requires achievement behaviors, which might include the behaviors of studiousness and compliance deemed by some of their peers as "acting White."

The identity struggles that students of color face are obviously more complex and complicated than the simple bifurcated choice of whether to participate in mainstream culture on one hand, or to claim one's own ethnic and racial heritage on the other hand. The teacher who expects to be effective with African American children must not only be able to read and recognize cultural expressions of children, but also incorporate them in the fabric of classroom life and discourse. That means that the practices of "doing" science, English, mathematics, or history should not be experienced as foreign or as merely another variation of "acting White." The additional challenge for teachers is to create the social and cultural system in their classrooms such that "doing science" and "doing English" seem natural, important, and valuable.

The questions at hand are, "What discourse practices will allow us to organize the social and intellectual life of the classroom in ways that are culturally receptive, socially responsive and organizationally supportive for African American learners?" In other words, in what ways do we need to use our understanding of language and culture to promote their achievement and development in domain(s) of academic practice?" How do we organize the culture of the school in ways that help young learners access those resources and acquire the tools empowered participation in the broader culture? What should we, as teachers, know about the tools (the practices) that enable them to operate well in the community of scientists, or community of writers or community of historians? The public school classroom is the critical place for systematic analysis of practice.

DISCOURSE PRACTICES IN A COMMUNITY OF MATHEMATICS LEARNERS

I have done some research on the learning of African American students in which I examined how knowledge and practices of the academic discipline of mathematics are shaped in and through the everyday talk of teachers and their learners (Murrell, 1993, 1999). I sought to establish the relationship between the teacher's discourse practices and the changes in the intellectual practices of students as they are represented their learning achievement in mathematics. What I found almost immediately was that the African American students construed both the purposes and the practices of mathematics learning differently than what was intended by the teacher as a consequence of using a new "math discourse."

The distinct patterns of discourse among learners I termed "math talk." The phenomenon of math talk denotes the types and amounts of discourse that occur during mathematics instruction, particularly the oral reasoning performances of learners during teacher-led mathematics inquiries in the classroom. It consists of students' public talk and public display of mathematics reasoning, in both on-task and off-task situations, as well as their sense of the purpose of mathematics discourse.

The primary discourse pattern of the teachers I worked with was a variation of the typical IRE discourse sequence described by Cazden (1988), who contends that nearly all classroom discourse can be interpreted according to a basic pattern of teacher questioning, student response, and teacher evaluation of the response. According to Cazden, the IRE sequence consists of: (I) teacher initiation, (R) learner response, and (E) teacher evaluation. The first step usually occurs in the form of a teacher's question about a solution to a problem; however, these questions most often are used to elicit from students a specific response. For example, a teacher might ask, "Is a fraction a ratio?" (I), to which the called-upon student might answer "Yes" (R), and obtain the teacher's evaluation of "Correct" or "Good" (E).

According to the sociocultural perspective I drew on for an African-centered pedagogy, the uses of language and forms of discourse are critical determinants of the degree to which children can participate in the social-interactional dynamics of learning. It therefore behooves us as teachers to understand how these new forms of classroom discourse may marginalize those who are not already regular participants in it. An important example is the relatively recent curricular standard of the NCTM (1989) calling for greater emphasis on the communication of mathematical reasoning. Mathematics instruction, perhaps more than any other subject area in school, has seen the infusion of constructivist teaching. That is, the community of mathematics educators has, for the most part, embraced an approach to learning mathematics that has emphasized understanding, reasoning, and inquiry initiated by the learning discourse practices in the classroom.

We have established that classroom learning is a social process requiring considerable communication, coordinated action, and common understanding on the part of teachers. We have also established that cultural and social class differences influence educational outcomes, and certainly show up when ever discursive performances (classroom talk) are required. Now it is time for me to get more specific about the sort of social practices and intellectual practices that we should be mindful of when working with African American children. Classroom discourse is becoming an increasingly important area of research in education.

Discourse processes are a large measure of how the practices (both social and intellectual and academic) become adopted and used by a community of learners. Our task right now is to identify those discourse processes that constitute culturally responsive teaching for African American children.

The African American sixth and seventh grade focus students in the study I reported (i.e., Murrell, 1994) participated in math talk, but not as a discourse of conceptualization and learning, as was intended by the NCTM standards of communication of mathematics ideas. For the presentations and oral reports of the focus students—the frame of "getting over" and "getting the right answer" predominated. They perceived the classroom math talk not as the means for deepening understanding (academic and intellectual practices of doing mathematics), but rather as social practice on how they were expected to comport themselves. As students acted on these perceptions, their learning performance differed dramatically from those intended by the curricular innovations. It is the purpose of an African-centered pedagogy to provide teachers with the means of recognizing that this is going on in his or her classroom, and then making modifications so that the discourse forms serve the acquisition of mathematics content.

What makes mathematics teaching responsive to African American children? Responsive teaching for any group of children depends on how well the teacher orchestrates a learning experience or event which incorporates: (1) an understanding and appropriate use of discourse frames; (2) instructional strategies which create particular discourse frames that optimize conversation for the purpose of understanding; and (3) purposeful, meaningful, and intellectually worthwhile learning goals that develop abilities. The metapurpose of instruction on this account could be characterized by promoting the internalization of "analytical talk" into "analytical thought"—the internalization of analytical discourse into analytical reasoning.

The central problem of nonresponsive teaching as exhibited in the study described above is appropriate use of framing of the instructional discourse. The African American focus students in the study (and probably most other students as well) construed or framed math talk and the instructional intent of the discourse differently from the teacher. To teach more responsively to these students, the teachers need to make explicit both the students' frame and frame of discourse-for-understanding. In particular, to the extent to which the focus students viewed math talk as a set of competencies, then the teacher should make learning math talk as competencies more explicit. Instructionally, this would entail commenting on the form of their presentations as well as the content—giving them credit (positive reinforcement) for what they may already do well while at the same time making clear that other criteria based upon substance are expected in the performance.

For those children, making explicit the rules, codes, and expected performances of math talk will help them develop it as an ability and means to moving toward greater conceptual understanding. Delpit (1988) makes exactly this point when she argues that if people marginal to a culture are explicitly taught the codes and rules for full participation, they are empowered. The teacher can make explicit the code and rules of math talk in her own discourse. The responsive teacher needs to be continuously aware that the relationship children construct with the teacher (as well as the subject matter) is shaped by the degree to which discourse routines and speech events promote interest, social participation, a sense of efficacy and industry, and sense of purpose.

The responsive teacher recognizes and capitalizes on the frames or discourse patterns of students. The ones I observe on a regular basis include:

1. "Show time!"—really showing off one's possession of information, or otherwise "holding the floor." This discourse pattern is better than nonparticipation, but the teacher has some work to do to make the discourse more instructionally and conceptually meaningful;
2. Giving information—responding to a request for information;
3. Getting information—asking a question to get specific piece of information;

4. Contentious talk—for confrontive verbal play, for delay, to control (usually by slowing down) the sequence of classroom events and activities;
5. Genuine instructional conversation—genuine inquiry discourse, happens most often in groups when students are truly engaged in problem solving or group learning activity;
6. Analytical talk or "here's my analysis"—extended explanation, most frequent setting is when students are asked to give a formal report.
7. "Cards on the table"—this is the signal from the teacher that what she wants is "the answer."

These six discourse patterns are not meant to be a catalogue for all African American youth. Patterns will vary from setting to setting. In fact, the major precept of my theory is to read cultural patterns in the situated contexts they occur. The awareness to not over-generalize is a pedagogical skill in itself. For example, it is an important achievement for my graduate students when they read Heath's (1983) now classic ethnography and learn not to generalize the figurative language patterns of the Trackton children to all working class Black children, and not to generalize the literal language patterns of Roadville children to working class White children. The point here is that the teacher needs to be able to read these cultural discourse patterns using what they know about the children's culture as well as what they understand about the immediate figured world of children.

The teacher who is aware of the different discourse patterns of analytical talk in his or her classroom is in a much better position to orchestrate learning. The need for both disciplinary control and making conceptual connections for students can be met more easily without diminishing the solidarity the teacher has with the students. For example, consider the exchange between a responsive teacher and a "troublesome" student in a seventh grade mathematics classroom. In her interaction with the student, she is explicit two frames exist: (1) math talk—time for listening, thinking, then talking; and (2) "pay attention—stay focused." In the example below she notices the student not paying attention:

Ms. Pye: Andre, what do you think?

Andre: (Had been talking to a neighbor and suddenly looks up in surprise.) Huh??

Ms. Pye: What do you think? Does her answer make sense?

Andre: I didn't hear.

Ms. Pye: I didn't think so. That's why I called on you. So anyway, Lacy says two blue rhombi make one-third. Do you agree?

Andre: (*Stares at the overhead for a moment*). Uh-uhn. Two green triangles make one-third.

The teacher in the above instance invokes two discourse frames, corresponding respectively to the participation and engagement practices and the community integrity practices of the African-centered. She invokes a directive, disciplinary frame ("pay attention!") and an inclusion frame ("We want you a part of this"). The teacher manages to communicate both frames because her action brings Andre back into the flow of the inquiry as he is about to drift out by not paying attention. By naming the "discipline control" frame ("You weren't paying attention and that's why I called on you") the teacher is not so much a warden punishing a misdeed, as she is a shepherd herding a stray back into the fold. Then, by pursuing the continuity of the instructional frame (i.e., updating Andre and then asking his view), she promotes the student's participation in math talk through both learning and acquisition. Had she simply moved quickly to another student for a response, her action would merely have been one of behavior management, thereby sacrificing the instructional connection she might have made with the student to draw him in. The fact that she restated the question so that Andre had something to respond to transformed the speech event from potentially one of mere admonishment to one of inclusion in the community of inquiry. The teacher's discourse practice gave Andre the opportunity to participate and correctly answer her query.

Obviously, there are a variety of ways of making discourse frames explicit and distinct, and the skillful teacher does so as a means of orchestrating meaningful and inclusive instructional conversations. The teacher operating from the African-centered pedagogical framework is more likely to recognize and respond to students' discourse patterns to probe for deeper understanding and better effort. For example, when a student who "holds the floor" launches into a long drawn out discourse to disguise the fact that he or she cannot answer a request for information, the accomplished teacher might say something like, "Hold up. I'm not asking you to think out loud right now. This is cards on the table. What I want to know right now is if you know how to multiply these two fractions right here!" Similarly, when a responsive teacher wants to encourage the participation and diminish students' escape in public math talk, she says something like, "I'm not going to call on someone else until you really put your mind to this. So you might as well stop guessing in hopes that I'll get exasperated and move on to somebody else and *think*." Finally, when a responsive teacher wants to encourage the process of sharing one's reasoning and group problem solving, she says something like, "You have done a good piece of work here, but why doesn't the rest of your team know this? What are you doing up here talking to me if the rest of your group doesn't know what you know?"

SUMMARY AND CONCLUSION

The key idea to take away from this discussion is the importance of discursive practices in organizing and orchestrating your classroom instruction. One aspect of that was illustrated in the mathematics classroom where the teacher learned to read the discourse patterns of children to assess their level of participation and understanding. The second aspect of discourse practice awareness is the development of those practices that are valued in the discipline. "Math talk" is valued among mathematicians, and the same kinds of inquiry discourse could be use in science classrooms.

Finally, if you are mindful of the instructional discourse you use you can shape the classroom culture. A good deal of the instructional conversation or instructional discourse is involved in shaping, directing, and scaffolding social practices in the urban classroom. There are many "in the flow" occasions where the teacher uses language to reorient behavior "Please take out your journals . . . Malik, what did I just say?" Culturally mainstream teachers are trained to think of this as discipline and that any occasion requiring that the teacher speak to a student about behavior is discipline. This is a different perspective from that of acccomplished practice among urban African American children. Rather than being seen as situations requiring "corrective discipline," the situations in which children are not at all times in compliance with the requirements of comportment are understood as a natural condition of young learners. This is merely a condition in which the young person is in "need of assistance" to get them back on track, easily provided by the power of the word.

CHAPTER NINE

Teaching for Understanding, Learning for Liberation

In accord with their revolutionary origins, Americans celebrate the rebels who created their Republic, naming cities, monuments, broad boulevards, endless highways and numberless schools in their honor. No city, boulevard, highway or public school appears to bear the name of any of the slave insurrectionists who struck violently for their liberty and that of their people, although they often brandished the same principles and employed the same tactics as the Republic's revolutionary founders. When attempts are made to honor them in the manner accorded others who rebelled in the name of liberty, they are denounced and compared to Herod, Attila and, inevitably, Hitler. Their stories tend to be "buried history," to borrow a phrase from the dust jacket of David Robertson's new study of Denmark Vesey, the Charleston, S.C., black who in 1822 organized what arguably was the largest and most intricate slave conspiracy in American history.

—Ira Berlin, *New York Times Book Review*

Those who profess to favor freedom, and yet depreciation agitation,
Are men who want crops without plowing up the ground.
They want rain without thunder and lightning.
They want the ocean without the awful roar of its waters.

> This struggle may be a moral one; Or it may be a physical one; Or it may be both moral and physical; but it must be a struggle.
> Power concedes nothing without a demand. It ever did and it never will.
>
> —Fredrick Douglass, Speech on West India Emancipation (In Hale-Benson, 1982, p. viii.)

This chapter develops the concept of a critical literacy in the African-centered pedagogy. The significance of "Blackness" in the White literary imagination—as well as in the symbols, emblems and icons of "Blackness" in popular culture—is examined in the context of development of literacy learning for African American children. This chapter extends the idea *teaching for understanding* and makes the most important "understanding performance" the exercise of critical literacy. Teachers will see ways of teaching for understanding in relation to critical literacy. As I have said, there are a number of descriptions of what an African-centered pedagogy should be like (Addae, 1996; Akoto, 1992; Ani, 1994; King, 1994; Lee, 1994; Murrell, 1993, 1997). The task now is to examine the literacy learning activities of an entire school as a community of practice that systematically enacts the pedagogy.

The case study to follow illustrates the conceptual underpinnings of an African-centered community of practice (Lave, 1988). The chapter first describes critical literacy in the African-centered pedagogy, then examines it in relation to literacy development, and then will finally illustrates the framework in the professional deliberations of educators who are appraising literacy instruction practices.

LITERACY LEARNING IN THE AFRICAN-CENTERED PEDAGOGY

The discourse practices of the teacher in the African-centered school of achievement should include the oral tradition in African American heritage and the competence of orality or discourse-in-use. Critical literacy in the African-centered pedagogical framework includes both literacy as traditionally defined and as orality. Gordon and Thomas (1990) argued the need for this expanded notion of literacy for African American education. Literacy on this account refers to both literacy as traditionally defined—the capacity to decode and interpret written language—and orality. They define orality as "the capacity to receive, generate, and express feelings, signals, descriptors, ideas and concepts through language" (p. 71). The broad range of critical literature and orality includes:

- Multicontextual and multilingual communication—the capacity to communicate in a variety of contexts using multiple symbols;
- Multicultural adaptive competence—the capacity to function in more than one culture;
- Tertiary signal system mastery of alphabetic and numeric formulae—the capacity to use symbols to represent symbols (in terms of literacy, this involves the more complex capacity to use symbols to represent symbols to the extent that an individual can generate alphabetic or numeric formulae, use metaphors, and use abstract phenomena to represent other abstract phenomena);
- Scientific and technological literacy—the capacity to read and understand scientific and technological material;
- Political economic literacy—the capacity to understand the interlocutory, systematic alignments which sustain and reinforce race, class, and gender biases within the larger society;
- Social and interpersonal literacy—the capacity to manipulate and interpret quantitative data;
- Cultural literacy—In contrast to the usages of conservative writers as knowing American culture, the more appropriate use of the term "cultural literacy" refers to an individual's command of information, problem-solving strategies, symbol systems, and currency.

An African-centered perspective on advanced reading is that of symbolically guided thinking (Gordon, & Thomas, 1990, p. 71). In my own theory, this symbolically guided thinking involves three processes: (1) the interpretation of symbols—ascription of meaning; (2) the appropriation of symbols—the reuse of these meanings in one's own discourse; and (3) the inventive reappropriation of symbols—the production of a new system, authoring a new meaning based on acquired symbols and meanings. An analogy for inventive reappropriation in the music industry is the long-standing practice of "sampling" in which artists will lift base-beats from earlier recordings of other artists.

As indicated in chapter 5, there are many instances where the African American community has taken charge of the educational lives of their children, such as the case of African American independent schools. Emancipatory educational practices do appear to be emerging whenever community agency and cultural affirmation have been asserted by community members in the schooling practices. But the symbolic culture in urban public schools is much less culturally responsive than they are in these independent schools. The effectiveness of the literacy learning curriculum depends on how "culturally appropriate curricular content" is constituted and whose perspective deems it "appropriate." It would seem that there is still a received curriculum that prefigures the subject positions of African American students, whether or not they are encouraged to critically question.

From the perspective of an African-centered pedagogy, recovering narratives is the work that the people themselves must do. The act of collective self-definition is a crucial part of the reconstruction of African American subjectivity. The act of recovering narratives of Blackness in America is neither radical nor new, and has always been a crucial aspect of collective self-determination and cultural identity among African Americans (Woodson, 1933). This theme is important to the critical consciousness of African Americans. The conflictive relationship between self and the Black collectivity is a theme that needs to be developed in the critical pedagogy of African American learners through the literature and cultural history of African Americans.

CRITICAL LITERACY AND LITERACY DEVELOPMENT

As a preface to examining literacy learning in the African-centered pedagogical framework, it will first be useful to make a few connections with research in literacy development. In particular, I want to first set the terms for our unit of analysis. In the framework this far, I have used the term *practice* to refer to the ongoing effective pedagogy of a teacher as accomplished practice and have defined accomplished practice in the African-centered framework as employing five cultural practices.

The legacy of the work of Heath (1983) and her notion of the *literacy event*, Hymes (1974) and his notion of the *literacy event* and more recently, Street's (1995) notion of the *language practice*. Bloome, Champion, Katz, Morton, and Muldrow (2001) expand the idea of a language practice, saying, "Almost all social and cultural practices can be viewed as language practices because almost all involve the use of language (p. 46, note 1)." These studies represent the growing sociocultural approach to literacy developed and is termed New Literacy Studies (Street, 1993). The characterization of language practices is one of the concerns of New Literacy Studies. On one hand Bloome et al. are concerned that the term *language practice* might give the impression that the practices are static and deterministic, noting that "people are continuously modifying established language practices, adapting them to new situations (p.47). On the other hand is the concern that the concept of a *language practice*, if it is something so modifiable and situationally contextualized, may be too labile to pin down as a useful description of anything. The resolution to this stability issue comes from a number of theorists who argue that a language practice is always situated, or embedded if you will, in an event (setting) in which the practice is performance (activity). This corresponds perfectly to my articulation of the activity setting in the African-centered pedagogical theory.

Different theorists in literacy development discussed by Bloome et al. (2001) have different ways of characterizing the activity setting. For example, for Benjamin (1969), the principal language practice is a *narrative*, and the narrative is situated in the event of its occurrence—the setting in which it is told—as well as by the events the narrative recounts. Solsken and Bloome (1992) note that there is a distinction among story, narrative, and story telling event. That Solsken and Bloome view *story*, *narrative*, and *story telling event* as inseparable is, I would argue, a perfect avowal of the situated activity of story telling, where the activity is the telling of the narrative (telling a story) and the setting is the story telling event (story time).

I digress to this New Studies Literature not merely because it parallels the epistemology of situated activity in the domain of literacy development studies, but mainly to seize upon the *narrative* as a central important language practice of particular relevance to African-centered pedagogy and to my conception of practice in the theory. For example, Bloome et al. (2001) recapitulate the tenets of situativity theory I base my theory on as they list the implications for this socioculturally situated view. For example, the idea that "a narrative must be analyzed within the context of the social events in which they occur" (p. 48) is a tenant of situativity theory. Similarly, the statement that "a narrative is not simply a result of what the speaker or writer has produced, but the result of a sort of authorship between speaker and writer" affirms the notion of a language practice as a conjoint productive activity—something for which there is a coparticipation in the language practice. Third, referring to Ochs they state that "the exploration of language development is an exploration of how children use storytelling to affiliate with their friends, families and teachers," which affirms the tenet of situativity theory that learning is a social activity (cited in Bloome et al., 2001, p. 48). This is what teachers and learners do in the community circle of practice. Finally, attributing Bakhtin they state that "narratives need to placed in historical time "as part of what has come before and what will, or is anticipated to, come later (cited in Bloome at al., 2001, p. 48)"

CASE THREE—
APPRAISAL OF LITERACY LEARNING PRACTICES

The following case study is included as an example of an application of African-centered pedagogy in a situation that is specifically pedagogy focused—a professional portfolio assessment in a humanities classroom. I thought it would be instructive to illustrate the African-centered pedagogical perspective with respect to a setting and a subject matter that does not specifically focus on African American culture or heritage. The case is fictional, but based on issues and situations that have actually occurred. The social scene of the case is a professional discussion of a teacher's multicultural pedagogy involving her instructional unit on Native Americans. The setting is a panel of teachers, administrators, and teacher educators who are reviewing the performance portfolio of the teacher submitted as a model of good multicultural practice. I will use this case to further illustrate African-centered pedagogy by demonstrating the distinction between pedagogical foundations and the curriculum content issues.

THE SETTING

The school district of a large urban city, in partnership with a half dozen universities in the state, has devised a portfolio standardization project. This project seeks to develop model portfolios that exemplify accomplished teaching practice for the state's newly adopted teaching standards. The project asks that schools nominate teachers based on their high quality teaching, and these teachers are asked to prepare a portfolio for one of the seven new performance standards. These portfolios are reviewed by a special panel of higher education representatives, teachers and administrators to determine whether it is a good enough model to disseminate as an exemplary practice model for the standard.

Ms. Quinn is one of several middle school teachers selected to prepare a portfolio for the teaching to diversity standard. This setting is one of increasing significance in contemporary educational practice—that of a teacher illustrating her best pedagogical work in a portfolio exhibition for the purposes of determining teaching quality. The procedure is already the basis of performance assessment designs used by both the Interstate Assessment and Support Consortium (INTASC) and the National Board of Professional Teaching Standards (NBPTS).

Ms. Quinn, the featured teacher in this case, has not only received accolades in her school, but from the assessors at screening panel as well. The final review panel, however, consisted of representatives from three different universities that work with the school district. The group of portfolio assessors included an African American male, a Hispanic female, three African American females, two white males, and two white females. All members where in higher education and associated with teacher preparation. With the exception of one person, an African American woman whom we will call Ms. Bethune, the entire group thought that the teacher had done a good job of multicultural teaching, and should be rated high on the diversity standard. That is, they all held this view until challenged by Ms. bethune, the assessor with a strong African-centered pedagogical perspective.

The teacher being reviewed, Ms. Quinn, is a woman in her thirties who has been teaching social studies and language arts in a city middle school for seven years. She has received commendations for her "multidisciplinary and multicultural" teaching. The portfolio exhibit she put together is designated as an exemplar of this teaching. The unit seeks to combine literature and social studies on Native Americans. She proudly gave her permission to have it reviewed by the assessor panel for consideration as a model to be disseminated.

After reviewing the materials and viewing the videotape, each assessor received an opportunity to comment. Comments were elicited serially from each assessor going around the table. The last one to speak was Ms. Bethune.

CRITICAL CONVERSATION

Ms. Bethune: I'm sorry to have to say this, but I have serious concerns about this unit. It is the most troublesome case of racism in pedagogy I have seen in a long time. And I don't know which has me more concerned—the experience of seeing this put forth as accomplished practice or the fact that nobody else picked up on the racism.

The others, visibly shaken by Ms. Bethune's remark began to start in on her. "What do you mean the teacher was racist? If she was racist, do you think that she would have chosen the selection of Lakota Woman?" Several other members of the review panel made similar comments to Ms. Bethune.

Ms. Bethune: Please try to understand what I am saying. I did not say Ms. Quinn is racist—I'm talking about the racism embedded in the pedagogy and what the children seem to be coming away with. (*She added with some irritation in her voice*): I wish people would learn the difference between institutional racism and individual expressions of bigotry. What we have here is a form of institutional racism—a hidden curriculum if you will of White privilege and normative White superiority. People are fully capable of participating and promoting racism despite their best intentions or scrupulous avoidance of "racially offensive" language or behavior. I'm talking here about the impacts on the children's learning and what they come away with. That impact is decidedly racist, and you-all would see that if you looked beyond what the teacher says and go to the actual learning of the children.

Wanting to diffuse the mounting adversarial tone of the interaction pitting Ms. Bethune against the rest of the group, the panel leader made a suggestion.

Panel Leader: Well, why don't we take a look at that—racism in the lesson, I mean. That's what we are here for, isn't it? To examine quality of this teaching with respect to diversity and multicultural teaching. Why don't we go through the material again? (*The panel leader turns to Ms. Bethune and asks*): Could you point out the places where you found the racially offense language?

Ms. Bethune: I think we do need to talk about this further, but once again you're tacitly equating racism with "racially offensive language." From an African-centered pedagogical perspective, we would recognize that meaning is conveyed in multileveled ways—particularly in practices and institutions that subtly, symbolically, yet powerfully, communicate White superiority and assert privilege. If you're willing to talk about *that*, I'll go on.

Assessor A: (One of the White males) Well wait a minute. I don't really see what the problem is here. Ms. Quinn is a teacher who has selected a work by a Native American, the story of Mary Crow Dog as told by herself. She is using literature of the people she is teaching about. She can't promote a hidden racism about Indians if she uses a work written by an Indian.

Ms. Bethune: (*Speaking to Assessor A*) Are you sure about that? Listen, before I go on, I want to make one thing perfectly clear. I'm not saying that there are "racially offensive" statements in the text of the portfolio materials for this teacher. I found no language in this portfolio exhibit that I would term "racially offensive." Nonetheless, had we examined the material from an African-centered perspective for instance, we would not have lost sight of the fact that the most virulent instances of racism in America are rarely expressed at the level of offensive language or other individual acts of bigotry, but rather inheres in institutional practices. In this case, it is the impact that the curriculum has on the children.

Assessor A: Well wait a minute. I don't get it. It almost sounds like you're saying that this White teacher shouldn't be teaching about Native Americans.

Ms. Bethune: She shouldn't if she gets the kinds of results we see here, where the children end up with a stronger sense of White superiority over Native Americans than they did at the beginning of the lesson. Don't get me wrong. The selection of a piece of literature from Native American culture was a great opportunity to examine the cultural intersection of the Lakota Sioux with mainstream American culture. But it is an opportunity missed for this teacher. Unfortunately, Ms. Quinn ended up essentializing the Sioux as the "exotic other"—complete with feathers and warrior tales. How representative are warrior tales among Native American writers?

Assessor B: (*Addressing* Ms. *Bethune*) So you're saying that unless a teacher can produce an antiracist outcome, or at least a nonracist outcome, that she should not tackle the content theme?

Ms. Bethune: That's exactly what I'm saying. From an African-centered perspective, we would consider it inappropriate to teach about something insufficiently understood—in this case, another group's culture and traditions. Ms. Quinn's expressed goal for the instructional unit exhibited in this portfolio is to teach about Native American culture. Knowing that your students have been filled with negative imagery, would you *really* chose a saga about the personal struggles of a young Lakota Sioux woman for meaning, and against drug and alcohol addiction and anger over the destruction of her people and her culture? Would you really contrast warrior tales of the past with reservation life of the present as a way of exploring culture?

Assessor A: (*Speaking to* Ms. *Bethune*) Okay, so maybe the literature selection wasn't the best choice. But your asserting racism here. I'm not sure I see it.

Ms. Bethune: (*Speaking to Assessor A*) Well, let me ask you this. Would you agree that racism exists in situations where people's stereotypical images and biases are reinforced?

Assessor A: Yes, of course.

Ms. Bethune: Well that's happening here. And you would agree that, given our society, many children in this community are likely to harbor negative images perpetuated in the popular media?

Assessor A: Well, yes I suppose so. How does that apply here?

Ms. Bethune: It applies here because a truly skilled teacher would have taken *that* into account in designing her instructional goals. My point is that the themes that the teacher chooses to focus on ought to anticipate the stereotypes children are likely to have about "wild Indians." If your goal was to educate them out of their distorted images towards a real consideration of culture, would you select the themes Ms. Q. selected? The themes of her unit are about how Mary Crow Dog needs to learn to "pull yourself up by the bootstraps" and that "there is no point in clinging to the heroes of the past"—a tacit rejection of the Sioux reverence for their ancestors and traditions. The admonition is to stop "freeloading off their legends" and make one's own legends. Whose interpretation of the Lakota Sioux is this? It's certainly not that of the Lakota Sioux. It's certainly not mine, as an African American.

Assessor A: Well, I guess I see now that you point out those themes, that this wasn't a very objective assessment of Native American culture.

Ms. Bethune: I would say that it need not be "objective" as much as it is at least contextualized historically. No where do we see in the portfolio evidence that Ms. Quinn contextualizes the experience of Native Americans in the oppressive conditions they experienced at the hands of the federal government and local communities. It's as if the current plight of many Native Americans somehow "just happened."

Assessor C: (The only Hispanic woman in the group) I see what you mean.

Ms. Bethune: It is clear that Ms. Quinn genuinely strives for cultural diversity in her curriculum and seems to want to provide her students access to ideas and meanings they might not otherwise be exposed to. For this intent, Ms. Quinn should be commended. But her pedagogy nonetheless fortifies stereotypes and the view of Indians as pathetic and tragic figures. I read the book she uses. I found at least two examples of the values of the Lakota culture that appear nowhere in her instructional materials. Let me read you these two excerpts:

> Even now, among traditionals, as long as one person eats, all other relatives eat too. . . . Feeding every comer is still a sacred duty, and Sioux women seem always to be cooking from early morning. (p. 13)
>
> Kids were never alone, always fussed over by not one but several mothers, watched and taught by several fathers. (p. 13)

Assessor A: Well, that's only one case. She probably left lots of things out.

Ms. Bethune: That's right, she did. But it is not so much that she left things out, but that she selected and fortified only those things that support her own unexamined frame—her biased lens that views the Lakota Sioux as the degenerative remains of a once "noble savage" culture.

Assessor A: Aren't you being a little extreme?

Ms. Bethune: I don't think so. Just look at what the students *actually say* in their productions. Almost everything they write about and talk about marginalizes, criminalizes, and pathologizes the Lakota Sioux. Let's start with Student A's moralizing about Mary Crow Dog's experience: "She was taught a valuable lesson, NEVER TO TAKE WHAT ISN'T RIGHTFULLY YOURS." This is the student's statement of the theme of the autobiography. Not only is this NOT the theme, but it is a particularly poignant example of the reverse impact we should expect from a unit on Native Americans. This girl actually comes away with a perspective exactly opposite the theme of the autobiography—namely Mary's growing consciousness of what has been taken from her people.

Assessor C: Yeah, I think that Ms. Quinn should have caught that.

Ms. Bethune: And here is where you see the seriousness of not contextualizing the lesson historically. How does this student's moralizing about shoplifting sit in relation to the real history of broken treaties and attempted genocide? And now look at Student A's conclusion about what she learned from the unit, where she writes: "It makes me see how lucky I am compared to her (Mary Crow Dog's) early life." Did this child learn anything meaningful about the Lakota Sioux or did she merely fortify her sense of privilege? And am I the only one who caught this?

Assessor C: Well, I see it now.

Ms. Bethune: None of us believe that this is what Ms. Quinn intended—the further "othering" of Native Americans by her students. Yet, through her selection of the reading material and her own inability to critically examine the goals of her lesson and children's remarks, this teaching sample is a classic case of the new racism. We shouldn't blame the kids. But we should hold the teacher responsible, as she is the one who positioned the Lakota Sioux as exotic—"noble savages" as suggested by the images and readings of warrior legends—and as people who are confused, depressed, and aimless in the current day.

Assessor C: Well, maybe she didn't make the best decisions about the reading material.

Ms. Bethune: It's more than just the selection of material. That's only one part of pedagogy. As I said, I think that the choices of literature *could have* actually been quite good. But it is her inability to build understanding and lead good inquiry that is problematic. She cannot lead children to where she herself has not been—a critical interrogation of race and power vis-à-vis the genocidal and shameless treatment of a people. The selections could have been great had she developed a perspective centered in the experience of the Sioux. What seemed absolutely natural to Ms. Quinn. was the pathetic and degenerative state of the Lakota Sioux. This is reflected in her unfortunate pairing of the warrior legends with *Lakota Woman* to purposely emphasize the contrast between the greatness that once was with the depressed life on the reservation that exists now. What she did with the literature fortifies students' perception of Indians as once great but now tragic and pathetic figures.

Assessor A: Well, couldn't she could fix all that?

Ms. Bethune: I don't think so, at least not unless she first has a discussion of her literacy practices like this. But on her own, how would she know what to fix? I don't think even at this point she could recognize what a "fixed pedagogy" would look like. Had she an African-centered or a Sioux-centered perspective of her pedagogy, "fixing" might be possible. But I have no confidence in that. This case has moved all the way down the line as "exemplary multicultural practice." She didn't think of it and YOU didn't think of it, either.

Ms. Bethune: Let's look at another example of student work. Students B and C in this sample write on their "inferences based on information in the text" page that "Mary Crow Dog was a lonely person, revealing that she couldn't relate to anyone, living in fear of different races." In the previous chapters Mary Crow Dog wrote of her horrible experience at the hands of the white nuns and school-people at the Indian School, but she *did* have friendships and relationships with other Indian children. Ms Q asks the girls why they made that judgment that Mary Crow Dog couldn't relate to *anyone*, noting that the interpretation was inaccurate based on information in the text. But Ms. Quinn makes no attempt to correct their biased and incorrect inference about the protagonist. So, despite the evidence in the novel, the students see the protagonist as a dysfunctional victim instead of viewing the narrative as a story about a struggle against overwhelming odds for personhood. Moreover, among other things recorded in their "facts sheet from the text," students noted that:

- Indians such as Mary mainly support themselves financially by shoplifting;
- Although reservation life is removed from most of the rest of American life it's drugs that Indians share among themselves.

Assessor B: Let me just say this in Ms. Quinn's defense . . .

Ms. Bethune: I don't want to make this about Ms. Quinn so let's not waste time defending her as if this was a stand-alone case—as if this was the only time anything like this ever happens. The tragedy here is not that she exhibited racist pedagogy. The tragic thing is that, not only did no one catch it, but if we weren't having this conversation right now, this performance would have "gone in the books" as exemplary teaching to diversity. This is why we ought to incorporate a critical pedagogical perspective. We ought to be talking about the framework of pedagogy that would not let this go unrecognized. For example, in the samples of students' work there are expressions of racism and pathetic regard toward Native Americans. This fact alone should not surprise us. But the fact that they were not addressed by Ms. Quinn *is* a concern.

Assessor D: I see what you mean. I can guarantee you that this kind of thing happens all the time with respect to African American children. And the boutique approach to diversity gets unbearable around February. Do you know what I mean? (*She directs this comment to the other African American panel members who are chuckling in recognition of the reference to Black History Month*).

Assessor A: I don't disagree with your analysis. But as to the missed opportunities of Ms. Quinn, couldn't she have come back to that later?

Ms. Bethune: Maybe she *could* have. But the evidence here suggests she did not. It neither evidenced in her self-analysis of this discussion nor in her feedback on that student's work. Moreover, Ms. Quinn herself states her view: that Mary Crow Dog writes about a period in Sioux history when there is little to be proud of. But let's look at another example of what students think as a result of this lesson, and you determine whether "coming back to it later," even if we presume she does it, will undo the damage. This student writes:

> Mary Crow Dog seemed to spend all of her time drinking, doing drugs and going to Native American rights marches with AIM. I spend my time on more worthwhile home oriented things than marches and equal rights.

While it may have been good to have students compare their lives with the protagonist in terms of how they spend their free time, the result here is "othering" Mary Crow Dog as a drug using activist with a not so subtle judgment that political activism for equal rights is not so worthwhile.

Assessor A: Well, maybe what this student came away with is problematic. But she can't teach everything, can she? She tried to give a flavor of what the Native American experience was like.

Ms. Bethune: No, she cannot teach everything—but do you see any worthwhile learning taking place here? Is there anything here that is worth the concomitant fortification of children's sense of superiority over the Lakota Sioux? What Ms. Quinn leaves out shapes children's imagination as much as what she puts in. From an African-centered perspective, how you contextualize knowledge or information has everything to do with how it is interpreted and understood. Where Ms. Quinn went wrong, from an African-centered perspective, is that she neglects to contextualize the narrative of Mary Crow Dog historically, and politically in the struggles of American Indians in the recent past. That is really what the autobiography is about, but that perspective doesn't show up in any of this instructional plan.

Ms. Bethune: Ms. Quinn's limited perspective is evident when she writes in her analysis of the preliminary discussion: "Without reading *Lakota Woman*, the students had a pretty good understanding of how depressed and directionless most Sioux were, and they recognized the causes of the Sioux state." Ms. Quinn seems to be satisfied with these so-called facts about the Lakota Sioux from the materials she selected. She even says here that she attributes students' allusions to the Sioux's "impoverished and oppressed life in other readings and films we viewed."

Panel Leader: (*Speaking to Ms. Bethune*) So what do you see this teacher needing?

Ms. Bethune: A Lakota perspective and, pragmatically, the sense to contextualize a people historically. She can talk about shame, but without historical contextualization, where does the notion of shame really reside? With Mary Crow Dog's personal habits or with the treatment of the Lakota Sioux at the hands of the U.S. government? Without meaning to, Ms. Quinn ends up framing "shame" so that it belongs only to the Sioux, rather than to the disgraceful and genocidal treatment of the Sioux at the hands of the United States Government.

Which framing do students come away with? All you have to do is look at their productions to find the answer. One example involves a piece of text from one of the students regarding the poem *Aimless*, in which she writes about Yellow Bird on page 14 of the document: "She did not like white people and was scared of them." Now, this is the child's take, drawing the inference perhaps from the biography. But if you read this poem you will not find anything indicative of dislike or fear of whites. Rather than helping the student sharpen her interpretation of the text, the teacher does nothing to challenge the child's interpretation and fortifies a poor interpretation. That's not good literary teaching.

Assessor B: Okay, you've convinced me that this teacher is not the diva of multicultural teaching. I realize, now that you have pointed out to me some of the student work that some pretty undesirable things have happened in her classroom. What does she need to become a better teacher?

Ms. Bethune: What this teacher was missing, and apparently what we in this group are missing, is pedagogical perspective independent of the culturally mainstream sensibilities of normative whiteness. I'm going to call the necessary critical perspective an African-centered pedagogical perspective, because multiculturalism doesn't capture it. Remember, this teacher has been nominated by her professional community as a good multicultural teacher.

Assessor B: You make it sound like that without an African-centered perspective or an "other-perspective," we can't effectively evaluate teaching performance in the manner we've been doing.

Ms. Bethune: That's exactly what I am saying. I'm not at all convinced that the necessary critical stance can be commodified into a set of teaching performance standards. Unless you already operate from an African-centered or other critical perspective, I'm not sure you could recognize the biased practice evidenced by Ms. Quinn. Her school didn't. The people who want to give her multicultural teaching awards didn't. YOU-ALL didn't. So you'll pardon me if I am skeptical that this sort of pedagogical expertise can be incorporated as criteria or standards without an African-centered perspective.

Assessor B: Well, I'm interested in this critical perspective, particularly the way you have characterized it as an African-centered pedagogical perspective. How can we begin to think about applying it in teachers' professional development, using Ms. Quinn as an example?

Ms. Bethune: Okay. Well, we'd start with student outcomes. From an African-centered perspective, you'd never assess the success of teaching and learning apart from actual learning outcomes. So the starting point for teacher professional development is to ask: What outcomes do we want from the children we're teaching? To her credit, Ms. Quinn reports being concerned with students "simply responding or interpreting from a visceral standpoint" but does nothing about it. It may be that my critique all boils down to an inappropriate selection of text material—and I wouldn't consider it appropriate for a teacher who had the capacity to effectively address the broader issues of social justice.

Let me give you a summary analysis of this portfolio of multicultural teaching practice from an African-centered perspective. To summarize, what presents in this portfolio is a candidate who has not given sufficient thought to the ideology and negative images she portrays in the selection of materials and themes. An example of this is the fore grounding of the "pull yourself up by the bootstraps" motif of the quote about not clinging to the heroes of the past, "freeloading off their legends," and making one's own legends. No where do we see in the portfolio material evidence that she contextualizes the experience of Native Americans in the oppressive conditions and broken treaties. No where in the artifacts is evidence of the values of the Lakota culture. This is a central issue of pedagogy. The other issue of pedagogy is the evidence of her inability to act and react responsibly towards her students' expressions of racism and class privilege. When students come up with negative interpretations of the Lakota Sioux that were not in the text, the teacher does not call them on it and in fact seems to concur with their biased attributions. She frames the protagonists in the texts—Mary Crow Dog and the author in of the poem—as victims and then asks students to note or identify aspects of Lakota life.

The issues and messages actually expressed by the autobiography are ignored. The ignorance and stereotypical thinking the teacher was ostensibly trying to reduce actually seemed to be reinforced, based upon students' work samples. We see missed opportunities to deal with the biased race-privileged comments they make, by failing to have the students examine the text deeply enough. I found this section in the book that reveals much of who Mary was as a person:

> In South Dakota, white kids learn to be racists almost before they learn to walk. When I was about seven or eight years old, I fought with the school principal's daughter. We were in the playground. She was hanging on the monkey bar saying, "Come on, monkey, this thing is for you." She also told me that I smelled and look like an Indian. I grabbed her by the hair and yanked her down from the monkey bar. (Crow Dog, 1990, p. 22)

It's interesting that Ms. Quinn selects one feature of Sioux culture that unfortunately reinforces the worst stereotypes that mainstream American culture has projected about Native Americans—the idea that they were good warriors, owing to their primitive and savage existence but now are reduced to drunken impotence as a people. So having chosen the most essentializing and exoticizing feature of the culture, she proceeds to make that the representative genre of Native American literature—the warrior legend. Out of this come the "othering" responses of the students. The goal of "exposure to a variety of culture which may be similar or quite different from their own" (Crow Dog, 1990, p. 3) is problematic if it ignores principles of teaching and learning and fortifies racism and class privilege in the process.

At what point should her practice be questioned in her selection of the literature, her unintentionally racist attributions

> of the Lakota Sioux as once brave warriors and now pathologic, lost, confused victims? From an African-centered perspective it is easy to see the teacher qualities that are missing. What other qualities important for teachers are being left out? What about the teacher's ability to culturally read classroom situations and interpersonal dynamics? What about the teacher's ability to maximize opportunities for developmental progress in prosocial behavior and/or identity development? What about building a character of social justice and democratic thought? What capacities in reasoning, analysis, problem solving, researching, composition, and so forth, is her unit supposed to promote among her learners?
>
> I think that we seriously need to rethink this enterprise from an African-centered or at least a critical-perspective. You cannot assess the effectiveness of a teacher independently of how well children are learning. Learning must be culturally and historically contextualized—something that is too easily overlooked and forgotten without a critical pedagogical perspective.

CONCLUSION

Ms. Bethune was enacting African-centered pedagogy in a professional setting that is becoming increasingly common and important. In the new national agenda for school reform that focuses on the performance assessment of teachers, performance assessment has taken center stage (Murrell, 2001). The professional activity setting in this case was the assessment of a teachers' practice through examination of a performance portfolio of her literacy and humanities instructional practice. The structured portfolio is a model of what is currently used by the Board of Teaching and Professional Standards (NBPTS) to select its board certified teachers. Ms. Bethune's analysis of the teachers' practice portfolio underscores the necessity of the deeper level interrogation of practice, despite the new innovation of performance assessment protocols.

Ms. Bethune's analysis reveals that without a deep appraisal of practice—one that spans micro-, meso- and macro-systemic aspects of practice—bad educational outcomes will emerge despite good intentions. The portfolio that had passed muster as an example of good multicultural teaching turned out to be deeply problematic from an African-centered perspective. Ms. Bethune's analysis revealed that, though the teacher incorporated a "multicultural" reading selection (i.e., Lakota Woman) to explore a "multicultural theme" (i.e., Native Americans), the unit did little to elevate the students' understanding. Despite the teacher's attempt at a good multicultural instructional setting, she not only does not add appreciably to students' literacy achievement, she actually ends up increasing racial bias and bigotry as evidence by what students actually end up saying about the Lakota Sioux. Ms. Bethune's appraisal of this practice from an African-centered perspective also reveals that it is not merely an African American perspective, but an American perspective.

CHAPTER 10

Appraising My Own Practice: African-Centered Pedagogy in Preparing Teachers

> Despite the pragmatic realization that knowledge entails lived practices and not just accumulated information, putting into operation educational plans that seriously consider students experiences remains a mysterious assignment for many educators. Indeed, ideas, socially reified, are enormously effective determinants of activity.
>
> —Kirshner & Whitson

Doing African-centered pedagogy involves research and development into Black culture and history as much as does planning a lesson; it involves critical analysis of standard practice as much as it does culturally responsive practice. The critical part, the *working* part, of African-centered pedagogy is the *appraisal of practice* in five critical areas of cultural activity and at three levels of analysis (micro, meso and macro), both of which require a deep read of culture, language, identity and history. As I argued in the introduction of this volume, there are at least two phases for developing a system of successful teaching and learning for African American learners. Phase one is developing responsiveness of the learners in front of us by inviting them into a figured world of inquiry. Our task as teachers in this phase is to create instructional settings that are culturally inviting and intellectually vibrant to all of our students. Phase two is the ongoing work of building the community of inquiry that will contest the hidden barriers and build the supports for learning and achievement. In this chapter, I describe my efforts doing phase two with graduate students.

There is an implicit research and development component of African-centered pedagogy that is no less vital than instructional delivery. There is a critical interrogation of policy and politics that is no less important than lesson planning. The following case description illustrates my own attempt to institute African-centered pedagogy in my graduate class module of African American teachers seeking certification. The course module, called *Learning and Teaching*, was designed to focus both on pedagogy and the instruction of American history. An additional goal, for reasons I will explain presently, was to provide the teacher participants with a solid grounding in African-centered pedagogy for their own practice. I offer this case illustration to provide concrete examples of the practices and the premises of African-centered pedagogy.

CASE FOUR — TEACHER PREPARATION

The following description of my experience of teaching a graduate course module to African American teachers is useful for several reasons. First, it offers a good example of the *application* of African-centered pedagogy — an explanation of how and what you *do in practice*. It describes the intellectual work and the outcomes for the learning and development for teachers and students alike. According to the framework, the pedagogy of the accomplished teacher is not simply what he or she does in the acts of teaching, but also inheres in the cultural research that the teacher does in anticipation of creating the intellectual, social and spiritual life of the classroom. Second, the analytic reflection on the experience of teaching the course offers a kind of assessment of the African-centered pedagogy as a framework for professional practice. I thought that it would be a strong demonstration of the impact of African-centered pedagogy if I could show that the African American participants in this alternative program became better teachers of African American children by virtue of having acquired specific culturally situated knowledge and skills for their practice.

Third, since the principal instructional aim of the course module was, in essence, to help teachers develop their African-centered pedagogy, it provides an example of the type of *community of practice* teachers would engage in to recreate connected pedagogy in their schools. The teacher participants in the course module were not merely seeking certification; they wished to become better teachers of their African American children. The pedagogy was something they were hoping to learn given their status as African American teachers in a state system of higher education that made it difficult for them to even complete their certification, much less develop abilities the for greater success in promoting the achievement of African American students. In that regard the goal of the pedagogy, the goal of the course, and the aims of the teacher participants were the same.

The module course on Learning and Teaching provides concrete examples of the abstract components of the African-centered pedagogy, including:

1. What it means to build a community of practice;
2. What it means to create an activity setting that promotes learning of all participants—teachers and learners alike;
3. What it means to historically and culturally *situate* one's instruction;
4. What it means to draw on local knowledge — cultural, historical, linguistic and political;
5. What it means to employ discursive practices in figuring a learning community;
6. What it means to employ the five cultural practices.

AFRICAN-CENTERED PEDAGOGY IN AN ADULT LEARNING COMMUNITY

For me, the experience of the course module represents a continuation of the sojourn into Black culture, history and heritage I described in chapter 2 and my focused attempt to become a better history teacher. The opportunity for teaching the course module in South Carolina came about because of intersection of several factors. It began with my need to get deeply immersed in pre-Civil War American history for the revision of the social studies methods course in the teacher preparation curriculum at my university. The irresistible opportunity presented itself for me to teach and research in a richly historical and cultural location for African Americans. The cultural appeal was the fact that course module was offered to a cohort of African American teachers on the South Carolina Sea Island of St. Helena, in the midst of Gullah culture. The Gullah people have retained more of their African heritage than any other group of Blacks in North America. Scholars have been able to document that this heritage was born in the part of West African now known as Sierra Leone. Another key aspect of the historical significance is that Beaufort is the site of the Port Royal experiment, the first large-scale government effort designed to assist newly freed Blacks in making the difficult transition from slavery to freedom. Finally, the opportunity to work with African American teachers who were in an alternative program for certification because of barriers created for them by the state laws of South Carolina was also irresistible.

The African-centered pedagogy was the framework I used to organize and tailor the course module for the teachers. It was my desire to have them learn the framework through immersion, experiencing the pedagogy first hand as the organizational structure of the course module. The course module examines several educational approaches for understanding ways of knowing among individuals including those with special needs, and among racially, culturally, linguistically and economically diverse groups. Participants are asked to critically examine the defining content curriculum standards for history and the social studies, as well as the corpus of multicultural children's literature, and the media representations and resources for the teaching of history. Successful completion is supposed to result in participants being able to articulate and apply frameworks for accomplished teaching practice for children in diverse, communities and use children's literature to do so. This meant that teacher participants in the course were to advance their pedagogical understanding in conjunction with their understanding of American History to sufficient levels to develop rich and effective history curriculum.

The educational approaches participants were to work with included *culturally responsive teaching, teaching for understanding, situated learning (cooperative learning)*, and critical pedagogy. The content frameworks were circumscribed by the state curriculum standards on South Carolina history. The sequence of American history began with colonial America and ended at the Civil War. Both content and pedagogical frameworks were to be applied as participants developed a curriculum plan (we called it a Curriculum Blueprint) that incorporated children's literature and media resources in the design of instructional activity. The *implicit* goal of the course module was for us to learn how to better educate our children in our way—to draw on those cultural resources, cultural practices, and intellectual traditions that maximize the learning and development of African American students.

The explicit goal was to convey the premises and practices of the African-centered pedagogy to these teachers. The activity settings were designed so as to replicate, in the learning of American history, the same sort of dual, multi-leveled learning that takes place for parents in effective intergenerational literacy projects, where adults' learning parallels the learning experiences of their children. The idea is that both student achievement and teacher development are worked on simultaneously and collaboratively in the daily practices of teaching and learning.

All of the 25 teachers, except for two, are Black. On the first evening, I offered my perspective on teaching and expressed it as the six points of African-centered pedagogy I described in the preface. Everyone seemed to resonate with my articulation of accomplished teaching for African American children as educators who:

1. Create a intellectual environment and cultural community in their classrooms that systematically provides the social, intellectual and cultural tools for rich and worthwhile learning and development;
2. Research the deep structure of African American culture, history, language and life well enough to appropriate it in the structuring of the classroom intellectual environment for African American children.
3. View themselves as responsible for promoting the intellectual, spiritual, ethical and social development of young people, and stewarding them into capable, caring and character-rich adulthood.
4. Critically appropriate contemporary curriculum, educational policy and instructional practice as a matter of *daily practice* by asking, "How does this practice or policy perpetuate the underachievement of African American learners?"
5. Critically appraise their own practice by recognizing and *deconstructing* the ways that traditional pedagogy and current instructional paradigms perpetuate underachievement of children of color.
6. Recognize the complexity of human development and identity development of African American children, and the possibility of conflict in three domains — the psychological or intrapersonal, the social or interpersonal, and the cultural.

After some discussion, we agreed that these six points would be our operating principles that would guide the development of their Curriculum Blueprints (American History and Literacy units) for the course module, and the five essential cultural practices (Table 3) would be the criteria by which we would evaluate the blueprints.

ENGAGEMENT AND PARTICIPATION PRACTICES

In instituting African-centered pedagogy, I asked the same type of questions as I mentioned earlier (in chapter 4) that an accomplished literacy teacher asks: What do I need to ensure that the participants get what they need in the way of history pedagogy? How do I make sure that everyone gets the support they need to reach proficiency in using the state curriculum frameworks for history? How do I organize, on a routine basis, the instructional activity over the course of five hours everyday to bring about these ends?

The key for instituting engagement and participation for the course module was designing a *generative task*. This was a challenge, because the course was organized to meet every day for ten days from 4:30 p.m. to 9:30 p.m. after the teachers put in a full day of work in their respective schools. What ever we chose to do as the modal instructional activity had to be *generative*—it had to generate interest, enthusiasm, and knowledge-in-use, as well as a "way in" for everyone to participate. With a group of 25 tired teachers, I knew that the model activity certainly was not going to be lecture. I decided to approach creating the instructional activity after deciding on an *instructional enterprise*—what we do together that would result in our meeting the course module goals as described above.

The enterprise in the course module of learning and teaching was one the participants and I shared. The enterprise was developing a pedagogical game plan for teaching the deep structure of American history using African American children's literature. We called this game plan a Curriculum Blueprint, and decided it should reflect American history as a narrative of "movement history" (McDowell & Sullivan, 1993) of African Americans powered by an inquiry into the genesis and legacy of America's trenchant contradiction: "life, liberty, and the pursuit of happiness" on one hand, and the institutions of bondage and oppression on the other hand. The appeal for the teacher participants completing their Curriculum Blueprints was the same appeal for me—to learn the richer narrative of American history made possible by a more detailed examination of the experience of Africans in America. All of us wanted to end the course with a product we could actually use in our teaching.

The best way to characterize our engagement and participation practices was a collective dedication to *narrative as a way of knowing*. We determined that our measure of understanding and mastery of factual, historical knowledge would be *narrative knowledge*. In other words, rather than merely learning the facts surrounding, for example, the Stono Rebellion, the type of knowledge "units" we all sought to maximize was that of telling the story of the Stono Rebellion and what it meant for America's struggles with its contradictions of freddom versus bondage slavery. We developed a number of "story starters" as calls to one another to evoke a narrative explanation of a particular episode in history.

One of the early story starters was called "Did you know that. . . ." As a recap of the previous evenings reading, we began sessions by sharing new knowledge—things that we had not learned in our history education coming up as students ourselves and that we found interesting. Retelling narratives became our practice. That is, our practice was not merely to tell about some epoch or episode, but to retell the events and say something about the global and personal significance in a way that contributes to the audience's deeper understanding of American history. In the first segment of our text, *Africans in America* (Johnson & Smith, 1998), the following were among the "Did you know that . . ." contributions:

- John Locke, the philosopher of American Liberty, was one of the major shareholders for the Royal African Company, chartered by the King of England to trade in African slaves as a lucrative business enterprise.
- Eleven million Africans stolen from Africa is the figure based upon the records that remain.
- Rebellions and insurrections in slave transport in the middle passage, like the *Amistad* happened frequently.
- The British system of slavery in Barbados, admired as a model of economy and profit throughout the British Empire and modeled by planters in South Carolina, was one where one out of every three Africans died because owners determined that it was cheaper to replace the slaves who were worked to death than to treat them humanely. Within the first 10 years of settlement of South Carolina, the largest influx of immigrants came from Barbados, planters who brought their slaves, their British culture, and a fully conceived idea of slavery that took root in America.
- By 1740, other than Charleston, no city in colonial America had a higher density of slave population than New York (out of eleven thousand city residents, 2 thousand were Black). Restrictions by the Common Council of New York in 1731 prevented assembly and required burials during the day.
- At the same time as the Stamp Act and the colonial petitioning for "liberty" from taxation without representation slaves themselves were petitioning the colonial government for their liberty. By law free Negroes were not allowed to walk the streets or travel the waterways after dark without a pass in New York. Connecticut's Black codes prevent its citizens from inviting a Black person or an Indian into their homes. In Boston, a free Black person could not even carry a stick or a cane unless they could prove they required it for an infirmity. There was always the threat of being kidnapped and sold into slavery.

By default of limited time and a tremendous amount of material, a major activity setting was the viewing and discussion of the *Africans in America* series, the Frontline edition entitled *Jefferson's Blood*, and *Tutu and Franklin: A Journey Toward Peace*, all of which originally aired on Public Broadcasting System. We viewed one segment of *Africans in America* per night (there were four segments) and allowed ample time for examination and discussion of the content. In that process, it wasn't until the second five hour session that I noticed that the participants had their books open and that there were long stretches of time that many were looking more at their books than at the video screen. This puzzled me at first because I thought, "How can they miss out on the rich visual accompaniment to the narrative? It is too hard to try to read to catch up when we are already viewing the video." But then I realized that what they were doing was actually following along on the narrative that was being presented in the video. I discovered that much of the narrative in the video was also reproduced in the text, providing the opportunity for encountering the text in the aural and visual modes. This meant that there was less pressure on people to "cover the material" and that they could devote more concentration on their narratives of explanation. Hence, the discussions we had of each segment included the many "Did you know that . . ." discoveries about significant episodes and events of American history. The effort of participants was sustained not merely by the very real experience of learning something new and interesting, but the eagerness to incorporate the new insight into their teaching and their own enriched narrative knowledge of American history. The test of understanding became that of telling or retelling the good story. Our credo became "what you can *narrate*, you can *explain*: and what you can explain you can *teach*."

Narrative became a speech event and a form of literacy performance with heightened importance as time went on in the course. We saw this as natural given the importance of narrative and the connection between oral and written literacy in the African American cultural heritage. Narratives are not merely products, but should also be regarded as a form of meaning resulting from coauthorship between writers/speakers and listeners/readers (Ochs, 1997). We began calling the literacy performance *retelling the narrative*. Retelling narratives became a way of articulating desired learning achievements—both for our students as well as for ourselves. For example, telling the story of the "Terrible Transformation"—how the fledging colonies went from pursuing a utopian vision of a new society to a bondage labor economy (first through indentured servitude and finally to slavery)—involves both content knowledge and literacy performance (orality).

IDENTITY DEVELOPMENT PRACTICES

Recall that identity development practices are those that attend to the identity work of individuals who participate in the instructional activity setting. The function of the teacher in this practice is to promote learners' interest in being a part of activity setting and seeking connection to the ongoing enterprise. The result of identity practices is that participants begin developing their association with the social setting and with the doings of the group. The success of this essential practice would manifest as learners actively seek participatory and contributive roles in the doings of the group—in this case, constructing a rich, movement history narrative of American history in the antebellum period.

What developing identity practices meant for me, as a Boston northerner coming to the South, was to do some homework. Before I went down to South Carolina, I read all I could about Gullah language and the culture of the people. A valuable resource was the video *Family Across the Sea* (1989) that documents the connection between Gullah culture and Sierra Leone, a video that I had actually viewed with this same cohort on an earlier visit to the area. Knowing that I would be working intensely with teachers from the African American community for ten days, nearly everyday, I wanted to be familiar with the cultural patterns, forms of talk and custom of the area.

The starting point of my identity practice was to figure out how to constitute the class more as a community of African American educators, and less as a structured seminar. I wanted folks to feel a membership to our enterprise. This I did both through the design of the instructional activity settings, to orchestrate the in-the-moment interactions so that we engaged in collective self-definition as a group of African American educators mutually assisting each other to become better teachers.

There is a long-term identity work like that which we do with our students and our children, and a short-term identity work we do when an individual seeks to become a legitimate participant in a social group or community of learners. My identity practices in the course module focused more on the latter type, as it was important for all participants to find a way in to the learning enterprise and feel membership in our cohort. Of course, both types of identity work are linked—the development of an individual's self-image and that individual's sense of place and belonging as collateral processes. I took into account participants' identities as teachers, and their desire to become *better* teachers, when designing the instructional activity settings. The participants had been developing a collective identity as a cohort beginning with the course they had taken the previous summer.

The African-centered pedagogy was my blueprint for how this identity work organized the classroom life. Certainly a major piece of this was the selection of the instructional focus—the text of *Africans in America* and the use of African American children's literature to teach an intellectually richer and more honest American history. We tried to be mindful of how we constructed ourselves in the community of learners. I made explicit the idea of a community of practice. I assumed the role of lead learner in this community, retaining the stance that what we all were experiencing the rediscovery of Black history as a means to becoming much more effective history and social studies teachers.

By assuming the positionality of a guide through various educational pathways that I'd traveled, rather than that of an "expert," I hoped to encourage the collegial relationships. It was important how people thought of themselves as *both learners and teachers* in relation to the enterprise. We fortified the point made by Holland, et. al. (1998) that identities are lived *in* and *through* activity. This allows us as teachers to support processes of identity development by the social products we expect, the social practices we encourage, and the social/intellectual props we provide. I was mindful that the positionality of "teacher" they accorded me was constructed and nourished by the positive and edifying learning experiences they had daily. I daily monitored our community building process with a variety of simple strategies (e.g., "pluses and wishes," a strategy for getting participants' feedback about what they liked and what they would like changed). The challenge for community integrity might have been the fact that two European American women had enrolled in the course. But the fact that we were mindful of how we built a congenial community resulted in a seamless connection between these two and the rest of the cohort.

COMMUNITY INTEGRITY PRACTICES

The whole notion of structured but informal assistance is a key part of African-centered pedagogy. The operating principle for African-centered pedagogy is that improving instructional practice is not something done in isolation, but in collaboration. The task for creating a school of achievement for African American children is one of building an African American cultural and intellectual community, one that nourishes a *community of culturally connected teaching practice* among the adults who support learning of children in school, at home and where ever children come together to learn. My task for the course module was to build community in a similar fashion among the cohort of 25 teachers. In doing so, I incorporated the knowledge traditions of African American culture by drawing on the experiences expressed in the narratives of Black people. This is where the infusion of African American children's literature in the course module became very important.

In a community designed for learning, the students themselves have a role in the construction of the group practices—for inquiry, for completing instructional tasks, for narrating, and for social engagement. The extent to which everyone in the community—teachers and learners—can co-own and share the enterprise is the extent to which the learning community has coherence and integrity. As the instructor for the course module, I experienced the challenge of organizing the events of the long (five hour) class periods as a task requiring an ecology—a system of balance for participants to establish new relationships to American History, to teaching through literature, and to each other.

The cultural value and historical themes were, thankfully, provided by the text of *Africans in America* (Johnson & Smith, 1998)—both in its oral/visual (video) form and in the form of the companion book that we used as the text. The meta narrative—the content portion of the course—was manifest in this title. The course is about the meta-narrative of Africans in America. The community integrity practice of the course module was to explicitly and repeatedly evoke the idea of a *figured world of Black achievement*—a community of learners and teachers whose meta-enterprise was learning the deep significance of the movement history of African Americans, using the richest literacy tools available—narratives and children's literacy.

Another aspect of community integrity emerged because of the cultural resources embodied in African American culture—fictive kinship. I was reminded that members of a community of practice might also be members of other cultural communities, and bring to the present setting their ways and practices. I remember the occasion when our academically grounded community of practice became a decidedly cultural African American community of practice. It was the end of a class, when the participants brought food as a celebration of accomplishment. As the setting shifted from an academic enterprise to a social one, I was no longer the "elder" presiding. In the shift to the social enterprise, one of the women "elders" took charge, organizing the proceedings from that point on. She directed several younger women to lay out the food and the place settings, instructed the young men on how and where to move the tables, and informed another "elder" to preside in saying grace. He was a lay minister and therefore had earned the distinction of 'reverend' and the responsibility for delivering the benediction.

This experience was both a little unsettling and comforting at the same time. As a professor, I am not used to having the proceedings completely determined by other participants in my class. On another level, this was comfortable and culturally familiar. In those moments I noticed how the cultural forms of African American culture were in play, shaping our interaction. In those moments I had a feeling of being a part of something bigger than myself, a membership created by virtue of my cultural and ethnic identity. It was a natural extension of an African American cultural activity setting.

MEANING MAKING PRACTICES—APPROPRIATION OF TEXT

According to my framework, meaning-making practices go beyond merely asking learners to do things that advance their understanding or knowledge. It also means doing something new and/or different with the understanding or knowledge gained. In other words, meaning-making practices result in *appropriation of knowledge*. I made explicit that we were working against the transmission model (what Freire called the "banking concept") where the manifest purpose of schooling in America is not really understanding anything, but rather accumulating factual information. Our chief meaning-making activity was narration (as described above) as we appropriated the rich meta-narrative provided by the PBS series *Africans in America*. This made it easier for the participants to *appropriate* (incorporate for their own instructional use) various pieces of children's literature (see Table Appendix I) and significant understandings about American history.

One prop that supported narration as a tool was the chronological chart —a chart showing the chronology of events for a particular historical epoch. Constructing these charts for our Curriculum Blueprints frequently involved the interactive speech event "And then what happened?" prompt, where the teacher prompts a student or a group of students to identify the sequence of events in a story or piece of historical text. We did this prompting for each other, and extended meaning by the additional prompt "And why is this important to know?" This interaction may be developed into a scripted event that the teacher evokes when he or she wants to assess or extend students' narrative understanding of events—by which I mean a level of understanding permitting a retelling of the story. All of this was focused on how we can develop our students' narrative ability.

Keying on knowledge narratives was, in some ways, a natural and expected meaning-making practice to emerge from this group of African American teachers. The intense, hours long sessions in an un-air-conditioned classroom on the Marine Corps Air Station in Beaufort, South Carolina, produced an *espirit de corps* and focused us on developing useful knowledge for our students. Narratives are a natural means for us to first ascertain and experience for ourselves that which we want the children to experience. This is an act of figuring a world with cultural and symbolic supports children need to construct the full meaning and significance of what they are learning. The group developed other visual and conceptual tools to support narration—including the use of a Venn diagram to identify differences and similarities, and the KWL chart in relation to literacy instruction.

We came together as a community that could appraise each others' practice—the practice of telling historical narrative. We appraised this practice by first determining the quality of the telling, then the quality of appropriation to teaching, and then its likely impact on the hearts and minds of the students. The literacy practices that the teachers prepared for their students included inventive reappropriation of slave narratives, using the written petitions of slaves and freedmen to the government that illustrated appropriation of the language and ideals of the constitution and the declaration of independence. Gabriel's last words, saying that he would say no more than when George Washington would say had he been captured and sentenced to death by the British, were:

> I have nothing more to say in my defense than what General Washington would have to offer had he been taken by the British and put to trial. I have devoted my life in endeavoring to obtain the liberty of my countrymen.

In addition to narration, a second meaning-practice I built into the course module was media analysis in general, and film critique in particular. There were two films that were particularly useful for our enterprise of creating a Curriculum Blueprint. Participants viewed with a critical and pedagogical eye the films *Amistad* and *Race to Freedom: The Story of the Underground Railroad* using a guide for evaluation (see Appendix II).

PRACTICES OF INQUIRY—INVENTIVE REAPPROPRIATION.

Effective practices of inquiry are animated by genuine curiosity and an authentic need to find the truth of something. The implicit purpose is always "what can we take from this?" or "What is the *lesson* here?" One interesting example is the retelling of an episode from history in the frame of a lesson. The learning goals of teacher participants all required narrative knowledge. An example from one submitted eighth grade Curriculum Blueprint titled "Gullah Culture, Gullah People, and the Making of South Carolina. The students were expected to tell multiple versions of the story of Gullah People "making" South Carolina. Their narrative was to include language, folklore, arts/crafts, and labor.

Selected scenes from *Amistad* provided excellent points of discussion representing inventive reappropriation. Interrogating symbolic devices in film was a major means of developing course content—especially negative or distorting images of Blackness (Lott, 1999). The film was the prop for exploring intertextuality of literature—as in the soliloquy made by John Quincy Adams (played by Anthony Hopkins) that recapitulates the lasting impacts of what he learned about African wisdom, culture and tradition through his ongoing interaction with Cinque, the de facto spokesperson for the Africans.

The film offered interesting dramatizations of the significance of narrative as the means by which humans make meaning, especially as it was set in the freedom struggle of Africans that turned out to be the crux of the nation's deliberation on the most profound contradiction of its existence. There were also key dramatization of cultural models, such as when Cinque struggled to communicate with John Quincy Adams how to prepare his people's defense in front of the Supreme Court. The teacher participants found ways to use the film to foreground Africanist cultural values—the power of narrative, reverence for ancestors, drawing our identity and life force from them. The teacher participants saw ways of reappropriating the media imaging of these values when we deconstructed the segment of the film that depicted the case going before the Supreme Court. The power of the word, the connection to our ancestors, and African wisdom became the anchors of John Quincy Adams' understanding and the foundations for his powerful argument that won the day.

An assessment of the actual impact on student performance this instructional experience has had on the teachers will have to await my visit to these classrooms in future work together. The primary indication of results at the time of this writing is the excellent Curriculum Blueprints. All meet the criteria specified on the Curriculum Blueprint evaluation sheet (see Appendix III).

CONCLUSION

As I argued in the beginning of this book, a pedagogy is more than just set of strategies and approaches, it entails a philosophy of education. African centered pedagogy is not characterized by strategies, but rather as a system of understanding and meaning making that all children should be exposed to and enriched by. A pedagogy engenders answers to the implicit question: What should be the function and purpose of public education in contemporary society? A pedagogy works well when it addresses this question appropriately for the children, family, and communities being served. Historically, the functions and purposes of education have played out differently for White mainstream America, and the pedagogical theory offered in this book responded to the African American experience. A pedagogy always engenders a direction and a purpose for learning, whether it is a formal one like the African-centered pedagogy presented in these pages, or a personal one incorporating some or all of the many educational frameworks discussed earlier.

In contemporary American education, there are, of course, many functions of education. Some are articulated, some implicit, and many are contradictory in practice. A good example is the articulated function of American education to produce a good workforce so that we can compete successfully in the world market. When put into practice, it is at odds with the articulated function of producing well-rounded, educated citizens with civic character. I am convinced of the necessity of a framework that affords mainstream America the means to see themselves in practice with new eyes. At the time of this writing, I had just attended a workshop for reading tutors at which Jerome Kagan spoke. In his address, he urged tutors to work first and foremost on creating a common category of membership. It sounded good, and he was, of course, absolutely right. However, as I looked around the room, and listened to the types of questions asked and assumptions made and biases revealed about African American families, I thought to myself how far these tutors would have to go and how much they would have to change in order to make those connections. The huge challenge is for these tutors, and the trainers of tutors, to overcome their cultural and ideological encapsulation.

It is in settings like these where a pedagogy can inform an ecology of educational ideas and practices, to provide a balanced system for how public education ought to serve future generations of our children. I have developed this African-centered pedagogy to provide that balanced system for a large segment of American society particularly underserved by public schooling. While the educational aim of pedagogy is to promote learners' growing proficiency and participation in adult systems of practice, there is also a critical and analytical perspective that is important.

The primary goal of African-centered pedagogy is a deep read on American culture, world culture, and the institutions within cultures so that the climate for learning can be created. As we saw in case three, this deep read is not just about, for, or by African Americans. Without the critical cultural lens provided by Ms. Bethune, the other teachers and administrators would have been all to willing to embrace as "multiculturally sound" decidedly problematic practice. The primary aim of education in this pedagogy is cultural learning to develop the critical knowledge, consciousness, and proficiencies of a fulfilled and productive citizen and an agent of social justice. The aim here is *cultural learning for a better world.*

The pedagogy presented in this volume is a set a seven *premises* (Table 2) and five *practices* (Table 3) designed to develop connected pedagogy for successful work with African American children. The premises explained the theoretical precepts; the practices articulated what teachers need to incorporate into their professional repertoire to be effective with African American children. When practices and premises come together as a system of practice, the teachers using that system of practice are equipped as *cultural learners.*

Cultural learning for a better world is valued in our educational debates and discussion, but rarely articulated in the terms needed to make it happen. People are content with the form, but not the substance of multicultural education. Unless we are willing to fully engage what it means to know the world through a widening understanding and read of human systems and cultures, the default approach of multiculturalism will continue to be a the boutique look at cultural differences. The requirements for teachers in the African-centered pedagogy included culture and cultural learning, not multicultural education as it is currently realized in public schools, is an important aim. It is my hope that this book has at least begun the critical work.

Table 6

GLOSSARY OF TERMS IN AFRICAN-CENTERED PEDAGOGY

Activity setting	A social configuration in which particular actions and activities are expected and carried out toward mutually understood goals. In the classroom, *instructional activity settings* include lectures, labs, debates, and group discussion when the instructional goals are clear and explicit. *Professional activity settings* include curriculum meetings, team meetings, and parent conferences, again when the aims and goals are explicit.
Assessment of practice	An assessment of professional performance, which always specifies criteria for successful outcomes for clients (i.e., students, parents), specifies how the professional conduct is situationally and culturally appropriate to the setting, and indicates how stable the professional performance and student achievement are over time.
Accomplished practice	A way of talking about the pedagogy of successful teachers that identifies the successful practice as an activity system that integrates teacher actions and student outcomes. It is a description of teaching practice that describes practice in terms of the consequential achievements of learners that result from the practice.
Community of practice	A social configuration in which groups of individuals are bound together in a mutual activity with mutual exchange of ideas, values and act toward a common purpose or set of purposes.
Community teacher	A teacher who develops the contextualized knowledge of culture, community, and identity of the children and families as the core of their teaching practice. In contrast to course-based teacher preparation curriculum, this is a special knowledge that shows up as effective pedagogy and work in diverse community settings. A significant part of this knowledge is the candidate's own cultural, political and racial identity. These determine how central or peripheral they are with respect to the core practices of a group or community that result in successful development of children and youth.
Generative task	A learner-focused instructional activity setting. A generative task is an intellectually stimulating, culturally significant, and scholastically valuable activity or series of activities that results in the achievement of learned performances we value most.
Practice	A practice is a pattern of professional activity or professional performance. The pattern is recognized by three things: (1) the design and enactment of professional activity; (2) the situational and cultural context of the activity; and (3) the consequential outcomes for the client.

Appendices

Appendix I
Book List for African Centered Graduate Module

NARRATIVES, STORIES AND PLAYS

Bradford, Sarah (1886, 1993). *Harriet Tubman: The Moses of Her People*. Bedford, MA: Applewood Books. Grades 5–6.

Chambers, Veronica (1998). *Amistad Rising: A Story of Freedom*. New York, NY: Harcourt Brace. Grades 3–4.

Collier, James Lincoln, & Collier, Christopher (1987). *War Comes to Willy Freeman*. New York, NY: Dell Publishing.

Davis, Ossie (1989). *Escape to Freedom: A Play About Young Frederick Douglass*. New York, NY: Puffin Books. Grades 4–6.

Hansen, Joyce (1994). *The Captive*. New York, NY: Scholastic. Grades 5–6 about an African Child captured in slavery

Hopkinson, Deborah (1993). *Sweet Clara and the Freedom Ouilt*. New York, NY: Alfred P. Knopf (Dragonfly). Grades 24, escape to freedom.

Johnson, Delores (1993). *Now Let Me Fly: The Story of a Slave Family*. New York, NY: MacMillan. (Begins in Africa and ends in the U.S.) Grades 2–4.

Johnson, Delores (1994). *Seminole Diary: Rememberances of a Slave*. New York, NY: MacMillan. (relationship between Seminole and African American's in the 1830s).

Petry, Ann (1955, 1983). *Harriet Tubman: Conductor on the Underground Railroad*. New York, NY: Harper Trophy. Grades 5–6.

Porter, Connie (1993). *Addy learns a Lesson: A School Story*. Middleton, WI: Pleasant Company.

Porter, Connie (1993). *Addy's Surprise: A Christmas Story*. Middleton, WI: Pleasant Company.

Porter, Connie (1993). *Happy Birthday. Addy! A Springtim Story*. Middleton, WI: Pleasant Company. (need book five and six).

Porter, Connie (1993). *Meet Addy: An American Girl*. Middleton, WI: Pleasant Company.

Rappaport, D. (2000). *Freedom River*. New York, NY: Hyperion. Read aloud grades 1–4, about the Underground Railroad.

Ringgold, Faith (1999). *The Invisible Princess*. New York, NY: Crown Publishers. Fantasy story about an enslaved princess, grades 1–3.

Rockwell, A. (2000). *Only Passing Through: A Story of Sojourner Truth*. New York, NY: Alfred A. Knopf. Grades 2–4

Schroeder, A. (1996). *Minty: A Story of Young Harriet Tubman*. New York, NY: Puffin. Read aloud grades 1–4, independent reading grades 3–4.

EXPOSITORY BOOKS

Haskins,J., & Benson, K. (2001) *Building a New Land: African Americans in Colonial America*. New York, NY: Harper Collins. Grades 4–6 (2 copies)

McKissack, P., & McKissack, F. (1987). *Frederick Douglass: The Black Lion*. Chicago, IL: Chicago Children's Press. Grades 4–6.

McKissack, P., & McKissack, F. (1996). *Rebels Against Slavery: American Slave Revolts*. New York NY: Scholastic. Grades 4–6.

Myers, Walter Dean (1997). *Amistad: A Long Road to Freedom*. New York, NY: Dutton Children's Books. Grades 4–6.

Myers, Walter Dean. (1996). *Toussaint L'Ouverture: The Fight for Haiti's Freedom*. New York, NY: Simon and Schuster. Grades 3–4, two copies.

Osagle, Folayan Iyunolu (2000). *The Amistad Revolt: Memory. Slavery, and the Politics of Identity in the United States and Sierra Leone*. Athens, GA: University of Georgia Press.

Pinkney, A. D. (2000). *Let it Shine: Stories of Black Women Freedom Fighters*. New York, NY: Gulliver Books. Three of the ten are of the time period—Sojourner Truth, Biddy Mason, Harriet Tubman.

PERSONAL NARRATIVES

Hansen, Joyce (1997). *I Thought My Soul Would Rise and Fly: The Diary of Patsy, A Freed Girl*. New York, NY: Scholastic. Grades 4–6.

McCurdy, Michael (Ed.)(1994). *Escape from Slavery: the Boyhood of Frederick Douglass in His Own Words*. New York, NY: Alfred A. Knopf.

McKissack, P. (1997). *A Picture of Freedom: The Diary Clotee, A Slave Girl*. New York, NY: Scholastic. Grades 4–6.

POEM

Lawrence, Jacob (1968, 1993). *Harriet and the Promised Land.* New York, NY: Aladdin. Grades 1–3.

LETTERS

Lyons, Mary (1996). *Letters of a Slave Girl: The Story of Harriet Jacobs.* New York, NY: Aladdin. Grades 4–6.

SONGS

McGill, Alice (2000). *In the Hollow of Your Hand: Slave Lullabies.* Boston, MA: Houghton Mifflin. (Priscilla and Arthur).

Lester, Julius (1998). *From Slave Ship to Freedom Road.* New York, NY: Dial Books.

Liddell, Janice (1994). *Imani and the Flying Africans.* Trenton, NJ: African Free Press.

Monjo, F. (1993). *The Drinking Gourd: A Story of the Underground Railroad.* New York, NY: Harper Trophy

Ringgold, Faith *Aunt Harriet's Underground Railroad in the Sky.*

Smalls, Irene (1998). *A Strawbeater's Thanksgiving.* Boston, MA: Little, Brown and Company.

Turner, Ann (1987). *Nettie's Trip South.* New York, NY: Aladdin Paperbacks, Simon & Schuster.

Winter, Jeanette (1988). *Follow the Drinking Gourd.* New York, NY: Dragonfly Books, Alfred A. Knopf.

Wright, Courtni C. (1994). *Jumping the Broom.* New York, NY: Holiday House.

Appendix II
Video Review Assessment Sheet

For this paper you are critically reviewing the video material from the perspective of using it for teaching history. You will either review the film *Amistad* or the film *Race to Freedom: The Story of the Underground Railroad*. Part of this effort replicates the work you do as a teacher, trying to be a good critical consumer of resources you use in teaching. The other part is just as important, a media analysis of the representations of people, ideas and events in the same way a good film critic might. Both of these aims are important to accomplished teaching, especially as based upon the five essential cultural practices that organize this course.

Due: End of the Sessions

1. __ Explained what was historically accurate and inaccurate.
2. __ Analyzed what symbols were used.
3. __ Provided an analysis as to whether portrayal of people was accurate.
4. __ Provided an analysis of the portrayal of Africans in the new world.
5. __ Provided an analysis of the portrayal of Europeans in the new world.
6. __ Specified at least one connection to a work of children's literature.
7. __ Specified historical content that supports use of the children's literature.
8. __ Explained how the film might be used to support student engagement.
9. __ Explained how the film might be used to support identity development.
10. __ Explained how the film might be used to build sense of community.
11. __ Explained how the film might be used build interpretation skills of children.
12. __ Explained how the film might be used to support inquiry skills.
13. __ Work submitted in timely fashion.

Point Total: ______

Please attach this sheet to the front of your paper. Be sure you work meets all of the criteria before

Appendix III
Evaluation Sheet for Curriculum Blueprint

1. __ Provided a diagram or outline of the unit content and benchmarks.
2. __ Provided an overview of the content, activities, goals and assessments.
3. __ Provided a statement of the "big idea" or key theme for the Curriculum Blueprint.
4. __ Provided a statement of what *content standards* were drawn upon.
5. __ Specified how students would demonstrate mastery of the big idea or theme.
6. __ Specified grade level and the historical ideas appropriate for that level.
7. __ Activities include worthwhile higher order ability (e.g., oral history, historiography, narrative writing).
8. __ Described an appropriate *media stimulus* to engage students.
9. __ Learning goals clearly specify expected student behavior or performance achievement.
10. __ Learning goals indicate performances that require understanding of content.
11. __ Learning goals are consistent with the planned activities.
12. __ Specified how understanding is assessed.
13. __ Specified criteria for each student performance of understanding.
14. __ Specified all of the assessments in terms of *understanding performances*.
15. __ Describes the performances that are assessed.
16. __ Specified the factual/declarative knowledge that is assessed.
17. __ Specified the skill/procedural that is assessed.
18. __ Specified at least one work of children's literature.
19. __ Clearly indicated how children's literature is incorporated into instruction.
20. __ Clearly explained how media materials are incorporated into learning.
21. __ Explained the day-by-day instructional sequence.
22. __ Explained what activities engaged students in *instructional discourse*.
23. __ Explained in the overview how instruction supports *participation and engagement*.
24. __ Described the indicators to assess student participation and engagement.
25. __ Explained how instruction supports *identity development*.
26. __ Described indicators to assess student identity development.
27. __ Explained how instructional settings build learning *community coherence*.

28. __ Described indicators of students' increase sense of community.
29. __ Explained how/where students' ability to interpret text and media is developed.
30. __ Explained how instruction builds students' *ability to interpret.*
31. __ Described the indicators used to assess each student's increased ability to interpret.
32. __ Explained how instruction builds *critical inquiry skills*.
33. __ Work appropriately typed double spaced in manuscript format.
34. __ Work submitted in timely fashion.

IMPORTANT: Be sure to attach this sheet to the front of your submitted paper.

References

Addae, E. K. (1996). *To heal a people: Afrikan scholars defining a new reality*, Erriel D. Roberson, (Ed.). Columbia, MD: Kujichagulia Press.

Akoto, K. A. (1992). *Nation building: Theory and practice in Afrikan-centered education.* Washington, DC: Pan-Afrikan World Institute.

Anderson, J. D. (1988). *The education of blacks in the south, 1860–1935*. Chapel Hill, NC: University of North Carolina Press.

Anderson, J. D. (1995). Literacy and education in the African American experience. In V. L. Gadsden & D. A. Wagner (Eds.), *Literacy among African-American youth: Issues in learning, teaching and schooling* (pp. 19–37). Creskill, NJ: Hampton Press.

Ani, M. (1994). *Yurugu: An African centered critique of European thought and behavior.* Trenton, NJ: Africa Free World Press.

Anwisye, S. (1993). Education is more than the three "R"s. *Harvard Journal of African American Public Policy*, 2, 97–101.

Bahktin, M. (1981). Discourse in the novel. In M. Holquist (Ed.) *The dialogic imagination*, (C. Emerson & M. Holquist, Trans.) (pp. 259–422). Austin, TX: University of Texas Press (Original work published in 1935).

Banks, J. (1988). *Multiethnic education: Theory and practice* (2nd ed.). Boston: Allyn Bacon.

Bateson, G. (1958). *Naven*. Stanford, CA: Stanford University Press.

Benjamin, W. (1969). *Illuminations*. New York: Schocken Books.

Berlin, I. (1999, November). *Conspiring Theorist*, (p. 202). New York Times.

Bloome, D., Champion, T., Katz, L., Morton, M. B., & Muldrow, R. (2001). Spoken and written narrative development: African American preschoolers as story-tellers and storymakers. In J. L. Harris, A. G. Kamhi, & K. E. Pollock (Eds.), *Literacy in African American communities* (pp. 45–76). Mahwah, NJ: Erlbaum

Bond, H. M. (1932). Negro education: A debate in the Alabama Constitutional Convention of 1901. *Journal of Negro Education*, 1, 49–59.

Bowers, C. A., & Flinders, D. J. (1990). *Responsive teaching: An ecological approach to classroom patterns of language, culture and thought.* New York: Teachers College Press.

Bourdieu, P., & Passerson, C. (1977). *Reproduction in education, society, and culture*. Beverly Hills, CA: Sage Publications.

Boykin, A. W. (1986). The triple quandary and the schooling of Afro-American children. In U. Neisser (Ed.), *The school achievement of minority children: New perspectives* (pp. 57–92). Hillsdale, NJ: Erlbaum.

Brofennbrenner, U. (1979). *The ecology of human development*. Cambridge, MA: Harvard University Press.

Brown, J. S., Collins, A., & Duguid, P. (1989). Situated cognition and the culture of learning. *Educational Researcher*, 18(1), 32–42.

Bruner, J. (1997). *The culture of education*. Cambridge, MA: Harvard University Press.

Cazden, C. (1988). *Classroom discourse*. Portsmouth, NH: Heineman.

Clarke, J. H. (1991). *African world revolution: Africans at the crossroads*. Trenton, NJ: Africa World Press.

Chaiklin, S., Hedegaard, M., Jensen, V. J. (Eds.). (1999). Activity theory and social practice: Cultural-historical approaches. Aarhus, OK: Aarhus University Press.

Cochran-Smith, M. (1996, April). Constructing a knowledge base for urban teaching. Presentation at the annual meeting of the American Educational Research Association, New York.

Cohen, C., Roelofs, A. & Battat, J. (n.d.). *Studying life stories in the classroom*. Unpublished manuscript.

Cohen, R. (1969). Conceptual styles, culture conflict and nonverbal tests of intelligence. *American Psychologist, 71*, 828–856.

Comer, J., & Poussaint, A. F. (1992). *Raising black children : Two leading psychiatrists confront the educational, social, and emotional problems facing Black children*. New York: Plume Books.

Comer, J. P. (1997). *Waiting for a miracle: Why schools can't solve our problems—and how we can*. New York: Dutton Publishers.

Cook, P. J., & Ludwig, J. (1997). Weighing the "burden of 'acting white'": Are there race differences in attitudes toward education. *Journal of Policy Analysis and Management, 61*(2), 256–278.

Council of Black Independent Schools (1998). <http://cibi.org/handbook/How-CIBI-defines-Afrikan-centered-education.html>.

Crow Dog, M. (1990). *Lakota Woman*. New York: Harper Perennial.

Darder, A. (1991). *Culture and power in the classroom: A critical foundation for bicultural education*. New York: Bergin Garvey Press.

Delpit, L. (1988). The silenced dialog: Power and pedagogy in educating other people's children. *Harvard Educational Review, 58*(3). 280–298.

Delpit, L. (1995). *Other people's children: Cultural conflict in the classroom*. New York: New Press.

Dewey, J. (1933). *How we think*. Boston: D.C. Heath.

Driscoll, M. P. (2000). *Psychology of learning and instruction*. Boston: Allyn and Bacon.

DuBois, W. E. B., (1903/1989). *The souls of black folk*. New York: Bantam Books.

Elmore, R. F. (1996). Getting to scale with good educational practice. *Harvard Educational Review*, 66(1), 1–26.

Fine, M. (1991). *Framing dropouts*. Albany, NY: SUNY Press.

Fordham, S. (1988). Racelessness as a factors in black students' success: Pragmatic strategy or pyrrhic victory. *Harvard Educational Review, 58*(1), 29–84.

Fordham, S., & Ogbu, J. U. (1986). Black students' school success: Coping with the burden of "acting white." *Urban Review, 18*(3), 176–206.

Foster, M. (1989). It's cooking now: A performance analysis of the speech events of a black teacher in an urban community college. *Language and Society, 18*(1) 1–29.

Foster, M. (1990). The politics of race: Through the eyes of African American teachers. *Journal of Education, 172*(3), 123–141.

Foster, M. (1992). Sociolinguistics and the African American community: Implications for literacy. *Theory in Practice, 31*(4), 303–311.

Foster, M. (1997). *Black teachers on teaching*. New York: New York Press.

Foster, M. (2001). Pay Leon, pay Leon, pay Leon palentologist: Using call-and-response to facilitate language mastery and literacy acquisition among African-American students. In S. L. Lanehart (Ed.) *Sociocultural and historical contexts of African American vernacular English*. Amsterdam: John Benjamins.

Foster, M. (2001, June). How can we improve instruction in literacy for urban youth in teacher education and in partnering schools? Keynote address at the Second Annual Institute of the Massachusetts Coalition for Teacher Quality and Student Achievement, Sturbridge, MA.

Fraser, J. W., Allen, H. L., & Barnes, S. (1979). *From common school to magnet school: Selected essays in the history of Boston's schools*. Boston: Trustees of the Public Library of the City of Boson.

Freire, P. (1970). *Pedagogy of the oppressed*. New York: Seabird Press.

Garrod, A., Ward, J. W., Robinson, T. L., & Kilkenny, R. (Eds.). (1999). *Souls looking back: Life stories of growing up black*. New York: Routledge.

Gay, G. (2000). *Culturally responsive teaching: Theory, research and practice* (multicultural education series). New York: Teachers College Press.

Gee, J. P. (1997). Thinking, learning and reading: The situated sociocultural mind. In D. Kirshner & J.A. Whitson (Eds.), *Situated cognition: Social, semiotic and psychological perspectives* (pp. 37–55). Mahwah, NJ: Erlbaum.

Goodlad, J. (1984). *A place called school: Prospects for the future*. New York: McGraw-Hill.

Gordon, E. W. & Thomas, K. H. (1990). Reading and other forms of literacy: Implications for teaching and learning. *Journal of Negro Education*, 59(1), 70–76.

Haberman, M. (1995). *Star teachers of children in poverty*. Bloomington, IN: Phi Delta Pi Publications.

Hale, J. E. (1994). *Unbank the fire: Visions for the education of African American children*. Baltimore: Johns Hopkins University Press.

Hale-Benson, J. E. (1986). *Black children: Their roots, culture and learning styles*. Baltimore: Johns Hopkins University Press.

Harre, R., & Gillett, G. (Eds.). (1994). *The discursive mind*. Thousand Oaks, CA: Sage Publications.

Heath, S. B. (1983). *Ways with words: Language life and work in communities and classrooms*. Cambridge, UK: Cambridge University Press.

Hedges, L. V., & Nowell, A. (1998). Black-white test score convergence since 1965. In C. Jenks and M. Phillips (Eds.), *The black-white test score gap* (pp. 149–181). Washington, DC: The Brookings Institution.

Hilliard, A. G., III (1996). Teacher education from an African American perspective. In J. J. Irvine (Ed.) *Critical knowledge for diverse teachers and learners*. Washington: American Association for Colleges of Teacher Education.

Holland, D., Lachicotte, W., Jr., Skinner, D., & Cain, C. (1998). *Identity and agency in cultural worlds*. Cambridge, MA: Harvard University Press.

Holland, D. & Quinn, N. (Eds.) (1987). *Cultural models in language and thought*. New York: Cambridge University Press.

Howard, J. (1990). *Getting smart: The social construction of intelligence*. Boston: Efficacy Institute.

Hymes, D. (1974) *The foundations of sociolinguistics: sociolinguistic ethnography*. Philadelphia: University of Pennsylvania Press.

Irvine, J. J. (1991). *Black students and school failure: Policies, practices and prescriptions*. Westport, CT: Praeger Publishers.

Karenga, M. (1980). *Kawaida theory: An introductory outline*. Inglewood, CA: Kawaida Publications.

Kirschner, D., & Whitson, J. A. (Eds.). (1997). *Situated cognition: Social, semiotic, and psychological perspectives*. Hillsdale, NJ: Erlbaum.

Kunjufu, J. (1985; 1996). *Countering the conspiracy to destroy black boys*. Chicago, IL: African American Images.

Ladson-Billings, G. (1994). *The dreamkeepers: Successful teachers of African American children*. San Francisco: Josey-Bass Publishers.

Lave, J. (1988). *Cognition in practice*. Cambridge, UK: Cambridge University Press.

Lave, J. (1991). Situated learning in communities of practice. In L.B. Resnick, J.M. Levine, & S.D. Teasley (Eds), *Perspectives on socially shared cognition* (pp. 63–82). Washington, DC: American Psychological Association.

Lave, J. (1997). The culture of acquisition and the practice of understanding. In D. Kirshner & J. A. Whitson (Eds.), *Situated cognition: Social, semiotic, and psychological perspectives* (pp. 17–36). Hillsdale, NJ: Erlbaum.

Lave, J. & Wenger (1991). *Situated learning & legitimate peripheral participation*. Cambridge, UK: Cambridge University Press.

Lee, C. D. (1994). African-centered pedagogy: complexities and possibilities. In M. J. Shujaa (Ed.), *Too much schooling, too little education: A paradox of Black life in white societies* (pp. 295–218). Trenton, NJ: Africa Free Press.

Lee, C. D. (1995). Signifying as a scaffold for literary interpretation. *Journal of Black Psychology, 21*(4). 357–381.

Lee, C. D. (2001). Is October Brown Chinese? A cultural modeling activity system for underachieving students. *American Educational Research Journal, 38*(1), 97–141.

Lemke, J. L. (1997). Cognition, context, and learning: A social semiotic perspective. In D. Kirschner & J. A. Whitson (Eds.), *Situated cognition: Social, semiotic and psychological perspectives* (pp. 37–55). Mahwah, NJ: Erlbaum.

Leontiev, A. N. (1981). *The problem of activity psychology*. In J. V. Wertsch (Ed.), *The concept of activity in Soviet psychology* (pp. 37–71). Amonk, NY: Sharpe.

Lott, T. L. (1999). *The invention of race: Black culture and the politics of representation*. Malden, MA: Blackwell.

Madhubuti, H. & Madhubuti, S. (1991). *African centered education: Its value, importance and necessity in the development of Black children*. Chicago: World Free Press.

Madhubuti, M. R. (1994). Cultural work: Planting new trees with new seeds. In M. Shujaa (Ed.), *Too much schooling too little education: A paradox of Black life in White societies* (pp. 1–6). Trenton, NJ: Africa World Press.

Mahiri, J. (1998). *Shooting for excellence: African-American and youth culture in new century schools*. New York: Teachers College Press.

Manguel, A. (1996). *A history of reading*. New York: Penuin.

McDowell, C. L. & Sullivan, P. (1993). To fight swimming with the current: Teaching movement history. In T. Perry & J. Fraser (Eds.). *Freedom's plow: Teaching in the multicultural classroom*. New York: Routledge.

McKissack, P. (1986). *Flossie and the fox*. New York: E. P. Dutton.

McLaren, P. (1989). *Life in schools: An introduction to critical pedagogy in the foundations of education*. New York: Longman.

Meier, D. (1995). *The power of their ideas: Lessons for America from a small school in Harlem*. Boston: Beacon Press.

Meier, T. (1982). Open admissions in Black and White colleges: A comparative review. Unpublished manuscript.

Meier, T. (2001). *What teachers need to know for effective literacy instruction in multilingual and multicultural urban communities*. Keynote presentation at the Early Childhood Summer Literacy Institute, Wheelock College, Boston.

Minick, N., Stone, C. A., & Forman, E. A. (1993). Integration of individual, social, and institutional processes in accounts of children's learning development. In E. Forman, N. Minick, & C.A. Stone (Eds.), Contexts for learning: *Sociocultural dynamics of children's development* (pp. 3–16). New York: Oxford University Press.

Mosely, W. (2000). *Workin' on the chain gang: Shaking off the dead hand of history*. New York: The Ballentine Publishing Group.

Moses, R. P. & Cobb, C. E. (2001). *Radical equations: Math literacy and civil rights*. Boston: Beacon Press.

Murrell, P. C., Jr., (1991). Cultural politics in teacher education: What's missing in the preparation of African-American teachers? In M. Foster (Ed.) *Readings on Equal Education* Vol. 11, (pp. 205–225). New York: AMS Press, Inc.

Murrell, P. C., Jr. (1993). Afrocentric immersion: Academic and personal development of African American males in public schools. In T. Perry & J. Fraser (Eds.), *Freedoms plow: Teaching in the multicultural classroom* (pp. 231–260). New York: Routledge.

Murrell, P. C., Jr. (1994). In search of responsive teaching for African American males: An investigation of students' experiences of middle school mathematics curriculum. *Journal of Negro Education*, 63(4), 556–569.

Murrell, P. C., Jr., (1997). Digging again the family wells: A Freirean literacy framework as emancipatory pedagogy for African American children. In P. Freire,

J. Fraser, D. Macedo, T. McKinnon, & W. Stokes (Eds.), *Mentoring the mentor: A critical dialog with Paulo Freire*. (pp. 19–58). Albany, NY: SUNY Press.

Murrell, P. C., Jr. (1998). *Like stone soup: The role of the professional development in the renewal of urban schools*. Washington, DC: American Associate of Colleges for Teacher Education.

Murrell, P. C., Jr. (2001). *The community teacher: A new framework for effective urban teaching*. New York: Teachers College Press.

Murrell, P. C., Jr., & Borunda, M. (1998). The cultural and community politics of educational equity: Toward a new framework of professional development schools. In N. J. Lauter (Ed.), *Professional development schools: Confronting realities*. (pp. 65–86). New York: National Center for Restructuring Education, Schools and Teaching (NCREST).

National Council of Teachers of Mathematics (1998). Curriculum and evaluation standards for school mathematics. Reston, VA: Author.

Newman, L. (1989). *Heather has two mommies*. London: Alyson Publications.

Nobles, W. (1998). Foreward. In Asa G. Hilliard, *SBA: The reawakening of the African mind* (pp. xiii–xvii). Gainesville, FL: Makare.

Noddings, N. (1992). *The challenge to care in schools: An alternative approach to education*. New York: Teachers College Press.

Oakes, J. (1985). *Keeping track: How schools structure inequality*. New Haven, CT: Yale University Press.

Ochs, E. (1997). Narrative. In T. A. Van Dyjk (Ed.), *Discourse as structure and process* (pp. 184–204). London: Sage.

Ogbu, J. U. (1978). *Minority education and caste: The American system in cross-cultural perspective*. New York: Academic Press.

Ogbu, J. U. (1981). Origins of human competence: A cultural ecological perspective. *Child Development, 52*, 413–429.

Ogbu, J. U. (1983). Minority status and schooling in plural societies. *Comparative Education Reveiw, 27*, 168–190.

Ogbu, J. U. (1986). The consequences of the American caste system. In U. Neisser (Ed.), *The school achievement of minority children: New perspectives* (pp. 19–56). Hillsdale, NJ: Erlbaum.

Ogbu, J. (1988). Black education: A cultural-ecological perspective. In H. P. McAdoo (Ed.), *Black families* (pp. 169–186). Beverly Hills, CA: Sage.

Ogbu, J. U. (1989). The individual in collective adaptation: A framework for focusing on academic underperformance and dropping out among involuntary minorities. In L. Weis, E. Farrar, & H. C. Petrie (Eds.), *Dropouts from school* (pp. 181–204). Albany, NY: SUNY Press.

Ogbu, J. U. (1992). Understanding cultural diversity and learning. *Educational Researcher, 21*(8), 5–14.

Ogbu, J. U. (1994). Racial stratification and education in the United States: Why inequality persists. *Teachers College Record*, 96(2), 264–298.

Perkins, D. (1992). Smart schools: From training memories to educating minds. New York: The Free Press.

Perrone, V. (1997). Why do we need a pedagogy of understanding? In M. S. Wiske (Ed.), *Teaching for understanding: Linking research with practice* (pp. 39–58). San Francisco: Jossey Bass Publishers.

Perry, T. & Delpit, L. (Ed.) (1998). *The real ebonics debate: Power, language and the education of African American children.* Boston: Beacon Press.

Phelan, P., Yu, H. C., & Davidson, A. L. (1994). Navigating the psychological pressures of adolescence: The voices and experiences of high school youth. *American Educational Research Journal, 31*, 415–447.

Phillips, M., Crouse, J. & Ralph, J. (1998). Does the black-white test score gap widen after children enter school? In C. Jencks & M. Phillips (Eds.), *The black-white test score gap* (pp. 229–272). New York: Basic Books.

Piestrup, A. M. (1973). *Black dialect interference and accommodation of reading instruction in the first grade* (Monographs of the Language Behavior Research Laboratory No. 4). Berkeley, CA: University of California.

Rawick, G. P. (1972). *From sundown to sunup: The making of the black community*. Westport, CT: Greenwood Publishing Company.

Resnick, L. B., Säljö, R., Pontecarvo, C., & Burge, B. (Eds.). (1991). *Discourse, tools, and reasoning: Essays on situated cognition*. Berlin: Springer.

Resnick, L. B., Levine, J. M., & Teasley, S. D. (Eds). (1991). *Perspectives on socially shared cognition*. Washington, DC: American Psychological Association.

Richards, D. M. (1989). *Let the circle be unbroken: African spirituality in the diaspora.* Trenton, NJ: Red Sea Press. (originally published in 1980)

Rogoff, B. (1990). *Apprenticeship in thinking*. New York: Oxford University Press.

Rogoff, B. (1995). Observing sociocultural activity on three planes: Participatory appropriation, guided participation, and apprenticeship. In J.V. Wertsch, P. del Rio., & A. Alvarez (Eds.), *Sociocultural studies of mind* (pp. 139–164). Cambridge, UK: Cambridge University Press.

Rogoff, B., & Lave, J. (Eds.). (1984). *Everyday cognition: Its development in social context.* Cambridge, MA: Harvard University Press.

Schon, D. A. (1984). *The reflective practitioner: How professionals think in action.* New York: Basic Books.

Scribner, S. & Cole, M. (1981). *The psychology of literacy.* Cambridge, MA: Harvard University Press.

Shade, B. (1982). Afro-American cognitive style: A variable in school success. *Review of Educational Research, 52,* 219–244.

Sheets, R. H., & Hollins, E. R. (1999). *Racial and ethnic identity in school practices: Aspects of human development.* Mahwah, NJ: Erlbaum.

Shore, B. (1996). *Culture in mind: Cognition, culture, and the problem of meaning.* New York: Oxford University Press.

Shujaa, M. J. (1992). Afrocentric transformation and parental choice in African American independent schools. *Journal of Negro Education, 61*(2), 148–159.

Shujaa, M. J. (1994). Education and schooling: You can have one without the other. In M. J. Shujaa (Ed.), *Too much schooling, too little education: A paradox of black life in white societies.* Trenton, NJ: Africa World Press, Inc.

Siddle Walker, V. (1996). *Their highest potential: An African American school community in the segregated South.* Chapel Hill, NC: University of North Carolina Press.

Sizer, T. R. (1996). *Horace's hope: What works for the American high school.* Boston: Houghton-Mifflin.

Solsken, J. & Bloome, D. (1992, April). *Beyond poststructuralism: Story and narrative in the study of literacy in the everyday world.* Paper presented at the meeting of the American Educational Research Association, San Francisco.

St. Jean, Y. & Teagin, J. R. (1998). *Double burden: Black women and everyday racism.* Armonk, NY: M. E. Sharpe.

Steele, C. (1997). A threat in the air. *American Psychologist, 52*(6), 613–629.

Steele, C. M., & Aronson, J. A. (1995). Stereotypic threat and the intellectual test performance of African Americans. *Journal of Personality and Social Psychology, 65*(5), 797–811.

Street, B. (1993). The new literacy studies: Guest editorial. *Journal of Research on Reading, 16*(2), 81–97.

Tharp, R. G. (1997). *From at-risk to excellence: Research, theory, and principles of practice* (Research Rep. No. 1). Washington, DC and Santa Cruz, CA: Center for Research on Education, Diversity, & Excellence.

Tharp, R. G., & Gallimore, R. (1991). *Rousing minds to life: Teach learning and schooling in social context.* Cambridge: Cambridge University Press.

Treisman, P. U. (1985). A study of the mathematics of achievement of Black students at the University of California, Berkeley. Unpublished doctoral dissertation, University of California, Berkely.

Tyack, D. (1974). *The one best system: A history of American urban education*. Cambridge, MA: Harvard University Press.

Vygotsky, L. (1962). *Thought and language*. (E. Hanfman & G. Bakar, Eds. and Trans.). Cambridge, MA: MIT Press.

Vygotsky, L. (1978). *Mind in society*. (M. Cole, V. John-Steiner, S. Scribner, & E. Souberman, Eds.). Cambridge, MA: Harvard University Press.

Weiner, L. (1993). *Preparing teachers for urban schools: Lessons from thirty years of school reform*. New York: Teachers College Press.

Weiner, L. (1999). *Urban teaching: The essentials*. New York: Teacher College Press.

Wertsch, J. V. (1985). *Culture, communication, and cognition: Vygotskian perspectives*. Cambridge: University Press.

Wertsch, J. V. (1991). *Voices of the mind: A sociocultural approach to mediated action*. Cambridge, MA: Harvard University Press.

Wenger, E. (1998). *Communities of practice: Learning, meaning and identity*. Cambridge, UK: Cambridge University Press.

Wiggins, G., & McTighe, J. (1998). *Understanding by design*. Alexandria, VA: Association for Supervision and Curriculum Development.

Williams, B. (Ed.) (1996). *Closing the achievement gap: A vision for changing beliefs and practices*. Alexandria, VA: Association for Supervision and Curriculum Development.

Wilson, B. G. (1996) Internet Reference. <http://www.cudenver.edu/~bwilson/dlc.html> and <http://www.cudenver.edu/~bwilson/metaphor.html>

Wilson, B. G. (1996). *Constructivist learning environments: Case studies in instructional design*. Englewood Cliffs, NJ: Educational Technology.

Wilson, B. G. (1996) <file:///Hardrive/Desktop%20Folder/Field%20Work/Learning%20Environments>.

Wilson, K., & Allen, W. R. (1987). Explaining the educational attainment of young black adults: Critical familial and extrafamilial influences. *Journal of Negro Education*, *56*, 64–74.

Wiske, M. S. (1998). *Teaching for understanding: Linking research with practice*. San Francisco: Jossey-Bass.

Witkin, H. A. (1967). A cognitive-style approach to cross-cultural research. International *Journal of Psychology*, *2*, 237–238.

Wittgenstein, L. (1953). *Philosophical investigations* (tr. G. E. M. Ansambe) Oxford: Blackwell.

Wood, F. G. (1968). *Black Scare: The racist response to emancipation and reconstruction.* Berkeley: University of Claifornia Press.

Woodson, C. G. (1916). *The education of the Negro prior to 1861: A history of the education of colored people of the United States from the beginning of slavery to the civil war*. Washington, DC: The Associated Publishers.

Woodson, C. G. (1933, 1990). *The miseducation of the Negro*. Washington, DC: African World Press.

Index

Ability, 83
Accomplished practice, 59
Accomplished teaching and teachers, xvii, 40
Achievement gap, xxiv, xxx, 7–8, 15, 17
Activity setting – instructional, 105, literacy learning activity setting, 68–70
Activity setting, 16, 62–64, 66–70, 87–88, 105, 138
Activity system, 62–63, 67–70, 97–101
Activity theory, 45
Addae, E. K., 136
Akoto, A., 37, 78, 136
Anderson, J., xv, 25–28
Ani, M., 34, 77, 136
Anwisye, S., 77
Apple, M., 22
Appraisal of practice, 51, 88, 103, 155
Appropriation of knowledge, 49, 165
Arsonson, J. A., 122,
Assisted performance, xv, 104

Bahktin, M., 49
Banks, J., 77
Bateson, G., 115
Battat, J., 114
Bell, D., 77
Benjamin, W., 139
Bethune, M., xxxiv
Bloom, B., 30
Bloome, D., 138
Borunda, M., 108
Bourdieu, P., 22
Bowers, C. A., xiv, 116
Boykin, A.W., 21, 83
Brown, J. S., 45
Bruner, J., 39, 46

Cain, C., 115–116
Cazden, C., 128
Chaiklin, S., 45
Champion, T., 138–139
Circle of practice, 65
Clark, J. H., xv, 77
Coalition for Essential schools, xi
Cochran-Smith, M., xix
Cohen, C., 114
Cole, M., 45
Collins, A., 45
Collins, P., 77
Comer, J., 11–12, 84
Common school, 26
Community of culturally connected teaching practice, 164
Community of learners, 37–38
Community of practice, xv, xxxiv, 32–33, defined 80–81, 86, 105, 116–118, 156
Community teacher, xxxiv
Connected pedagogy, xv, xxxiii–xxxiv, 38–40
Constructivist teaching, xi–xii
Critical pedagogy, 76, 158
Cross, W., xiv
Cultural capital, 14
Cultural competence, 65, 80
Cultural congruity – synchrony, compatibility, 65, 12–14, 115
Cultural deficits, 10
Cultural ecology, 119
Cultural identity, 101
Cultural knowledge, 123
Cultural learning, 55
Cultural literacy, 30
Cultural model, 34–35, 83–84
Cultural norms, 84
Cultural patterns, 23, 34–35, 83, 116
Cultural practice, 34, 71–73
Cultural reproduction theory, 22
Cultural system, 35

Culturally interpreted inquiry, 80
Culturally relevant pedagogy, 12–17
Culturally responsive teaching, xxxiv–xxxvi, 12–13, 158
Curriculum blueprint, 160, 179

Darder, A., 77
Deficit model, 11
Delpit, L., xxiii, 37, 40, 130
Dewey, J., 88
Diop, C. A., xv
Disconnection and disengagement, xix–xx
Discourse frames, 132
Discourse patterns, 131
Discourse practices, 33, 133, 136
Double vision, double consciousness, 5, 10
Douglass, F., xv, 77, 136
Driscoll, M., xiv
DuBois, W.E.B., xv, 77
Duguid, P., 45

Ecological model, 11–12
Ecosocial perspective, xxvi–xxix
Elmore, R., 84
Erickson, F., xiv
Essential cultural practices of the African-centered pedagogy, 51–56, 61
Essential practices, 95

Figured world of black achievement, 165
Figured world of inquiry, 118
Figured world, xxxiv, 5, 10
Fine, M., xxix
Flinders, D., xiv, 116
Folk theories, 83
Fordham, S., xxix, 119–121
Foreman, E. A., 45
Foster, Michéle, xi, xxiii, 42, 103
Framework - Generative framework 59–60, Interpretive framework, 23, 59–60
Fraser, J., 24
Freire, P., xxxii, 22

Gallimore, Ronald, xi, 87–88, 105–107
Garrod, A., xiv
Gay, G., xi, xxiii
Gee, J., 34, 83–84
Generative question, 91
Generative task, 95, 100, 159–160
Generative topic, 101
Gillett, G., 45
Giroux, H., xxxii–xxxiii
Gordon, E., 136–137
Green, M., 22, 77

Haberman, M., 81
Habit of mind, 64
Hale, J., xxiii, 84, 103, 105
Harre, R., 45
Harris, K., 22
Heath, S. B., 131
Hedegaard, M., 45
Hilliard, A., 105
Holland, D., 115–116
hooks, b., 22
Hymes, D., 138

Improvisation, 120
Instructional enterprise, 160
INTASC, 140
Interpretive frame, 84
Interpretive traditions, 83
Irvine, J., xxiii, 38, 65

Jensen, V. J., 45

Karenga, M., 77
Katz, L., 138–139
King, Joyce, xxiii, 136
Kinship, 117–118
Kirshner, D., 39
Knowledge-in-practice, x, 60–61
Kunjufu, J., 10

Lachicotte, W., 115–116
Ladson-Billings, G., xxiii, 38, 40, 44, 103
Language practice, 138
Lave, J., xi, 32, 39, 45, 59, 79, 116, 136

Learner-centered teaching, 84
Learning communities, xi–xii, 32, 70
Learning styles, xxvii–xxviii, 105
Lee, Carol, 7, 3, 103, 136
Lemke, J., 45
Leontiev, A. N., 45
Literacy for freedom, 24–25, 30
Lomotey, K., 103
Lourde, A., 77

MAAFA, 31
MAAT, xv, xxi–xxii
Macedo, D., 77
Mahiri, J., 34, 40, 42
McDowell, C., 76, 160
McLaren, P., xxxix
McTighe, J., xi
Meier, T., 79
Minick, N., 45
Morton, M., 138–139
Mosley, W., 19
Movement history, 76
Muldrow, R., 138–139
Multicultural education, xx–xxi, 41, 117
Multiple intelligences, xi–xii
Murrell, P. C., Jr., 108, 128, 136

Narrative – as a way of knowing, 160, narrative knowledge, 160, retelling the narrative, 160
NBPTS, 140
Nobles, W., 21, 75

Obgu, J., xxix, 13, 119–121
Oppositional identity, 13

Participation structures, 119
Pedagogy, xxxii–xxiii
Perkins, D., xi
Perrone, V., 29
Perry, T., 40
Piestrup, A. M., 110
Practice defined, 50
Practice, x, 50–53, core practices, 66
Praxis, xi, 76, 85

Racelessness, 119–121, 123
Racism, 34, 76
Recursive reappropriation, 80
Resnick, L., 46
Responsive pedagogy, 117
Richards, D., 77
Ritual of resolve, 44–45
Robinson, T., xiv
Roelofs, A., 114
Rogoff, B., 45
Root, M., xiv
Rugged individualism, xxxi

Schon, D., 88
Schultz, S., 24
Scribner, S., 45
Shade, B., 105
Sheets, R., xiv
Shore, B., 45
Shujaa, M., 3, 45, 78, 103
Situated cognition, 45
Situated cultural theory, 83–85
Situated identity, 125
Situated learning theory, xi, xxiii, 39
Situated learning, 158
Sizemore, B., xxiii
Skinner, D., 115–116
Social context of cognition, 45
Social practice, 64, 82
Sociohistorical or sociocultural theory, xv, 39–40
Steele, C., xxix, 50, 122
Stereotypic threat, 122, 124
Stone, C. A., 45
Story starters, 160
Sullivan, P., 160
Symbolic culture, 123, 125
Symbolic self, 120
Systems of practice, xxxi

Teaching for understanding, xi, 29, 158
Teaching-in-practice, 59
Tharp, R., xi, 87–88, 103, 105–107
Thomas, K., 136–137
Treisman, P. U., 80

Triadic analysis, 106–108
Tyranny of the mundane, 108

Understanding performance, 99

Vygotsky, L., 39, 46, 48, 64, 86

Walker, V. S., 103, 120–121, 123
Ward, J., xiv
Weiner, L., xxx, 84
Wenger, E., xv, 39, 48, 54, 79, 82, 116
Wertsch, J., 39, 46
Whitson, J., 39
Wiggins, G., xi, 64, 96
Wilson, B. G., 68, 70
Wiske, J., xxxix, 95, 99, 101
Wittgenstein, L., 46, 48
Woodson, C., xv, 77

Zeichner, K., xxx
Zone of proximal development, 47